# Student Study Art Notebook

to accompany

*Vander's*

# Human Physiology

## The Mechanisms of Body Function

### Tenth Edition

**Eric P. Widmaier**
*Boston University*

**Hershel Raff**
*Medical College of Wisconsin–*
*St. Luke's Medical Center*

**Kevin T. Strang**
*University of Wisconsin–Madison*

Boston   Burr Ridge, IL   Dubuque, IA   Madison, WI   New York   San Francisco   St. Louis
Bangkok   Bogotá   Caracas   Kuala Lumpur   Lisbon   London   Madrid   Mexico City
Milan   Montreal   New Delhi   Santiago   Seoul   Singapore   Sydney   Taipei   Toronto

**The McGraw·Hill** Companies

Student Study Art Notebook to accompany
*VANDER'S* HUMAN PHYSIOLOGY: THE MECHANISMS OF BODY FUNCTION,
TENTH EDITION
ERIC P. WIDMAIER, HERSHEL RAFF, AND KEVIN T. STRANG

Published by McGraw-Hill Higher Education, an imprint of The McGraw-Hill Companies, Inc.,
1221 Avenue of the Americas, New York, NY 10020. Copyright © 2006 by The McGraw-Hill
Companies, Inc. All rights reserved.

 This book is printed on recycled, acid-free paper containing
10% postconsumer waste.

3 4 5 6 7 8 9 0 QPD/QPD 0 9 8 7 6

ISBN-13: 978-0-07-321120-6
ISBN-10: 0-07-321120-6

www.mhhe.com

# DIRECTORY OF NOTEBOOK FIGURES

## TO ACCOMPANY
### WIDMAIER/RAFF/STRANG
#### VANDER'S
#### HUMAN PHYSIOLOGY
#### The Mechanisms of Body Function 10/e

## Chapter 14

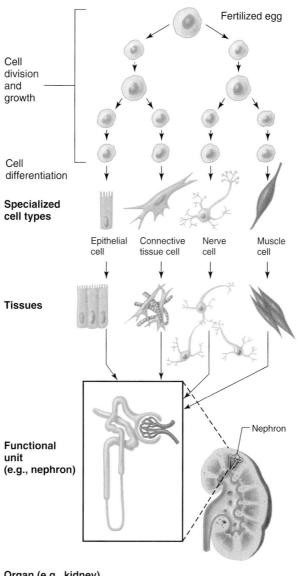

Fertilized egg

Cell division and growth

Cell differentiation

**Specialized cell types**

Epithelial cell | Connective tissue cell | Nerve cell | Muscle cell

**Tissues**

**Functional unit (e.g., nephron)**

Nephron

**Organ (e.g., kidney)**

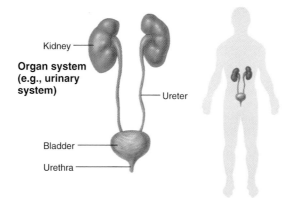

Kidney

**Organ system (e.g., urinary system)**

Ureter

Bladder

Urethra

**Total organism (human being)**

## Levels of cellular organization
Figure 1.1

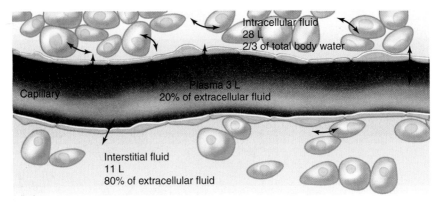

**Fluid compartments of the body**
Figure 1.2

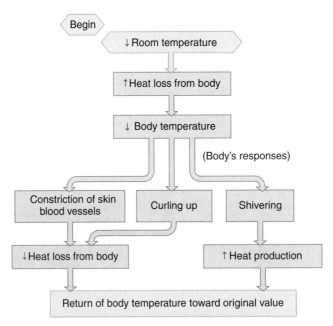

**The homeostatic control system**
Figure 1.3

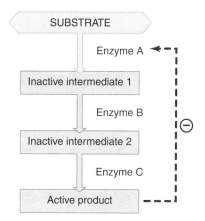

**Hypothetical example of negative feedback**
Figure 1.4

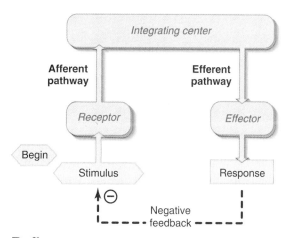

**Reflex arc**
Figure 1.5

INTEGRATING CENTER

Specific nerve cells in brain
Altered rates of firing

AFFERENT PATHWAY
(Nerve fibers)

EFFERENT PATHWAY
(Nerve fibers)

RECEPTORS

Temperature-sensitive
nerve endings

↑ Signaling rate

Smooth muscle in
skin blood vessels

↑ Constriction

Skeletal muscle

Contraction

Shivering

Begin

STIMULUS

Body
temperature

⊖

↓ Heat loss

↑ Heat
production

**Reflex control of body temperature**
Figure 1.6

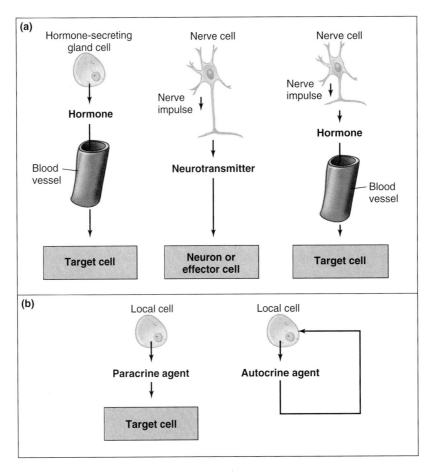

**Categories of chemical messengers**
Figure 1.7

4

## Circadian rhythms of a human subject
Figure 1.8

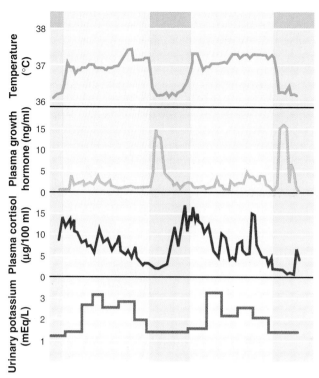

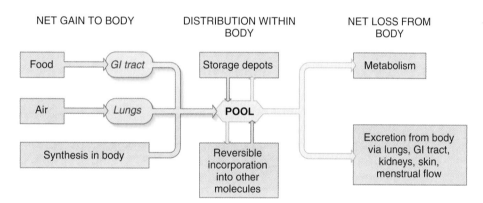

NET GAIN TO BODY    DISTRIBUTION WITHIN BODY    NET LOSS FROM BODY

## Balance diagram for a chemical substance
Figure 1.9

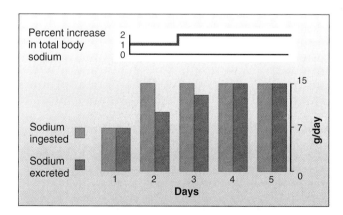

## Effects of a continued change in the amount of sodium ingested on sodium excretion and total-body sodium balance
Figure 1.10

| | Neutrons | Protons | Electrons |
|---|---|---|---|
| Carbon | 6 | 6 | 6 |
| Hydrogen | 0 | 1 | 1 |

Methane
(four covalent bonds)

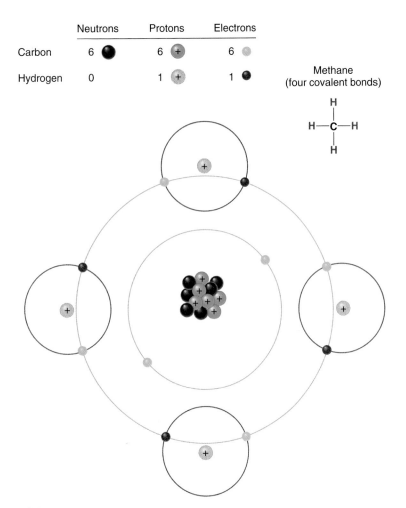

**Covalent bonds in Methane**
Figure 2.1

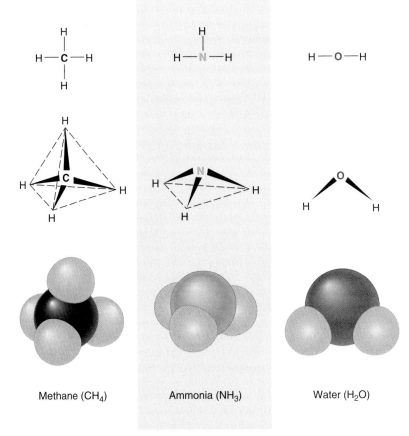

**Three different representations of covalent bonds**
Figure 2.2

Methane (CH₄)    Ammonia (NH₃)    Water (H₂O)

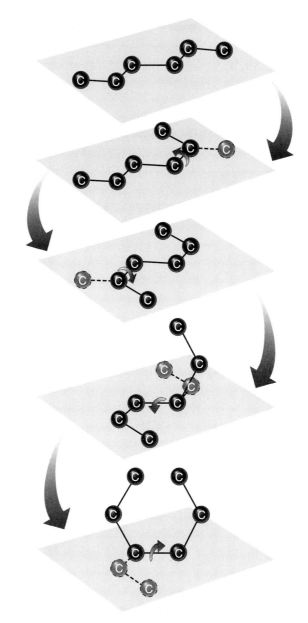

**Changes in molecular shape**
Figure 2.3

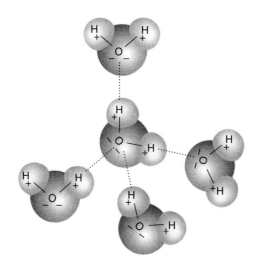

**Hydrogen bonding in water**
Figure 2.4

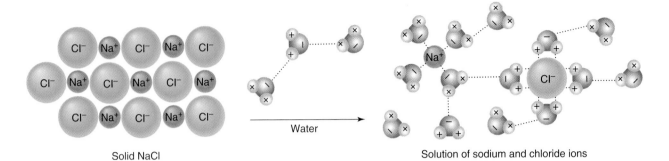

Solid NaCl

Water

Solution of sodium and chloride ions

**Organic molecules**
Figure 2.5

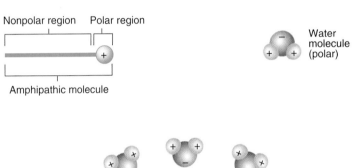

Nonpolar region    Polar region

Amphipathic molecule

Water
molecule
(polar)

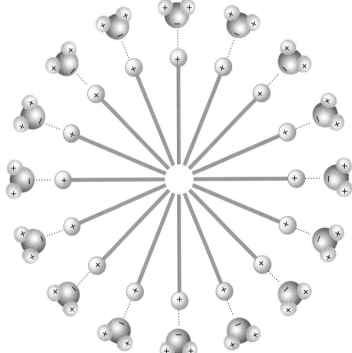

**Amphipathic molecules in water**
Figure 2.6

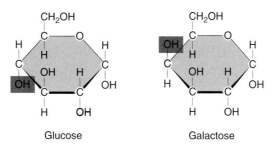

Glucose

**Two ways of diagraming monosaccharide glucose**
Figure 2.7

Glucose          Galactose

**Structural difference between monosaccharides glucose and galactose**
Figure 2.8

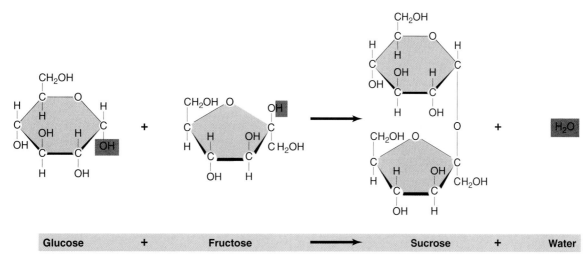

| Glucose | + | Fructose | → | Sucrose | + | Water |

**Disaccharide formation**
Figure 2.9

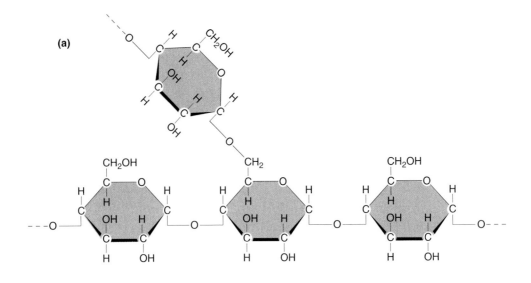

(a)

(b)

Glucose subunit

Glycogen

**Glycogen formation**

Figure 2.10

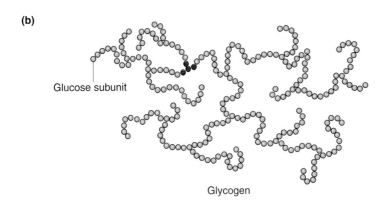

Glycerol

Saturated fatty acid

Polyunsaturated fatty acid

Triglyceride (fat)

Phospholipid (phosphatidylcholine)

**Major lipids**

Figure 2.11

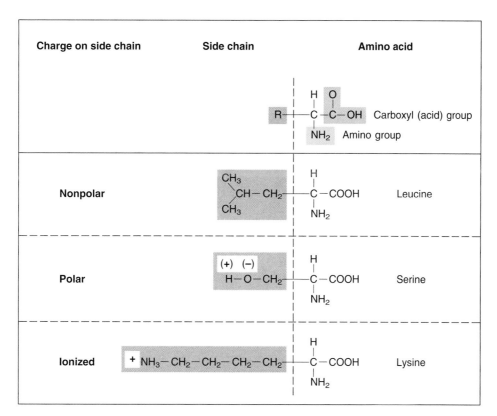

**(a)**

Steroid ring structure

**(b)**

Cholesterol

## Steroid ring structure
Figure 2.12

| Charge on side chain | Side chain | Amino acid |
|---|---|---|
| | | R—C—C—OH  Carboxyl (acid) group<br>NH₂  Amino group |
| Nonpolar | CH₃—CH—CH₂ / CH₃ | C—COOH  Leucine |
| Polar | (+) (−)  H—O—CH₂ | C—COOH  Serine |
| Ionized | ⁺NH₃—CH₂—CH₂—CH₂—CH₂ | C—COOH  Lysine |

## Representative structures of amino acids found in proteins
Figure 2.13

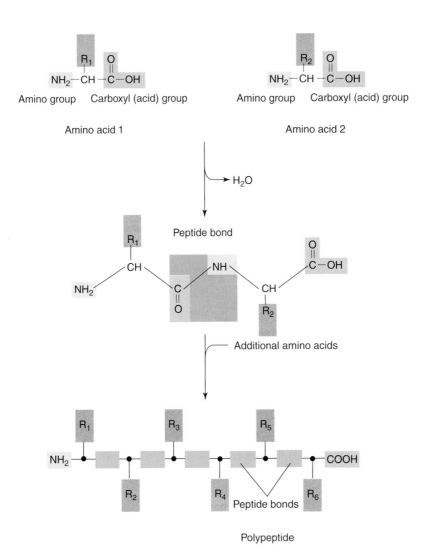

**Amino acids and peptide bonds**
Figure 2.14

**A polypeptide chain**
Figure 2.15

**Shape of the protein molecule myoglobin**
Figure 2.16

13

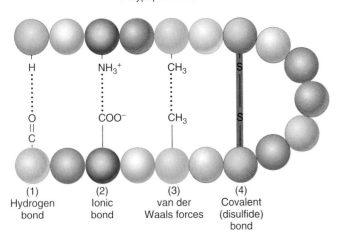

## Factors that contribute to the folding of polypeptide chains
Figure 2.17

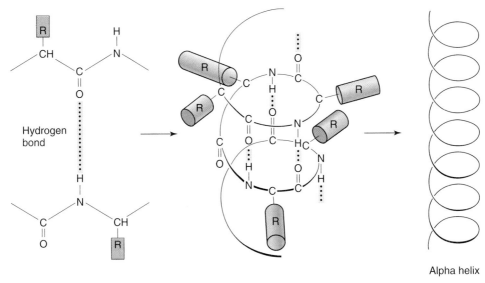

Alpha helix

## Helical conformation in a polypeptide chain
Figure 2.18

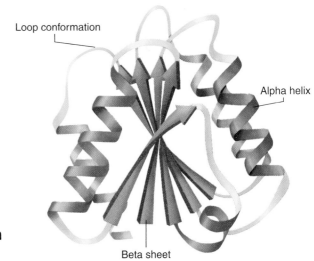

Loop conformation

Alpha helix

Beta sheet

## Ribbon diagram
Figure 2.19

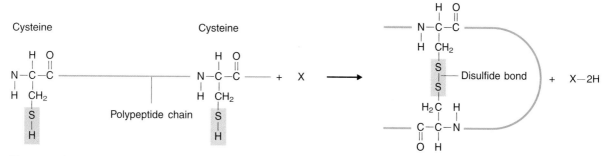

**Formation of a disulfide bond**
Figure 2.20

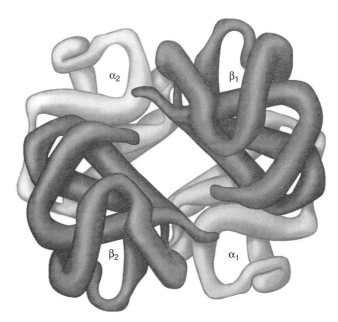

**Three-dimensional folding of hemoglobin**
Figure 2.21

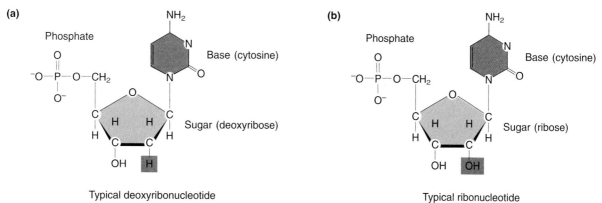

**Nucleotide subunits of DNA and RNA**
Figure 2.22

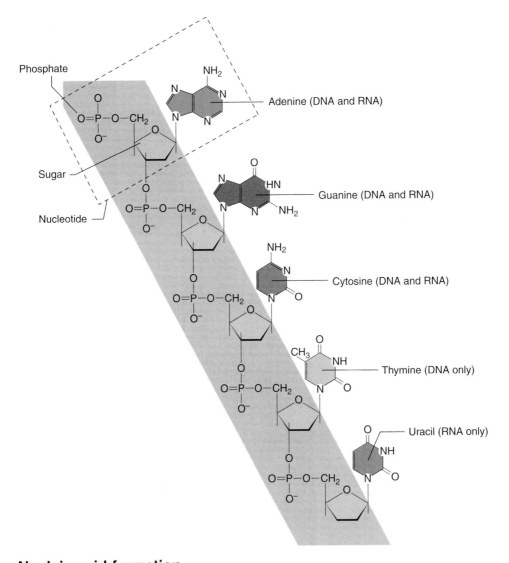

**Nucleic acid formation**
Figure 2.23

**Links between
strands in a DNA
double helix**
Figure 2.24

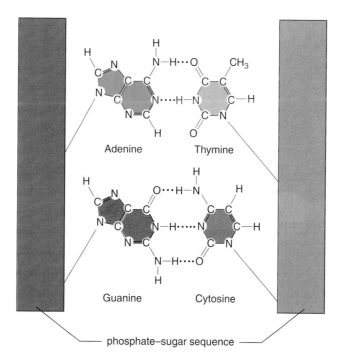

Adenine          Thymine

Guanine          Cytosine

phosphate–sugar sequence

**Hydrogen bonding in DNA**
Figure 2.25

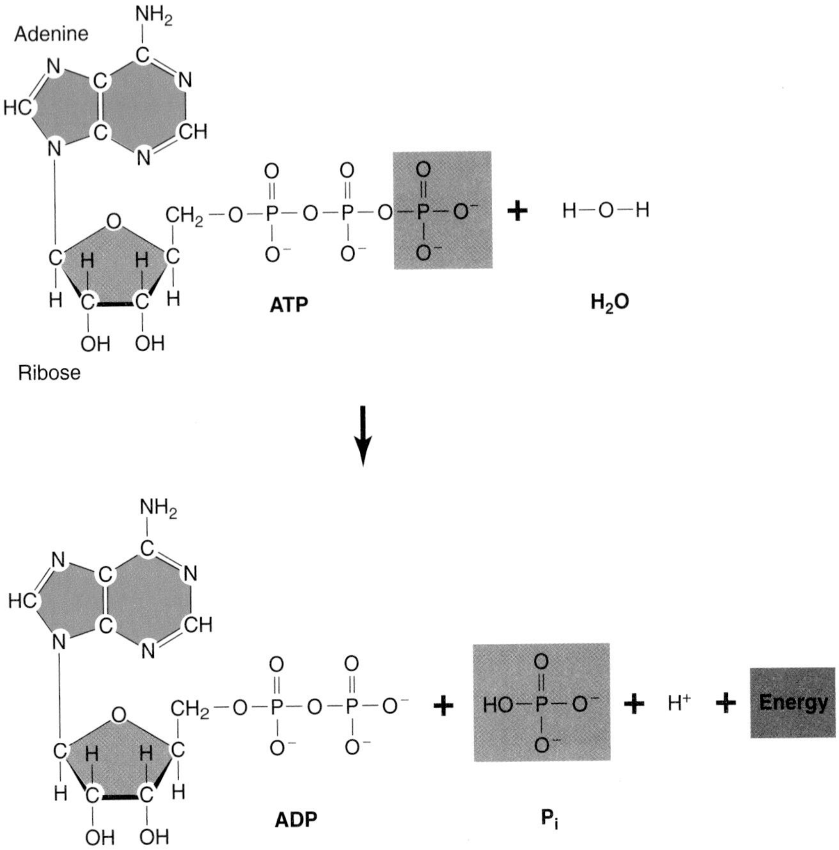

**Chemical structure of ATP**

Figure 2.26

ATP + H₂O → ADP + Pᵢ + H⁺ + energy

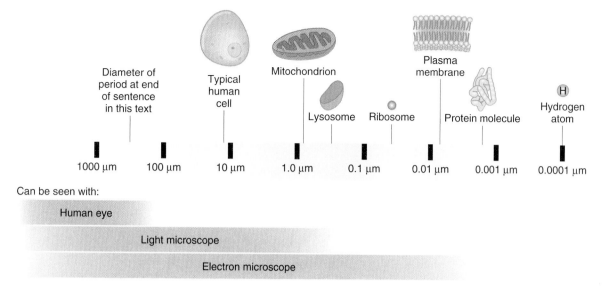

**Sizes of cell structures (logarithmic)**
Figure 3.2

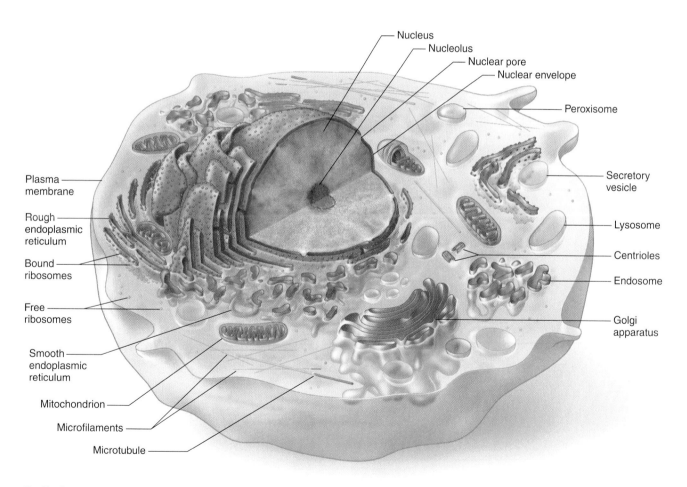

**Cellular structures**
Figure 3.4

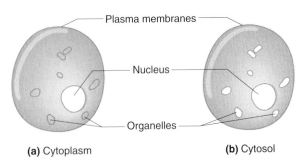

Plasma membranes

Nucleus

Organelles

**(a)** Cytoplasm  **(b)** Cytosol

## Comparison of cytoplasm and cytosol
Figure 3.5

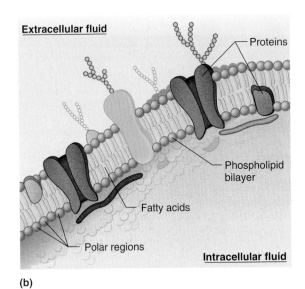

**Extracellular fluid**

Proteins

Phospholipid bilayer

Fatty acids

Polar regions

**Intracellular fluid**

(b)

## Plasma membrane
Figure 3.6

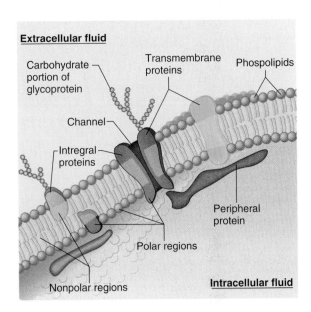

**Extracellular fluid**

Carbohydrate portion of glycoprotein

Transmembrane proteins

Phospolipids

Channel

Intregral proteins

Peripheral protein

Polar regions

Nonpolar regions

**Intracellular fluid**

## Membrane components
Figure 3.7

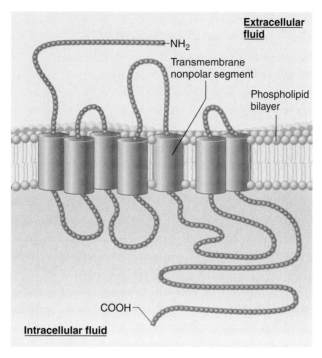

## A typical transmembrane protein
Figure 3.8

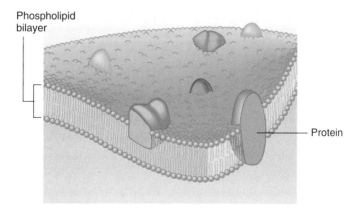

## Fluid-mosaic model of cell membrane structure
Figure 3.9

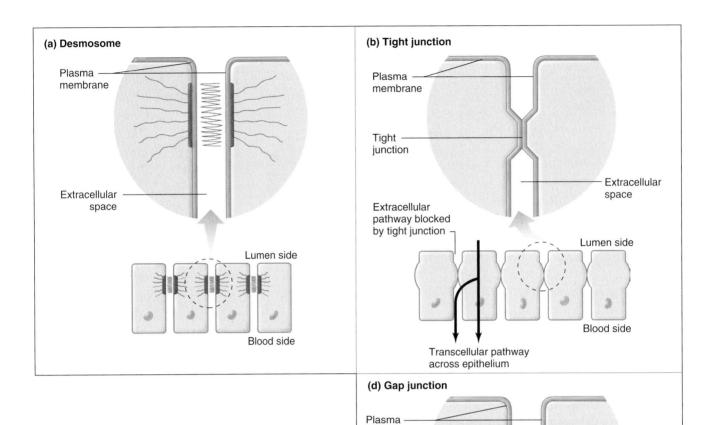

**Three types of specialized membrane junctions**
Figure 3.10

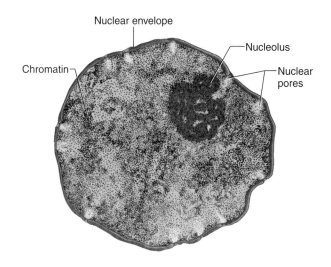

Nuclear envelope

Nucleolus

Chromatin

Nuclear pores

**Nucleolus**

*Structure:* Densely stained filamentous structure within the nucleus. Consists of proteins associated with DNA in regions where information concerning ribosomal proteins is being expressed.

*Function:* Site of ribosomal RNA synthesis. Assembles RNA and protein components of ribosomal subunits, which then move to the cytoplasm through nuclear pores.

## Nucleolus
Figure 3.11

**Rough endoplasmic reticulum**

*Structure:* Extensive membranous network of flattened sacs. Encloses a space that is continuous throughout the organelle and with the space between the two nuclear-envelope membranes. Has ribosomal particles attached to its cytosolic surface.

*Function:* Proteins synthesized on the attached ribosomes enter the lumen of the reticulum from which they are ultimately distributed to other organelles or secreted from the cell.

**Rough endoplasmic reticulum**   **Smooth endoplasmic reticulum**

Ribosomes

**Smooth endoplasmic reticulum**

*Structure:* Highly branched tubular network that does not have attached ribosomes but may be continuous with the rough endoplasmic reticulum.

*Function:* Contains enzymes for fatty acid and steroid synthesis. Stores and releases calcium, which controls various cell activities.

## Endoplasmic reticulum
Figure 3.12

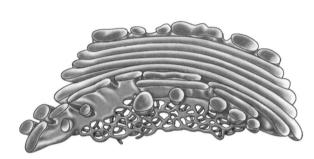

## Golgi apparatus
Figure 3.13

**Golgi apparatus**

*Structure:* Series of cup-shaped, closely apposed, flattened, membranous sacs; associated with numerous vesicles. Generally, a single Golgi apparatus is located in the central portion of a cell near its nucleus.

*Function:* Concentrates, modifies, and sorts proteins arriving from the rough endoplasmic reticulum prior to their distribution, by way of the Golgi vesicles, to other organelles or to secretion from the cell.

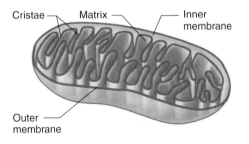

Cristae — Matrix — Inner membrane

Outer membrane

## Mitochondrion
Figure 3.14

**Mitochondrion**

*Structure:* Rod- or oval-shaped body surrounded by two membranes. Inner membrane folds into matrix of the mitochondrion, forming cristae.

*Function:* Major site of ATP production, $O_2$ utilization, and $CO_2$ formation. Contains enzymes active in Krebs cycle and oxidative phosphorylation.

| Cytoskeletal filaments | Diameter (nm) | Protein subunit |
|---|---|---|
| Microfilament | 7 | Actin |
| Intermediate filament | 10 | Several proteins |
| Microtubule | 25 | Tubulin |

**Cytoskeletal filaments**
Figure 3.15

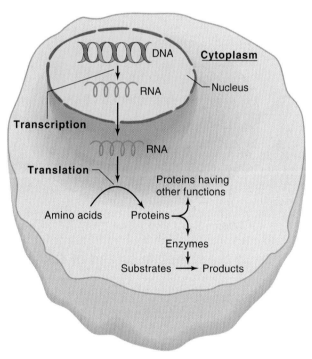

**Transfer of genetic information**
Figure 3.16

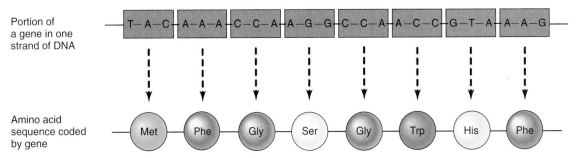

**Portion of a gene in one strand of DNA**

T–A–C  A–A–A  C–C–A  A–G–G  C–C–A  A–C–C  G–T–A  A–A–G

**Amino acid sequence coded by gene**

Met  Phe  Gly  Ser  Gly  Trp  His  Phe

**The sequence of three-letter code words in a gene determines the sequence of amino acids in a polypeptide chain**
Figure 3.17

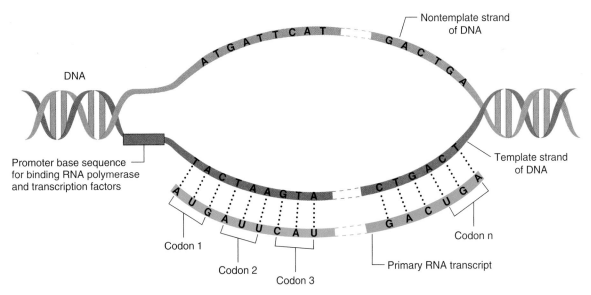

Nontemplate strand of DNA

DNA

Promoter base sequence for binding RNA polymerase and transcription factors

Template strand of DNA

Codon 1

Codon 2

Codon 3

Codon n

Primary RNA transcript

**Transcription of a gene from the template strand of DNA to a primary RNA transcript**
Figure 3.18

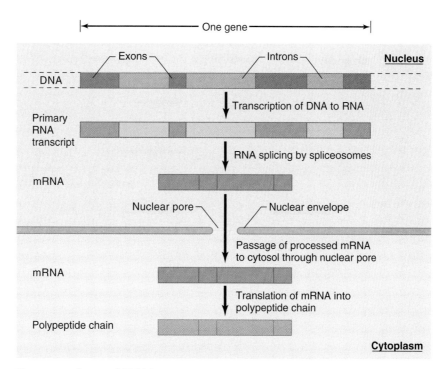

**Processing of DNA**
Figure 3.19

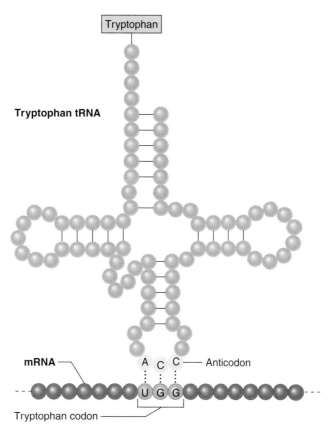

**Base-pairing between anticodon and corresponding codon regions**
Figure 3.20

27

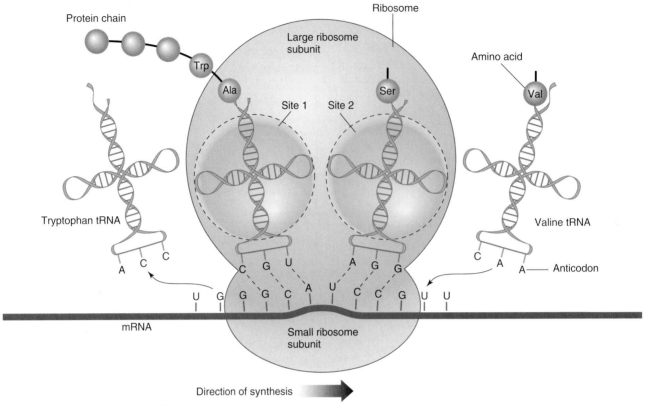

**Protein synthesis in ribosome**
Figure 3.21

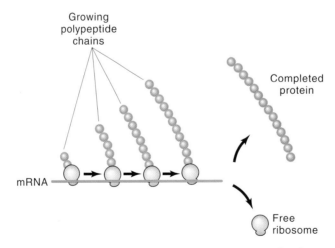

**Ribosome movement along a strand of mRNA**
Figure 3.22

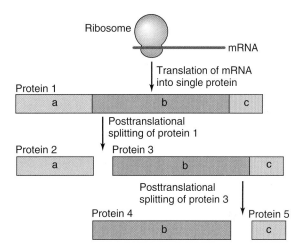

**Posttranslational splitting of a protein**
Figure 3.23

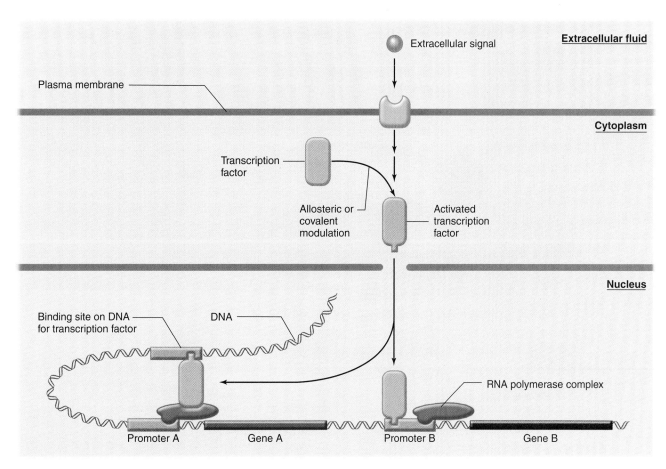

**Transcription and modulation of genes**
Figure 3.24

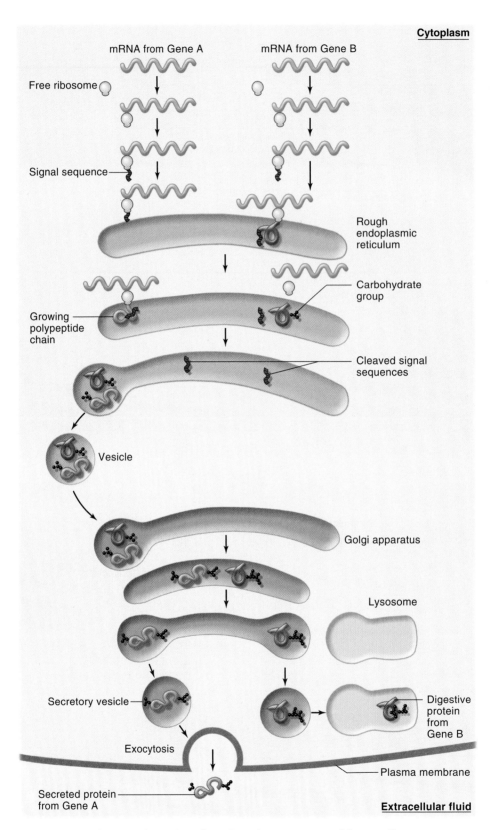

**Pathway of proteins destined to be secreted by cells or transferred to lysosomes**
Figure 3.25

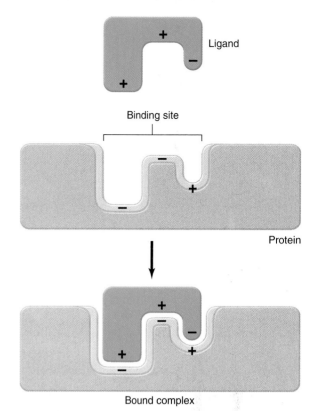

**Complementary shapes of ligand and protein binding site determine the chemical specificity of binding**
Figure 3.26

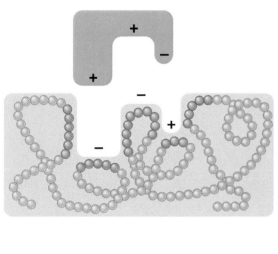

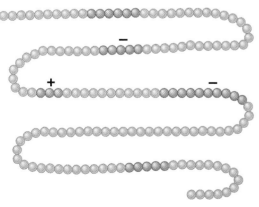

**Protein interactions**
Figure 3.27

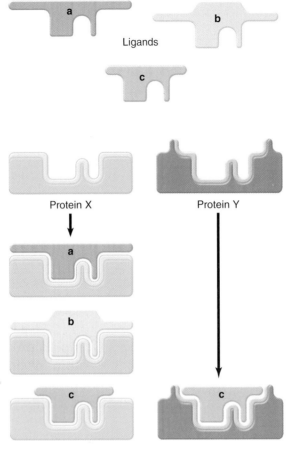

**Binding specificity**
Figure 3.28

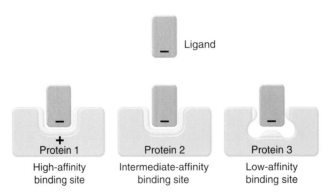

**Three binding sites with the same
chemical specificity for a ligand but
different affinities**
Figure 3.29

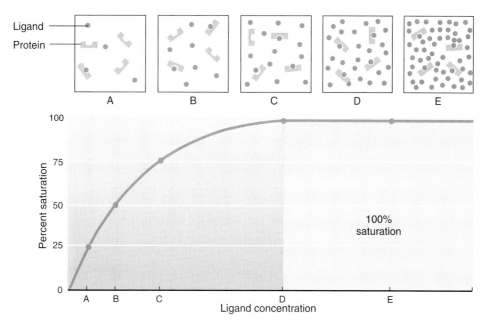

**Saturation binding**

Figure 3.30

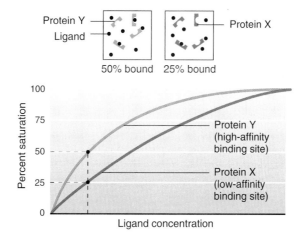

**Binding differences of proteins**

Figure 3.31

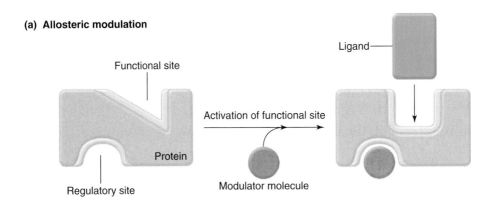

**(a) Allosteric modulation**

Functional site

Protein

Regulatory site

Activation of functional site

Modulator molecule

Ligand

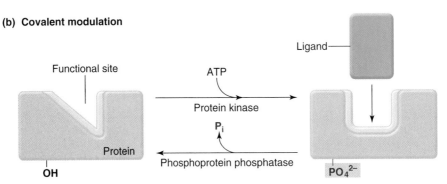

**(b) Covalent modulation**

Functional site

Protein

OH

ATP

Protein kinase

$P_i$

Phosphoprotein phosphatase

Ligand

$PO_4^{2-}$

**(a) Allosteric modulation and (b) covalent modulation of a protein's functional binding site**
Figure 3.32

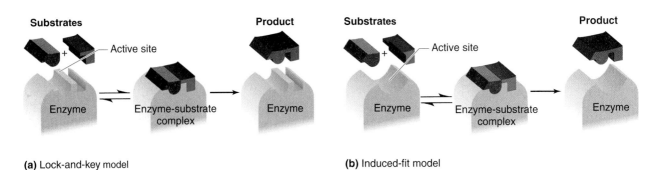

Substrates

Product

Active site

Enzyme

Enzyme-substrate complex

Enzyme

Substrates

Product

Active site

Enzyme

Enzyme-substrate complex

Enzyme

**(a)** Lock-and-key model

**(b)** Induced-fit model

**Binding of substrate to the active site of an enzyme catalyzes the formation of products**
Figure 3.33

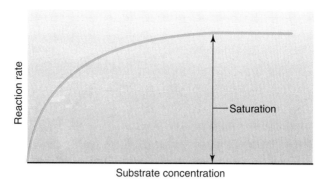

**An enzyme-catalyzed reaction**
Figure 3.34

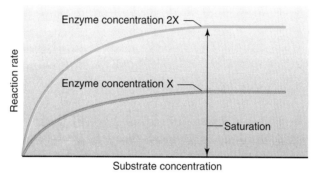

**Reaction rates and substrate concentration**
Figure 3.35

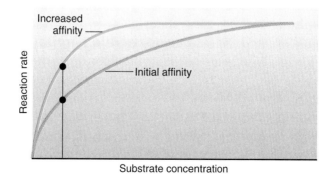

**Enzyme affinity and substrates**
Figure 3.36

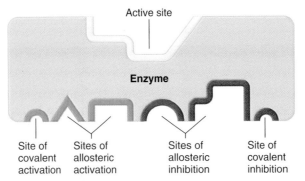

**Multiple sites on a single enzyme**
Figure 3.37

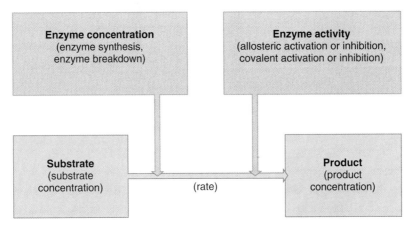

**Factors that affect the rate of enzyme-mediated reactions**
Figure 3.38

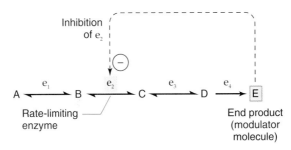

**End-product inhibition**
Figure 3.39

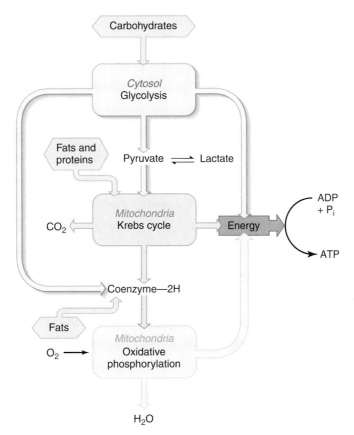

**Pathways linking energy release**
Figure 3.40

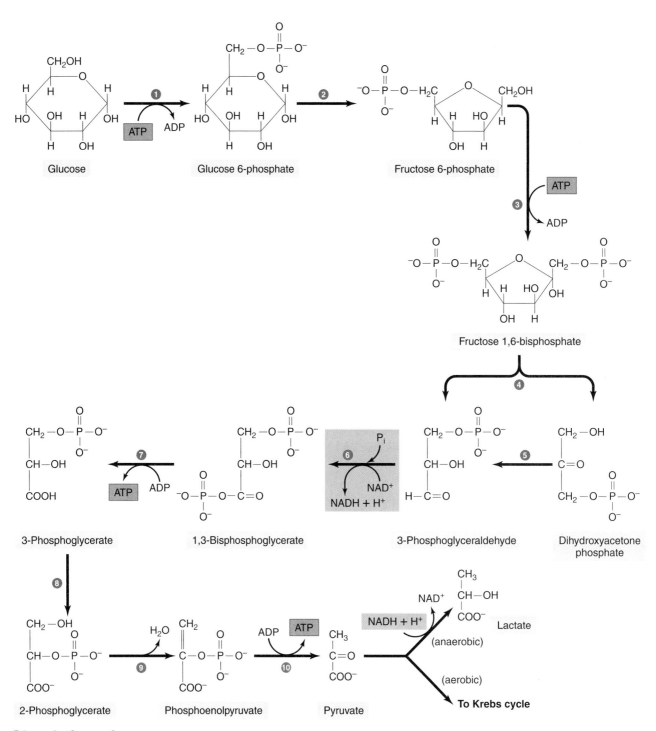

**Glycolytic pathway**
Figure 3.41

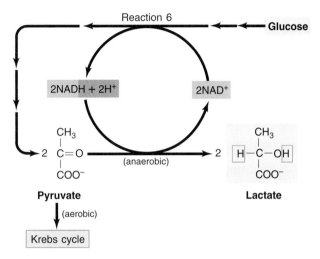

**Lactate formation under anaerobic conditions**
Figure 3.42

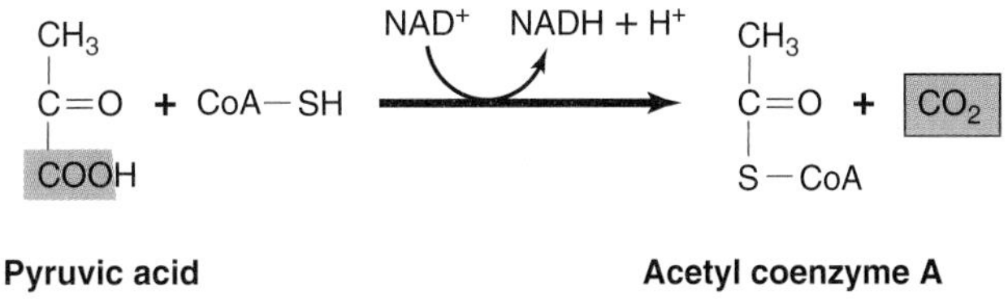

$$CH_3$$
$$C=O + CoA-SH \xrightarrow{\quad\quad\quad} C=O + CO_2$$
$$COOH \quad\quad\quad\quad\quad\quad\quad\quad S-CoA$$

NAD$^+$   NADH + H$^+$

**Pyruvic acid**                    **Acetyl coenzyme A**

**Formation of acetyl coenzyme A from pyruvic acid with the formation of a molecule of carbon dioxide**
Figure 3.43

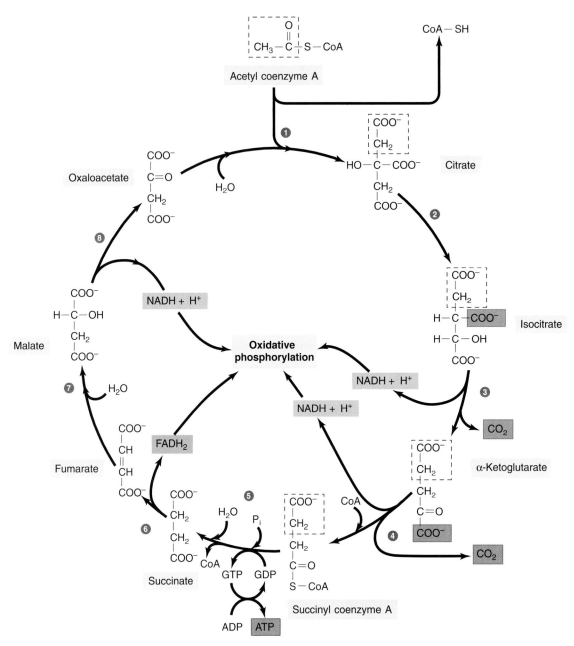

**Krebs cycle**
Figure 3.44

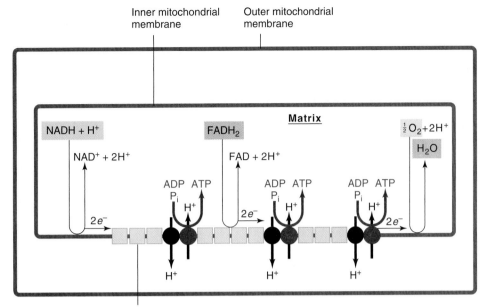

## ATP formation during oxidative phosphorylation
Figure 3.45

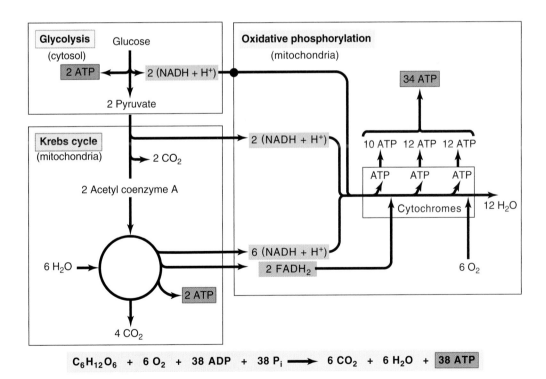

## Pathways of aerobic glucose catabolism
Figure 3.46

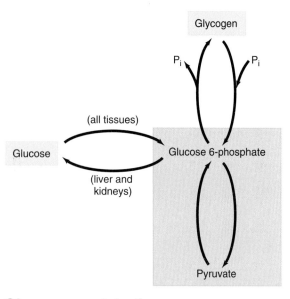

**Glycogen metabolism**
Figure 3.47

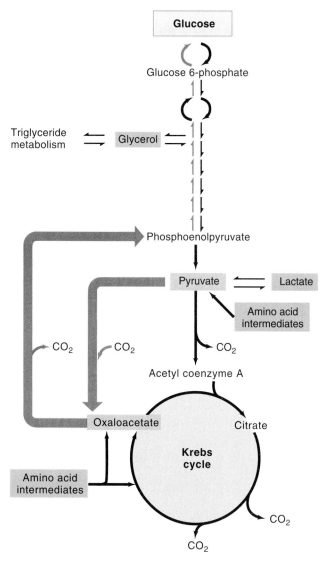

**The liver's gluconeogenic pathway**
Figure 3.48

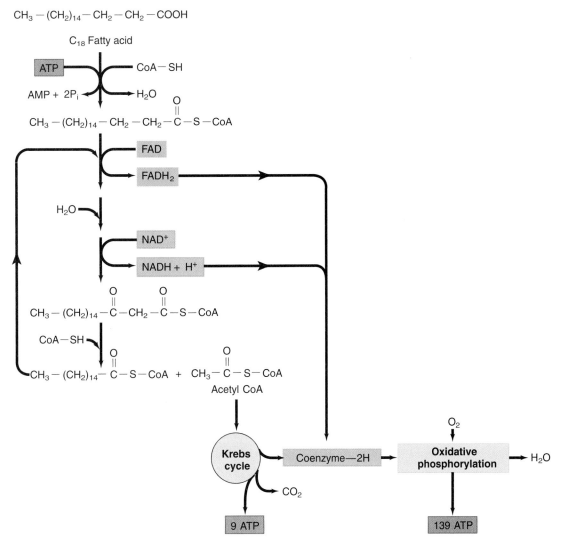

**Pathway of fatty acid catabolism**
Figure 3.49

$$R-\underset{\underset{\boxed{NH_2}}{|}}{CH}-COOH + H_2O + coenzyme \longrightarrow R-\overset{\overset{O}{\|}}{C}-COOH + \boxed{NH_3} + coenzyme-2H$$

Amino acid            Keto acid    Ammonia

Transamination

$$R_1-\underset{\underset{\boxed{NH_2}}{|}}{CH}-COOH + R_2-\overset{\overset{O}{\|}}{C}-COOH \rightleftharpoons R_1-\overset{\overset{O}{\|}}{C}-COOH + R_2-\underset{\underset{\boxed{NH_2}}{|}}{CH}-COOH$$

Amino acid 1     Keto acid 2          Keto acid 1     Amino acid 2

**Oxidative deamination and transamination of amino acids**
Figure 3.50

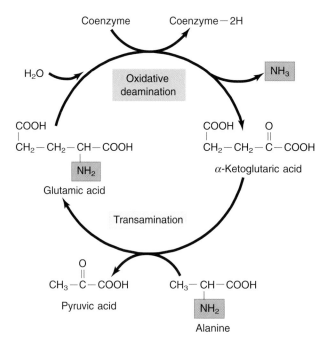

**Oxidative deamination and transamination of amino acids**
Figure 3.51

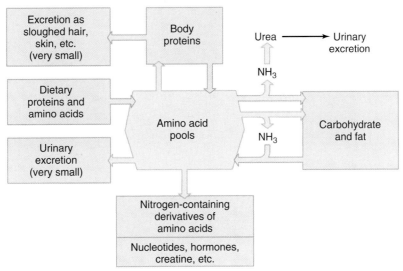

**Amino acid metabolism**

Figure 3.52

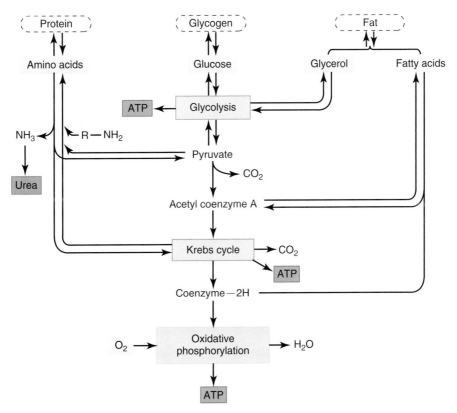

**Interrelations between the pathways for the metabolism of carbohydrate, fat, and protein**

Figure 3.53

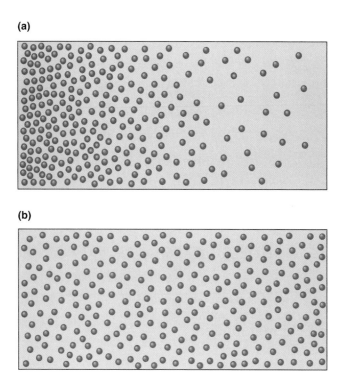

**Diffusion and random thermal motion**
Figure 4.1

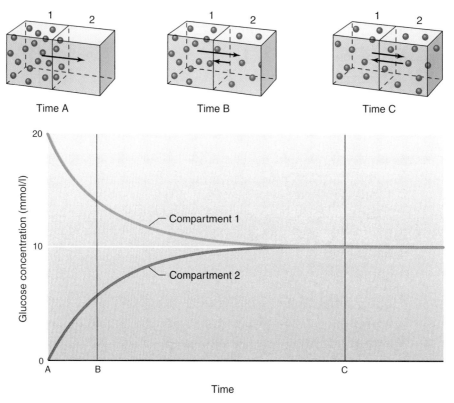

**Diffusion between compartments**
Figure 4.2

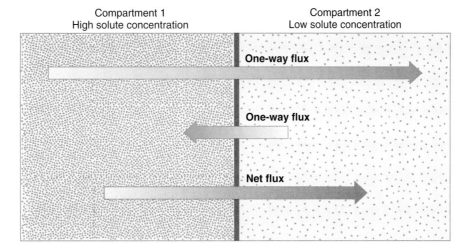

**Net flux**
Figure 4.3

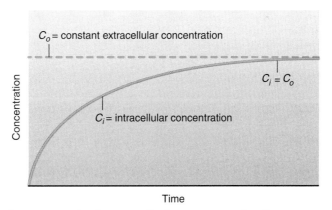

**Increase in intracellular concentration**
Figure 4.4

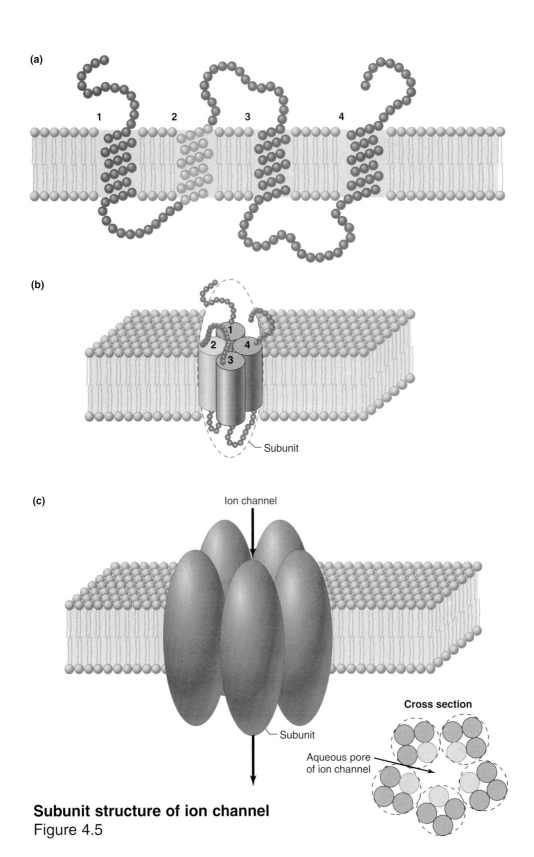

(a)

1  2  3  4

(b)

1
2  4
3

Subunit

(c)

Ion channel

Subunit

Cross section

Aqueous pore of ion channel

**Subunit structure of ion channel**
Figure 4.5

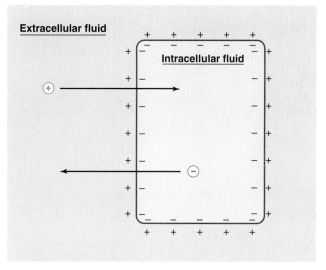

**Charge separation across membrane**
Figure 4.6

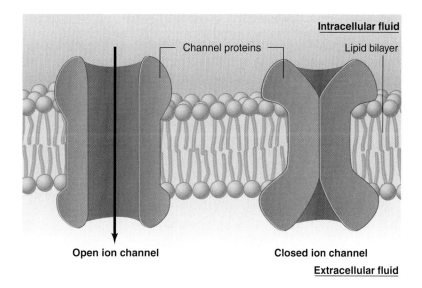

**Channel conformations**
Figure 4.7

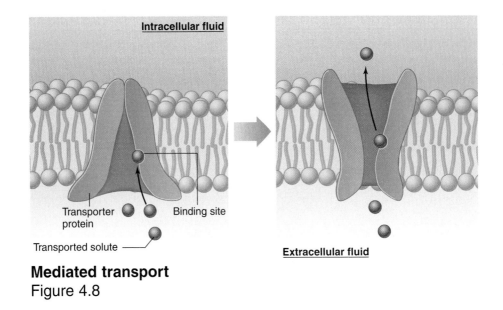

**Mediated transport**

Figure 4.8

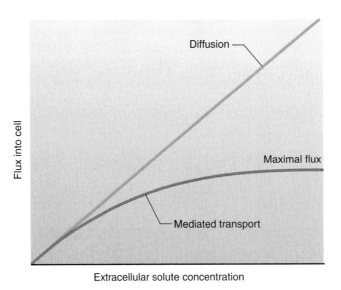

**Flux of molecules diffusing into a cell**

Figure 4.9

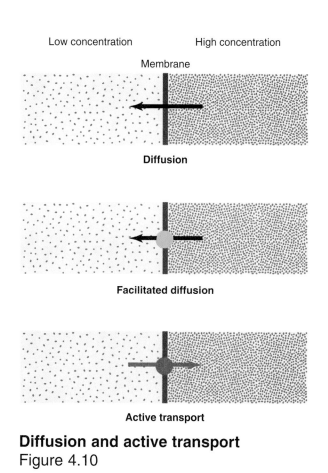

**Diffusion and active transport**
Figure 4.10

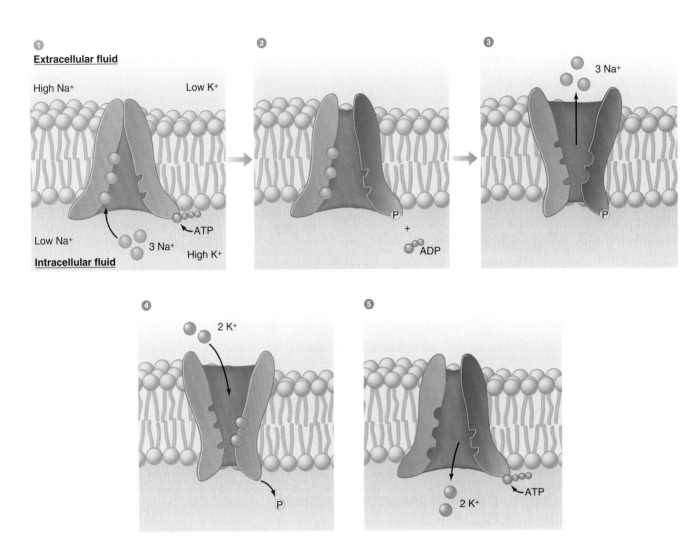

**Model of primary active transport**
Figure 4.11

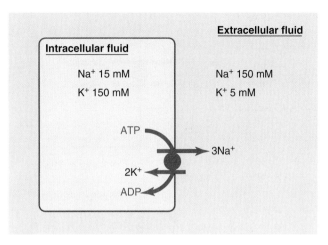

**Primary active transport of sodium and potassium ions**
Figure 4.12

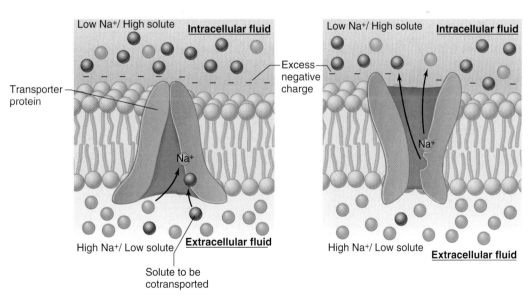

**Model of secondary active transport**
Figure 4.13

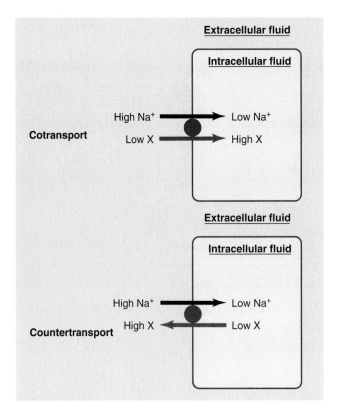

**Coupled transport**

Figure 4.14

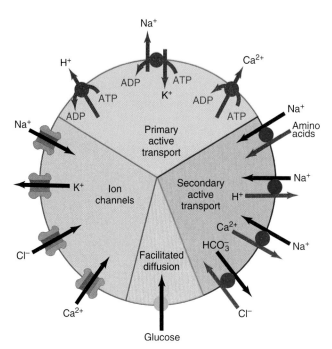

**Movements of solutes across a typical plasma membrane**

Figure 4.15

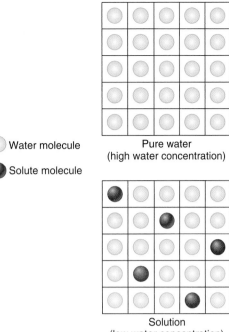

○ Water molecule

● Solute molecule

Pure water
(high water concentration)

Solution
(low water concentration)

**Addition of solute molecules to
pure water**
Figure 4.16

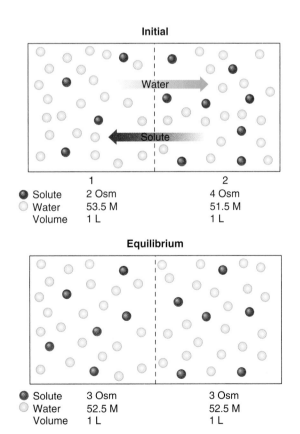

Initial

Water

Solute

|  |  | 1 | 2 |
|---|---|---|---|
| ● | Solute | 2 Osm | 4 Osm |
| ○ | Water | 53.5 M | 51.5 M |
|  | Volume | 1 L | 1 L |

Equilibrium

|  |  |  |  |
|---|---|---|---|
| ● | Solute | 3 Osm | 3 Osm |
| ○ | Water | 52.5 M | 52.5 M |
|  | Volume | 1 L | 1 L |

**Diffusion of water and solute across
a membrane permeable to both**
Figure 4.17

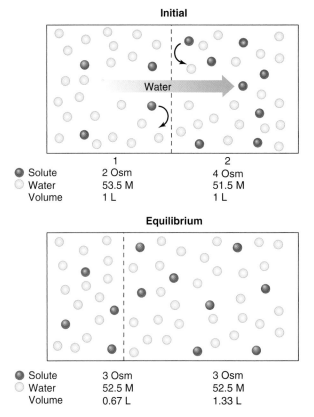

**Initial**

|  | 1 | 2 |
|---|---|---|
| ● Solute | 2 Osm | 4 Osm |
| ○ Water | 53.5 M | 51.5 M |
| Volume | 1 L | 1 L |

Water

**Equilibrium**

|  |  |  |
|---|---|---|
| ● Solute | 3 Osm | 3 Osm |
| ○ Water | 52.5 M | 52.5 M |
| Volume | 0.67 L | 1.33 L |

**Water movement across semi-permeable membrane**

Figure 4.18

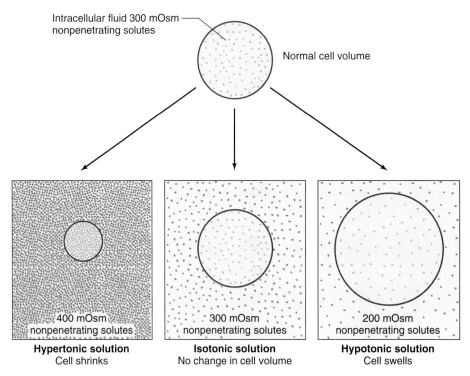

Intracellular fluid 300 mOsm nonpenetrating solutes

Normal cell volume

400 mOsm nonpenetrating solutes

**Hypertonic solution**
Cell shrinks

300 mOsm nonpenetrating solutes

**Isotonic solution**
No change in cell volume

200 mOsm nonpenetrating solutes

**Hypotonic solution**
Cell swells

**Tonicity and cell shape**

Figure 4.19

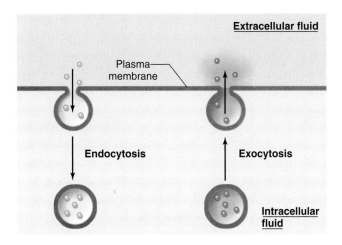

**Endocytosis and exocytosis**
Figure 4.20

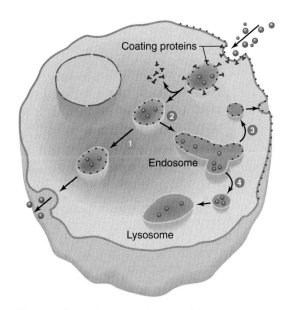

**Fate of endocytotic vesicles**
Figure 4.21

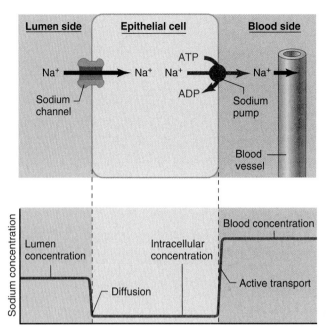

**Active transport of sodium across an epithelial cell**

Figure 4.22

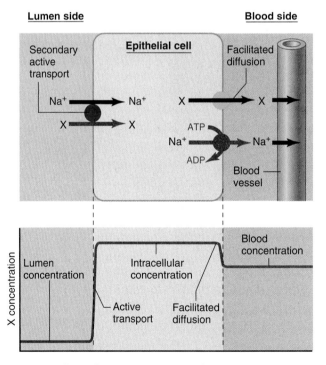

**Transepithelial transport of most organic solutes**

Figure 4.23

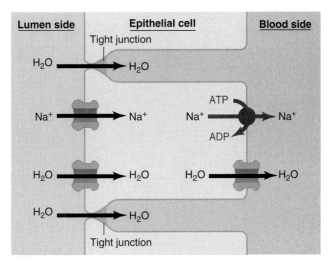

**Net movements of water across an epithelium**
Figure 4.24

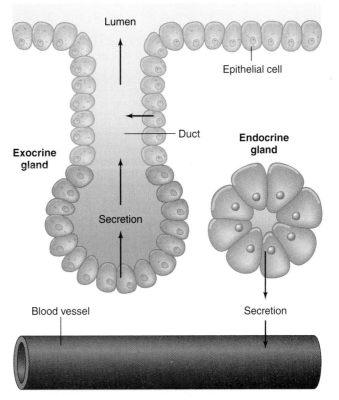

**Exocrine and endocrine glands**
Figure 4.25

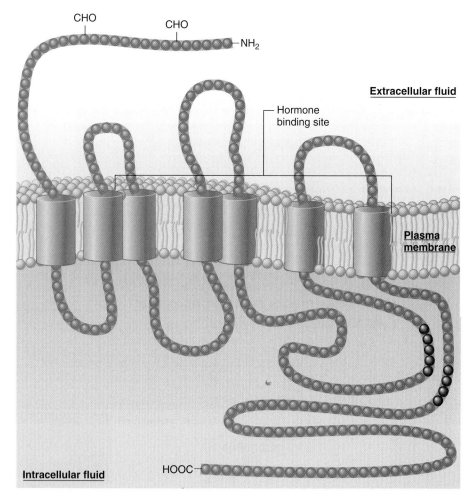

CHO          CHO
                —NH₂

Extracellular fluid

Hormone
binding site

Plasma
membrane

Intracellular fluid          HOOC

**Membrane receptor structure**
Figure 5.1

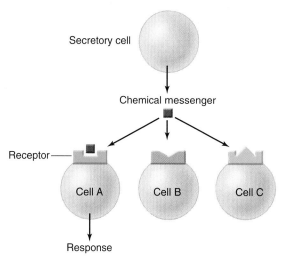

Secretory cell

Chemical messenger

Receptor

Cell A        Cell B        Cell C

Response

**Specificity of receptors for chemical messengers**
Figure 5.2

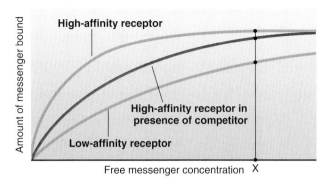

## Characteristics of receptor binding to messengers
Figure 5.3

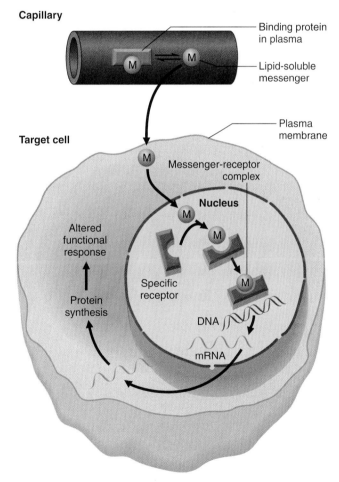

## Action of lipid-soluble messengers
Figure 5.4

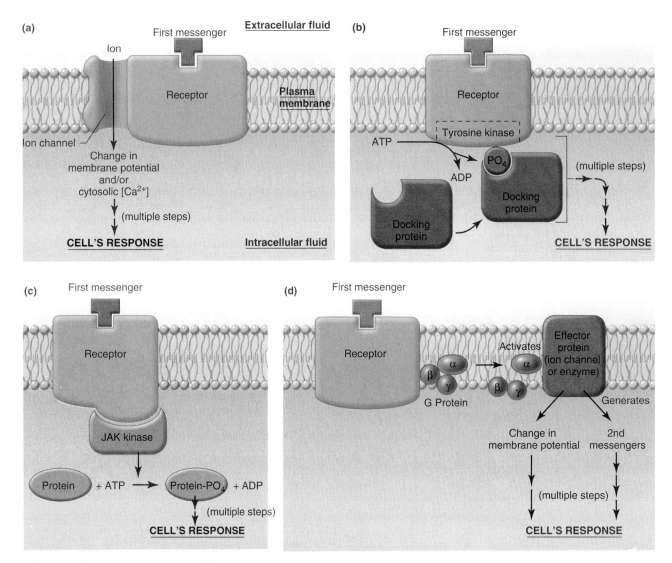

**Mechanisms of action of lipid-insoluble messengers**
Figure 5.5

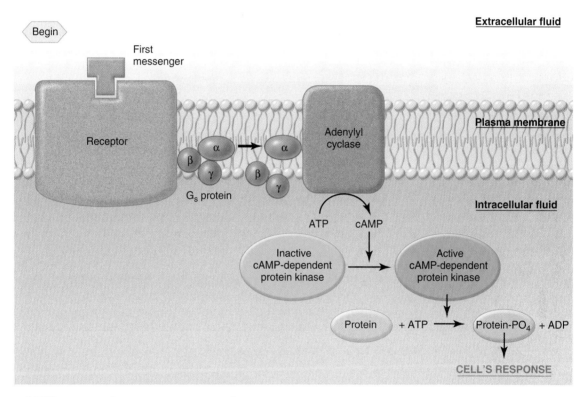

**cAMP second-messenger system**
Figure 5.6

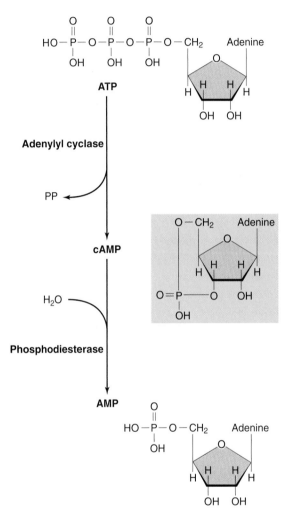

**Structure of ATP, cAMP, and AMP**
Figure 5.7

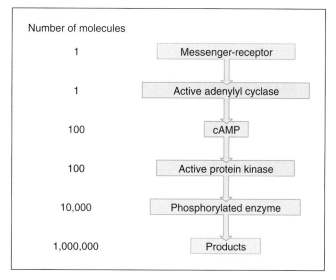

**Example of amplification in the cAMP system**
Figure 5.8

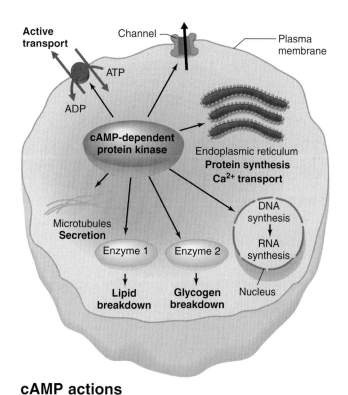

**cAMP actions**
Figure 5.9

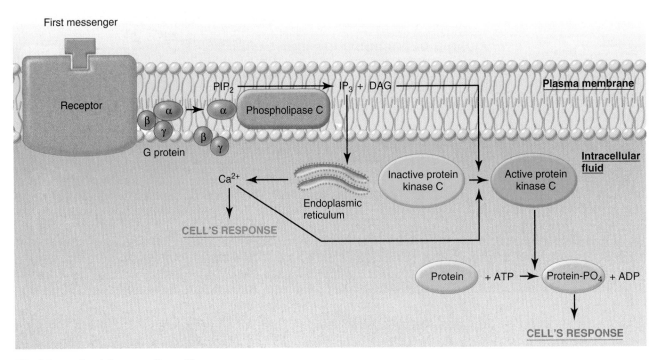

**IP₃/Protein kinase C pathway**
Figure 5.10

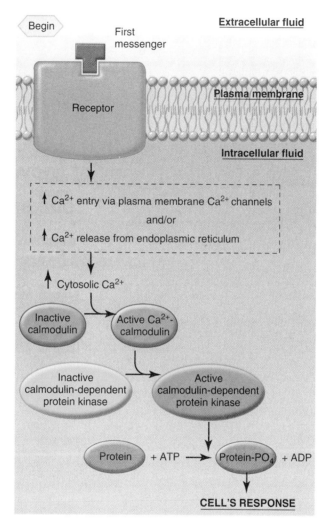

**Calcium, calmodulin, and the calmodulin-dependent protein kinase system**

Figure 5.11

## Pathways for the synthesis of eicosanoids
### Figure 5.12

Begin

First messenger

Receptor

Phospholipase A₂
⊕

Membrane phospholipid

↓

Arachidonic acid

Cyclooxygenase

Cyclic endoperoxides

Lipoxygenase

Prostaglandins    Thromboxanes

Leukotrienes

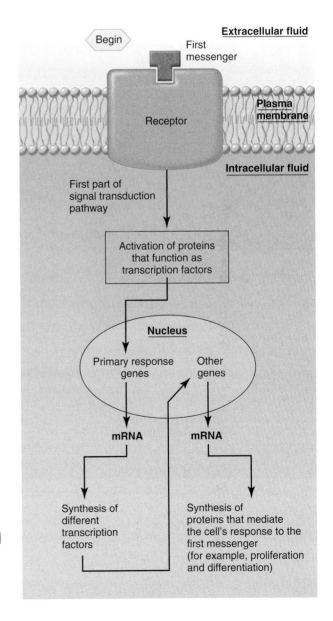

## Role of multiple transcription factors and primary response genes in mediating protein synthesis
### Figure 5.13

Begin

First messenger

Extracellular fluid

Receptor

Plasma membrane

Intracellular fluid

First part of signal transduction pathway

Activation of proteins that function as transcription factors

**Nucleus**

Primary response genes        Other genes

mRNA                           mRNA

Synthesis of different transcription factors

Synthesis of proteins that mediate the cell's response to the first messenger (for example, proliferation and differentiation)

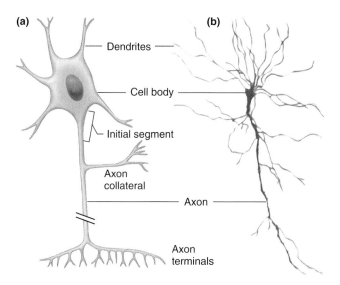

**Features of neurons**
Figure 6.1

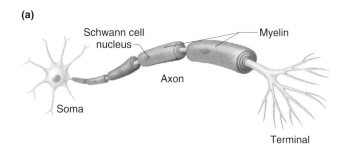

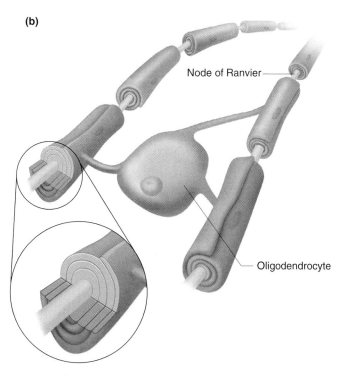

**Myelin formation**
Figure 6.2

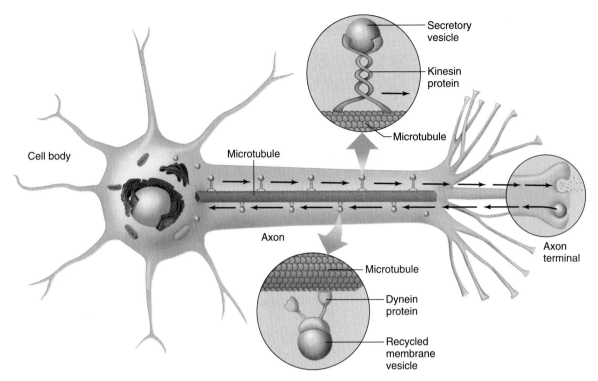

**Axonal transport along microtubules by dynein and kinesin**
Figure 6.3

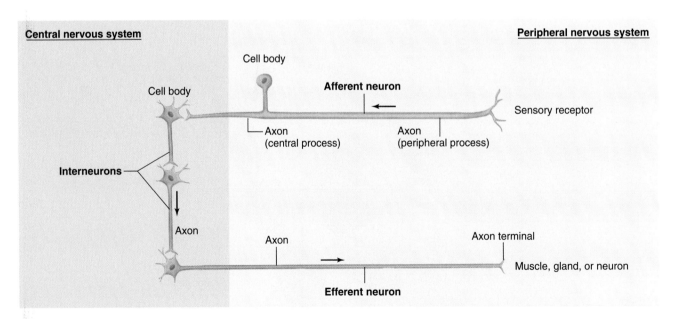

**Types of neurons**
Figure 6.4

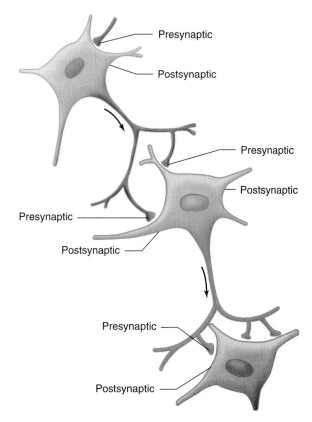

Presynaptic

Postsynaptic

Presynaptic

Postsynaptic

Presynaptic

Postsynaptic

Presynaptic

Postsynaptic

**A neuron postsynaptic to one cell can be presynaptic to another**
Figure 6.5

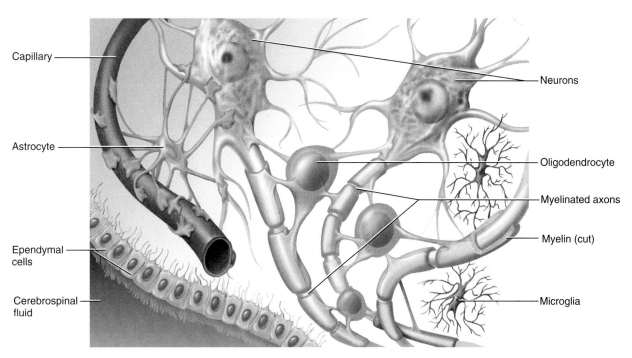

Capillary

Astrocyte

Ependymal
cells

Cerebrospinal
fluid

Neurons

Oligodendrocyte

Myelinated axons

Myelin (cut)

Microglia

**Glial cells of the central nervous system**
Figure 6.6

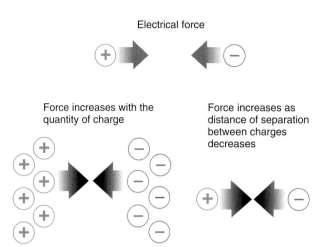

Electrical force

Force increases with the quantity of charge

Force increases as distance of separation between charges decreases

**Attraction between positive and negative charges**
Figure 6.7

(a)

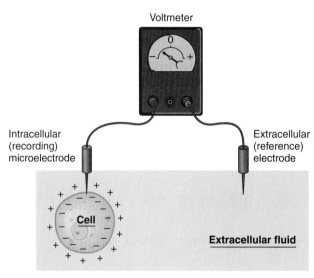

Voltmeter

Intracellular (recording) microelectrode

Extracellular (reference) electrode

Cell

**Extracellular fluid**

(b)

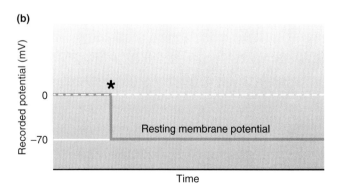

Recorded potential (mV)

0

*

−70

Resting membrane potential

Time

**(a) Apparatus for measuring membrane potentials (b) The potential difference across a plasma membrane**
Figure 6.8

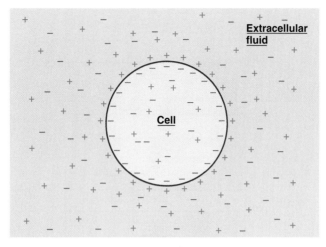

**Excess of positive and negative charges and the cell's plasma membrane**
Figure 6.9

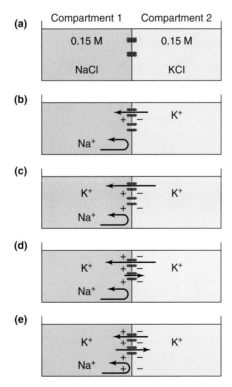

**Generation of diffusion potential**
Figure 6.10

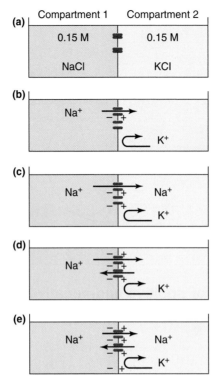

**Generation of a potential across a membrane**

Figure 6.11

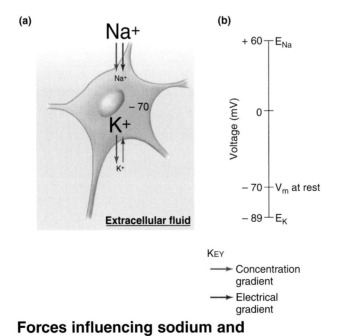

**Forces influencing sodium and potassium ions at the resting membrane potential**

Figure 6.12

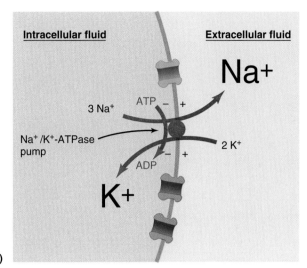

**(a)**

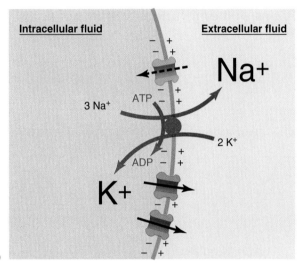

**(b)**

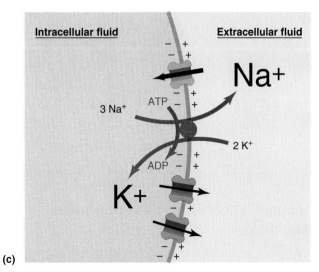

**(c)**

# Summary of steps establishing the resting membrane potential
Figure 6.13

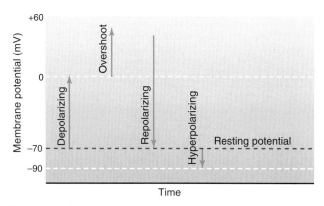

**Types of membrane potentials**
Figure 6.14

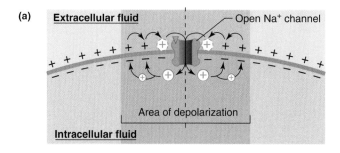

**(a)**

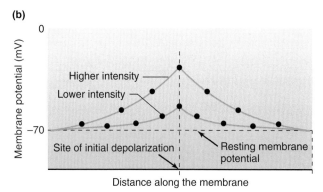

**(b)**

**Depolarization of a cell's membrane potential**
Figure 6.15

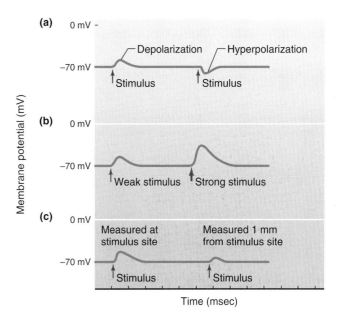

**Graded potentials**
Figure 6.16

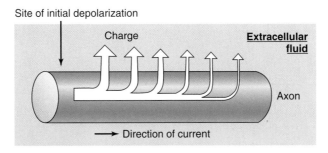

**Leakage of charge**
Figure 6.17

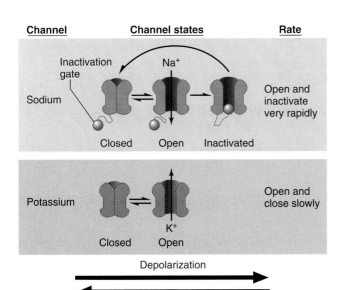

**Behavior of voltage-gated sodium and potassium channels**
Figure 6.18

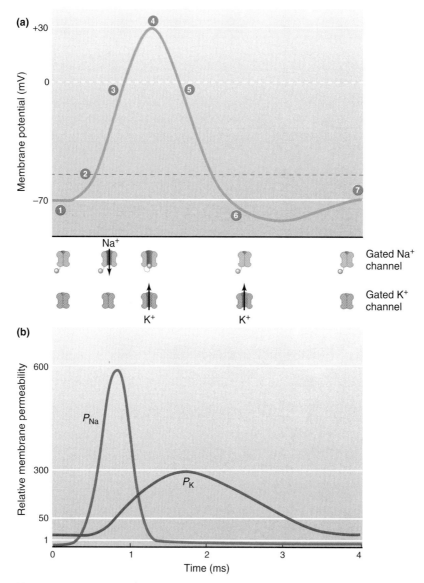

**The changes in (a) membrane potential (mV) and (b) relative membrane permeability (P) to sodium and potassium ions**

Figure 6.19

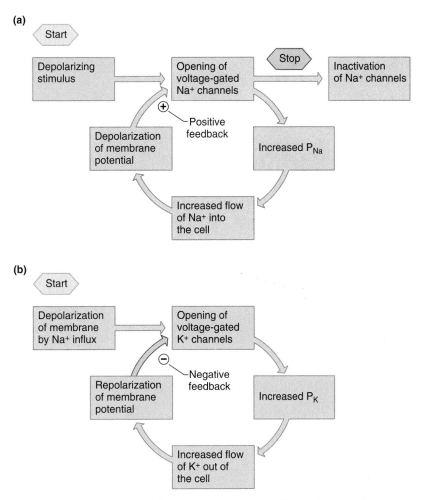

**Feedback control in voltage-gated ion channels**
Figure 6.20

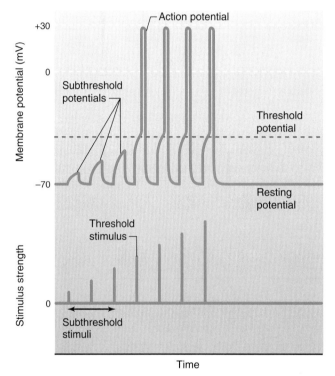

**Membrane potentials and stimulus strength**
Figure 6.21

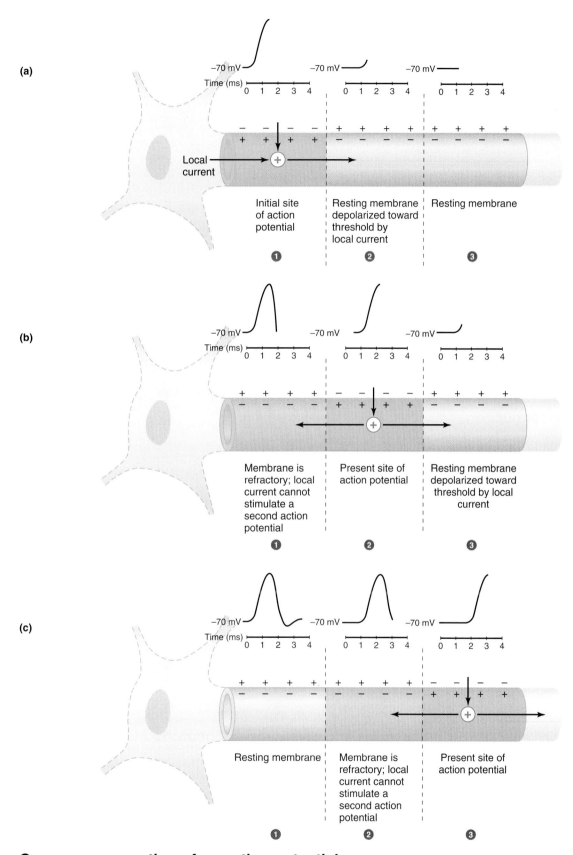

**One-way propagation of an action potential**
Figure 6.22

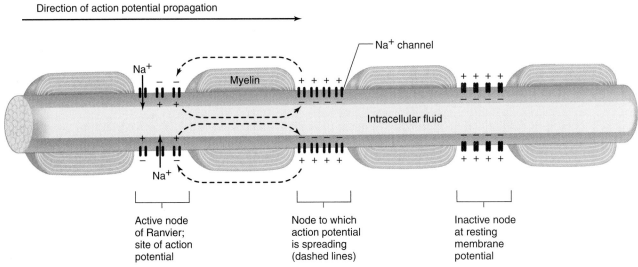

Direction of action potential propagation

Na⁺ channel

Na⁺

Myelin

Na⁺

Intracellular fluid

Active node
of Ranvier;
site of action
potential

Node to which
action potential
is spreading
(dashed lines)

Inactive node
at resting
membrane
potential

**Saltatory conduction**
Figure 6.23

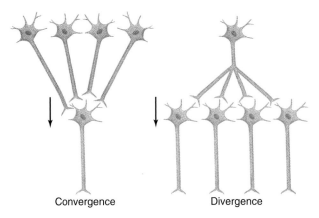

Convergence

Divergence

**Convergence and divergence of neurons**
Figure 6.24

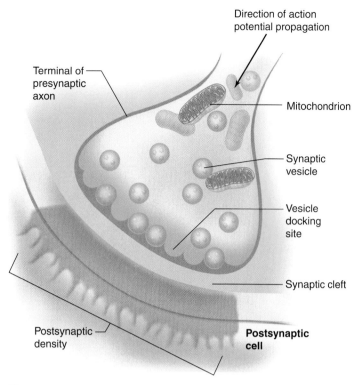

Direction of action
potential propagation

Terminal of
presynaptic
axon

Mitochondrion

Synaptic
vesicle

Vesicle
docking
site

Synaptic cleft

Postsynaptic
density

**Postsynaptic
cell**

**Synapse**
Figure 6.25

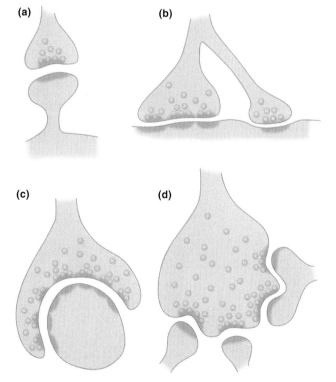

(a)

(b)

(c)

(d)

**Neurotransmitter storage and secretion**
Figure 6.26

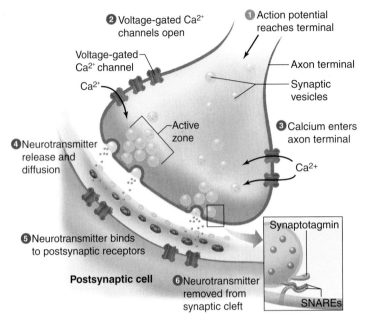

**Neurotransmitter storage and release**
Figure 6.27

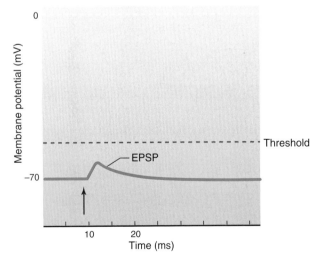

**Excitatory postsynaptic potential (EPSP)**
Figure 6.28

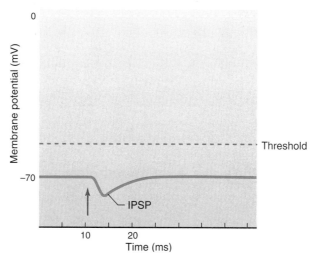

**Inhibitory postsynaptic potential (IPSP)**
Figure 6.29

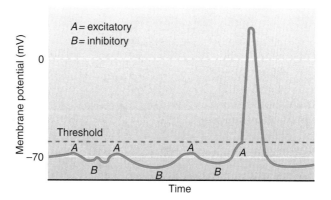

**Intracellular recording from a postsynaptic cell**
Figure 6.30

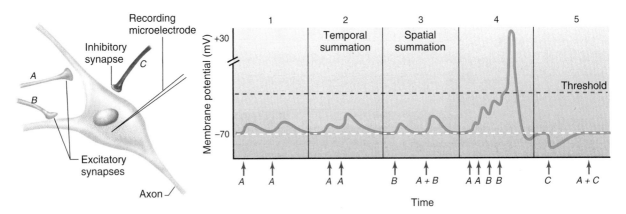

**Interaction of EPSPs and IPSPs at the postsynaptic neuron**
Figure 6.31

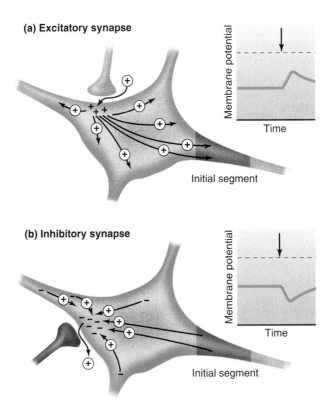

**Excitatory and inhibitory synapses**
Figure 6.32

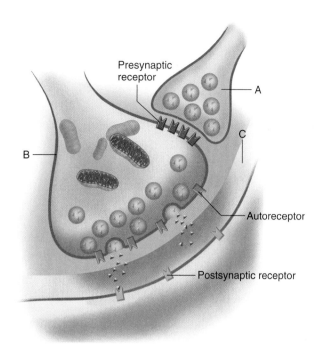

**A presynaptic (axo-axonic) synapse**
Figure 6.33

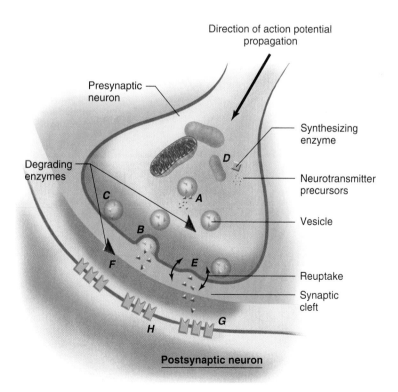

**Possible actions of drugs on a synapse**
Figure 6.34

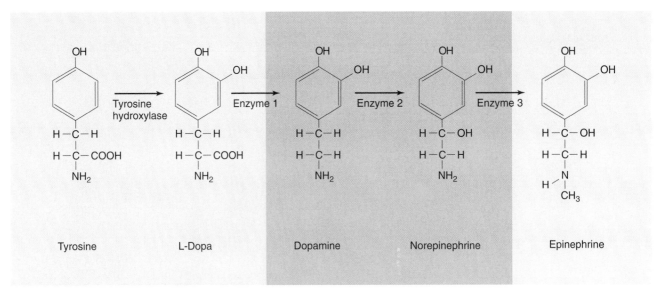

**Catecholamine biosynthetic pathway**
Figure 6.35

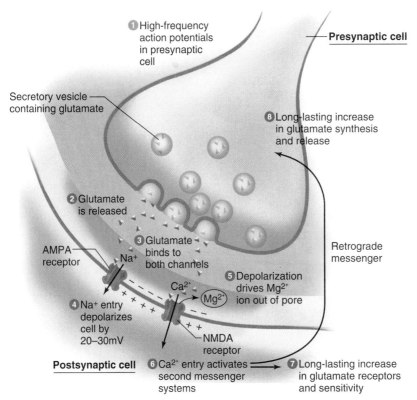

**Long-term potentiation at glutamatergic synapses**
Figure 6.36

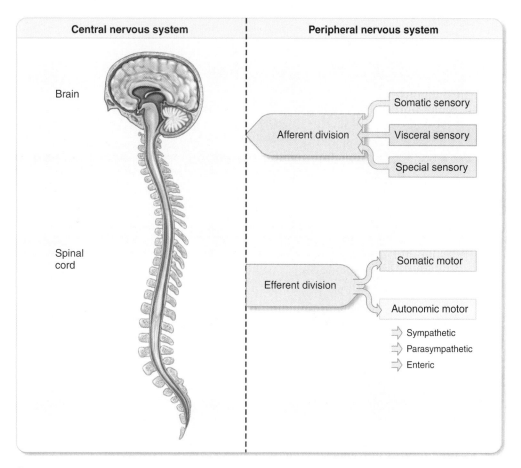

| Central nervous system | Peripheral nervous system |
|---|---|

Brain

Spinal cord

Afferent division
- Somatic sensory
- Visceral sensory
- Special sensory

Efferent division
- Somatic motor
- Autonomic motor
  - Sympathetic
  - Parasympathetic
  - Enteric

**Overview of the structural and functional organization of the nervous system**
Figure 6.37

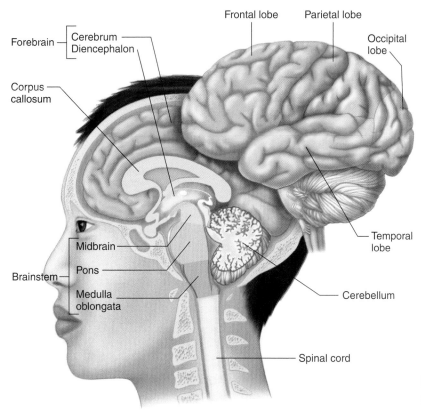

Forebrain
- Cerebrum
- Diencephalon

Frontal lobe

Parietal lobe

Occipital lobe

Corpus callosum

Midbrain

Pons

Brainstem

Medulla oblongata

Temporal lobe

Cerebellum

Spinal cord

**Overview of brain structure**
Figure 6.38

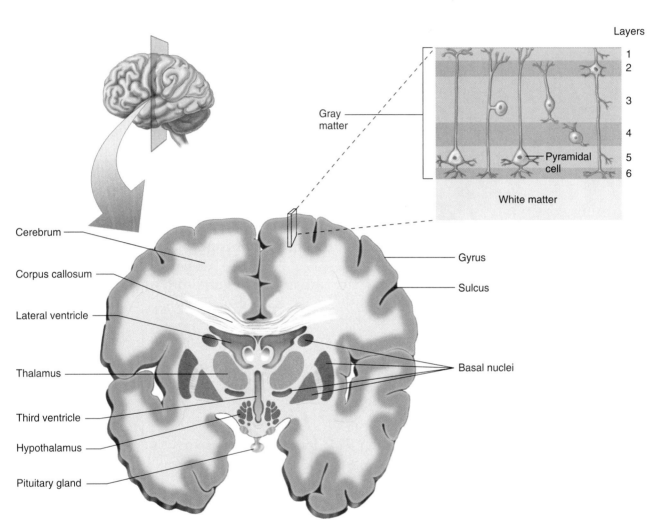

**Frontal section of the forebrain showing interior structures and the six-layer organization of the cerebral cortex**

Figure 6.39

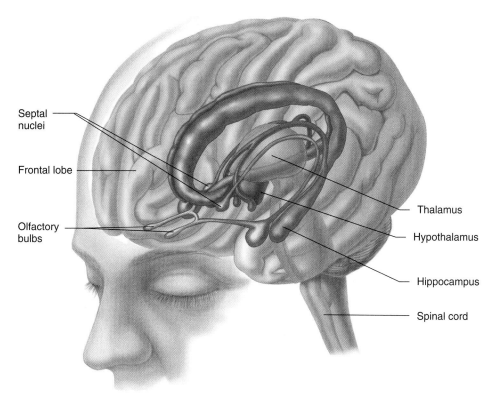

Septal
nuclei

Frontal lobe

Olfactory
bulbs

Thalamus

Hypothalamus

Hippocampus

Spinal cord

**Limbic system**
Figure 6.40

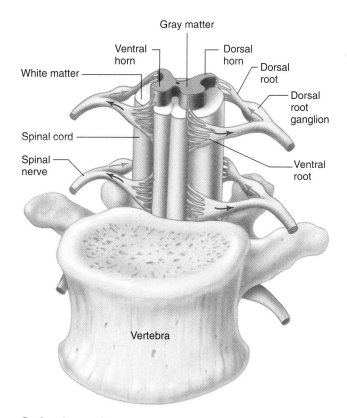

Gray matter

Ventral
horn

Dorsal
horn

White matter

Dorsal
root

Dorsal
root
ganglion

Spinal cord

Spinal
nerve

Ventral
root

Vertebra

**Spinal cord**
Figure 6.41

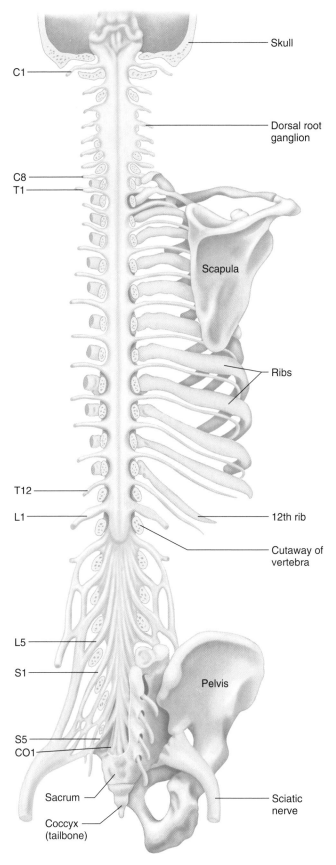

**Dorsal view of spinal cord**
Figure 6.42

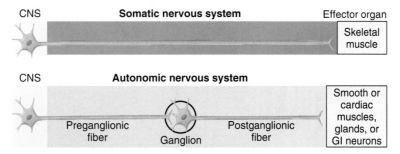

**Efferent division of peripheral nervous system**
Figure 6.43

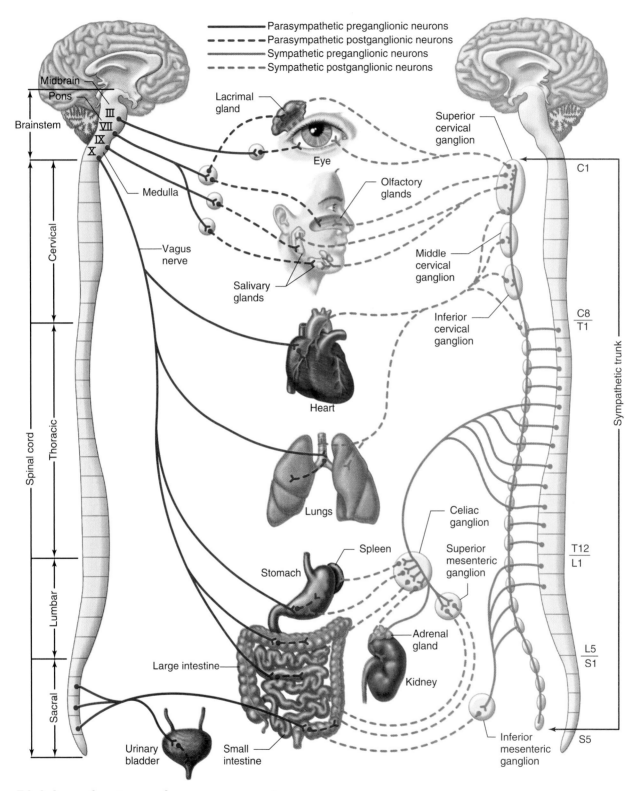

**Division of autonomic nervous system**
Figure 6.44

94

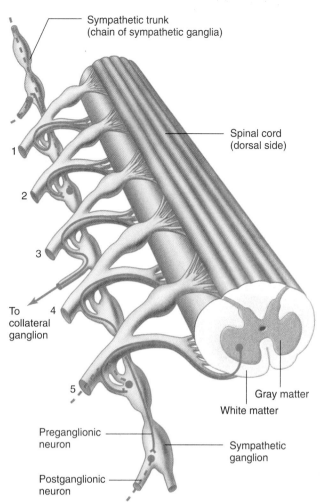

Symparthetic trunk
(chain of sympathetic ganglia)

Spinal cord
(dorsal side)

1

2

3

To
collateral
ganglion

4

5

Gray matter

White matter

Preganglionic
neuron

Sympathetic
ganglion

Postganglionic
neuron

**Relationship between a sympathetic
trunk and spinal nerves**
Figure 6.45

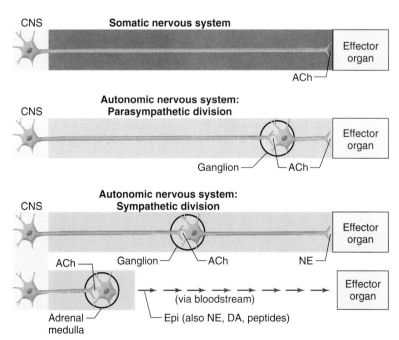

CNS

**Somatic nervous system**

Effector
organ

ACh

CNS

**Autonomic nervous system:
Parasympathetic division**

Effector
organ

Ganglion — ACh

CNS

**Autonomic nervous system:
Sympathetic division**

Effector
organ

Ganglion — ACh

NE

ACh

Effector
organ

(via bloodstream)

Adrenal
medulla

Epi (also NE, DA, peptides)

**Transmitters used in the various components
of the peripheral efferent nervous system**
Figure 6.46

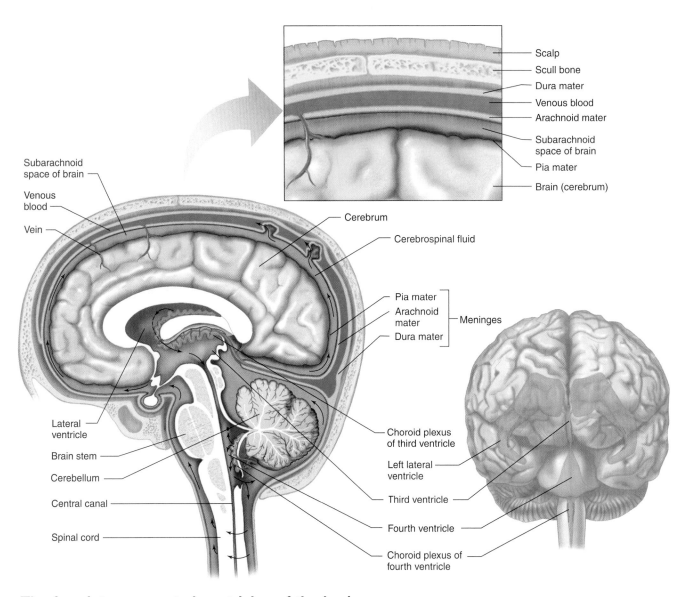

**The four interconnected ventricles of the brain**

Figure 6.47

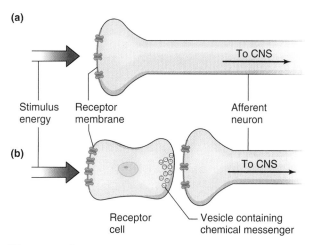

(a)

To CNS

Stimulus energy

Receptor membrane

Afferent neuron

(b)

To CNS

Receptor cell

Vesicle containing chemical messenger

## Types of sensory receptors
Figure 7.1

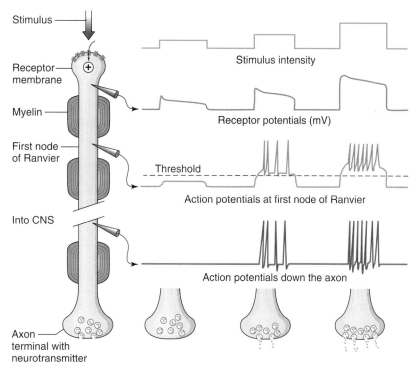

Stimulus

Receptor membrane

Stimulus intensity

Myelin

Receptor potentials (mV)

First node of Ranvier

Threshold

Action potentials at first node of Ranvier

Into CNS

Action potentials down the axon

Axon terminal with neurotransmitter

## Stimulation of an afferent neuron with a receptor ending
Figure 7.2

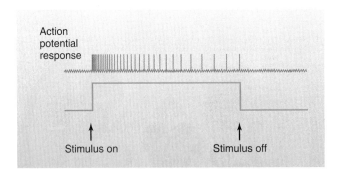

**Action potentials in a single afferent
nerve fiber**
Figure 7.3

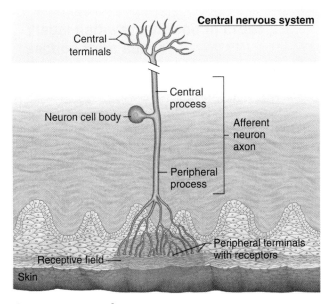

**A sensory unit**
Figure 7.4

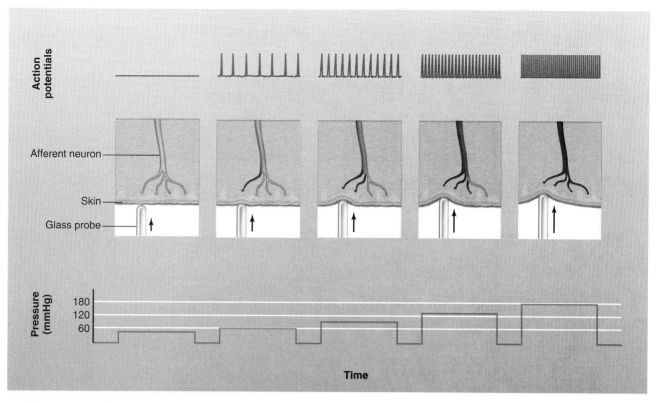

**Action potentials**

Figure 7.5

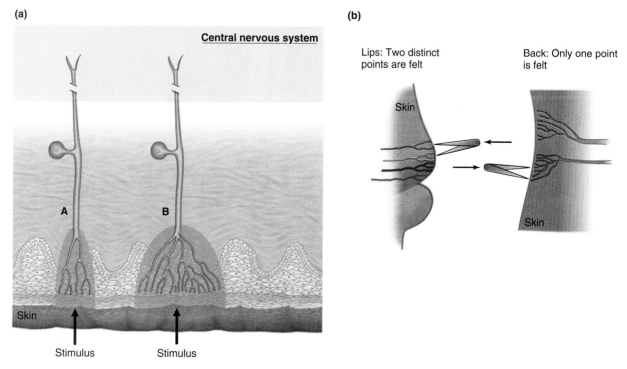

**The influence of sensory unit size and density on acuity**

Figure 7.6

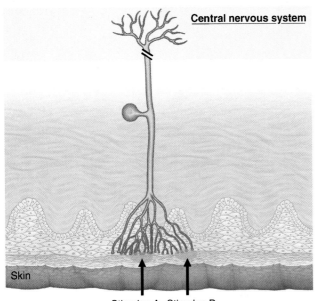

**Two stimulus points**
Figure 7.7

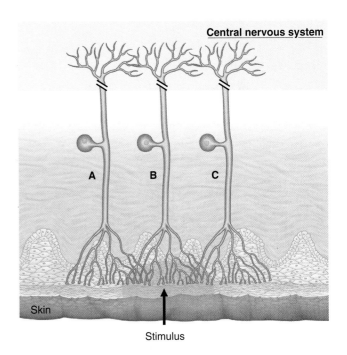

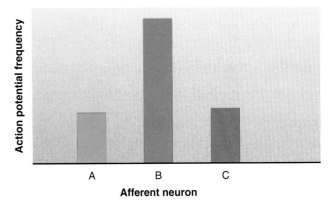

**A stimulus point in overlapping receptive fields**
Figure 7.8

## Afferent pathways showing lateral inhibition
### Figure 7.9

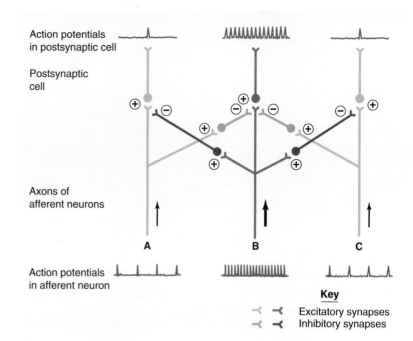

Action potentials in postsynaptic cell

Postsynaptic cell

Axons of afferent neurons

A    B    C

Action potentials in afferent neuron

**Key**
Excitatory synapses
Inhibitory synapses

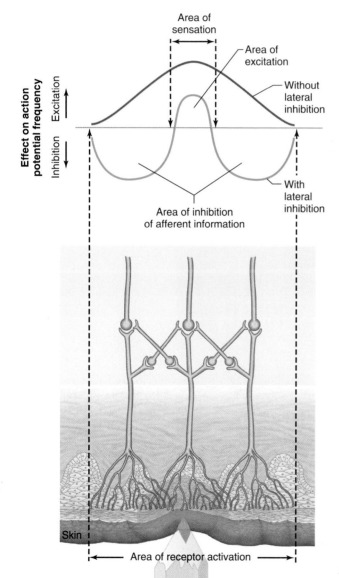

Area of sensation

Area of excitation

Without lateral inhibition

Effect on action potential frequency

Excitation

Inhibition

Area of inhibition of afferent information

With lateral inhibition

Skin

Area of receptor activation

## A pencil tip pressed against the skin
### Figure 7.10

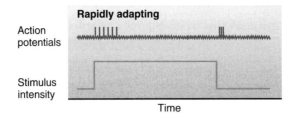

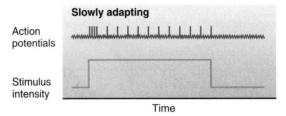

**Rapidly and slowly adapting receptors**

Figure 7.11

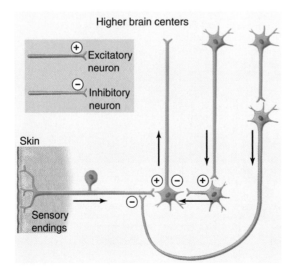

**Descending pathways may influence sensory information**

Figure 7.12

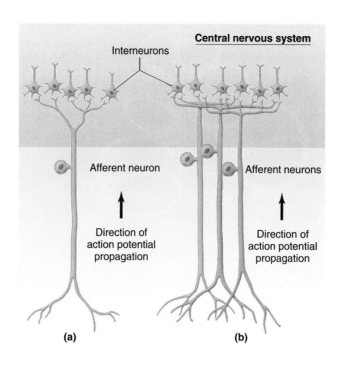

**Divergence and convergence of an afferent neuron**
Figure 7.13

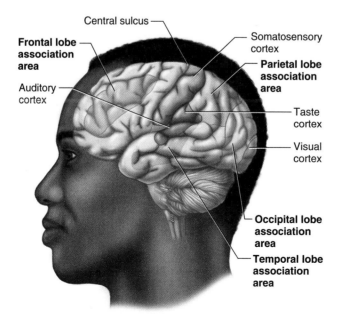

**Sensory areas of the brain**
Figure 7.14

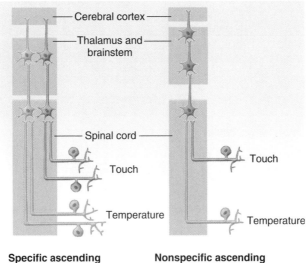

**Specific and nonspecific sensory pathways**
Figure 7.15

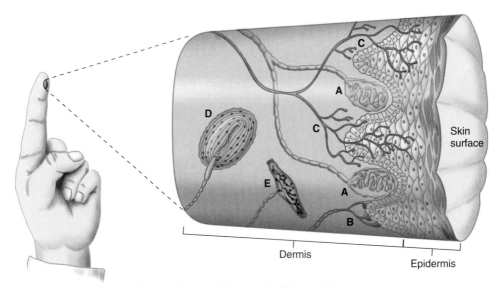

A – Tactile (Meissner's) corpuscle  (light touch)
B – Tactile (Merkle's) corpuscles  (touch)
C – Free nerve ending  (pain)
D – Lamellated (Pacinian) corpuscle  (vibration and deep pressure)
E – Ruffini corpuscle  (warmth)

**Skin receptors**
Figure 7.16

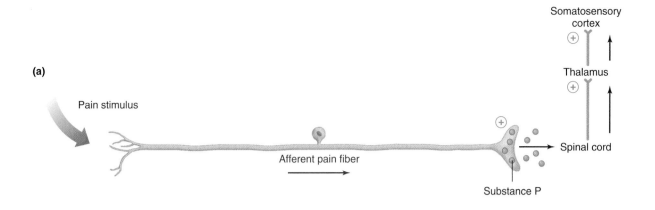

(a)

Pain stimulus

Afferent pain fiber

Substance P

Spinal cord

Somatosensory cortex

Thalamus

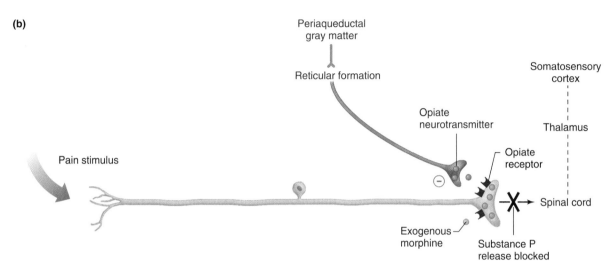

(b)

Periaqueductal gray matter

Reticular formation

Opiate neurotransmitter

Opiate receptor

Pain stimulus

Somatosensory cortex

Thalamus

Spinal cord

Exogenous morphine

Substance P release blocked

**Cellular pathways of pain transmission and modulation**
Figure 7.17

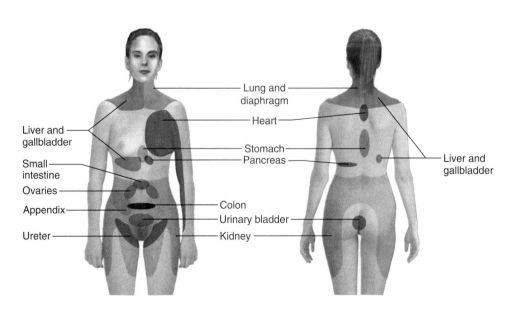

Lung and diaphragm

Heart

Liver and gallbladder

Stomach

Pancreas

Liver and gallbladder

Small intestine

Ovaries

Appendix

Colon

Urinary bladder

Ureter

Kidney

**Regions of the body surface where we typically perceive referred pain from visceral organs**
Figure 7.18

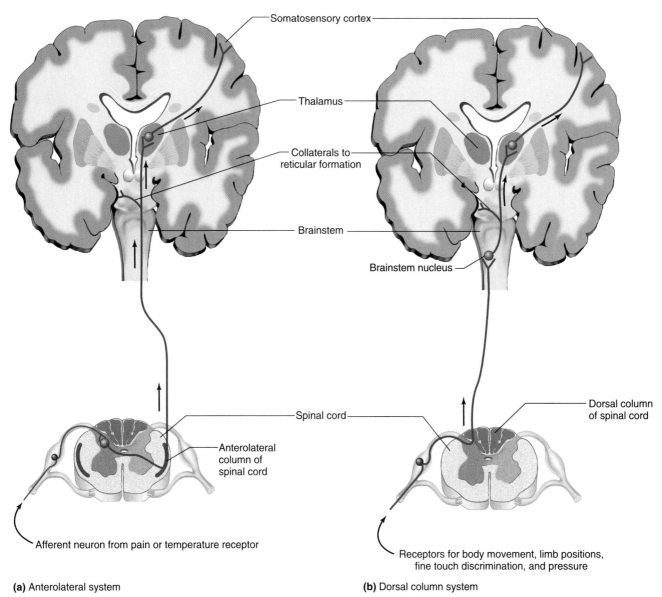

**(a) The anterolateral system (b) The dorsal column system**
Figure 7.19

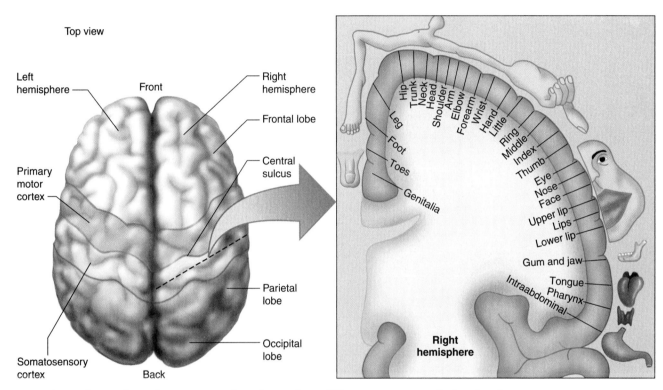

**The location of pathway terminations for different parts of the body**
Figure 7.20

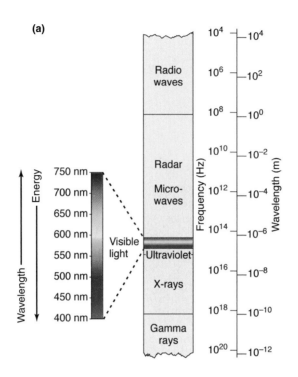

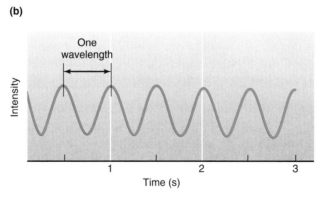

**Electromagnetic spectrum**
Figure 7.21

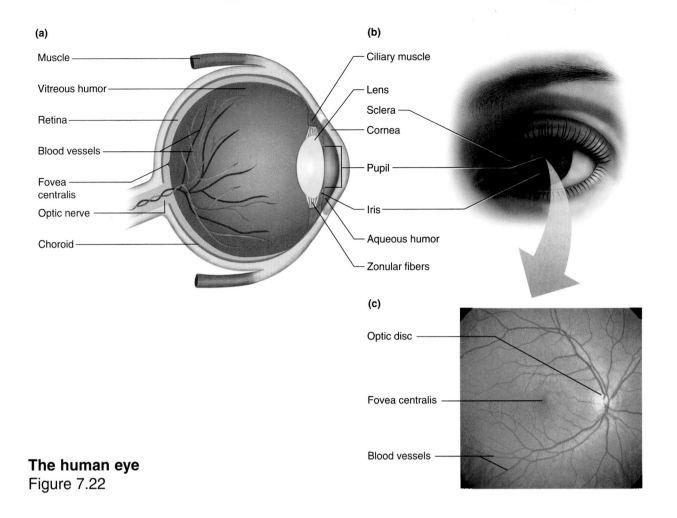

**(a)**

Muscle

Vitreous humor

Retina

Blood vessels

Fovea
centralis

Optic nerve

Choroid

**(b)**

Ciliary muscle

Lens

Sclera

Cornea

Pupil

Iris

Aqueous humor

Zonular fibers

**(c)**

Optic disc

Fovea centralis

Blood vessels

**The human eye**
Figure 7.22

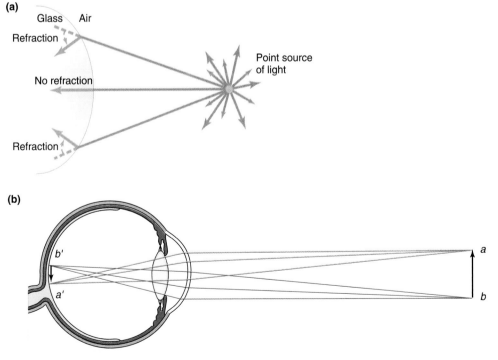

**(a)**

Glass    Air

Refraction

No refraction

Point source
of light

Refraction

**(b)**

b'

a'

a

b

**Focusing point sources of light**
Figure 7.23

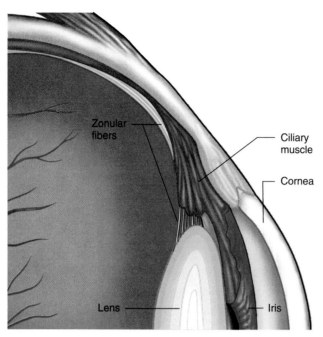

**Ciliary muscle, zonular fibers, and lens of the eye**
Figure 7.24

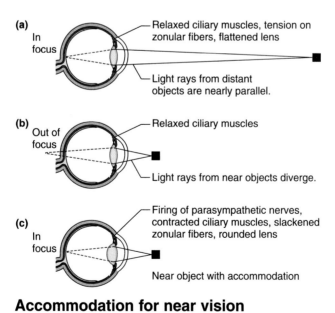

**(a)**
In focus

Relaxed ciliary muscles, tension on zonular fibers, flattened lens

Light rays from distant objects are nearly parallel.

**(b)**
Out of focus

Relaxed ciliary muscles

Light rays from near objects diverge.

**(c)**
In focus

Firing of parasympathetic nerves, contracted ciliary muscles, slackened zonular fibers, rounded lens

Near object with accommodation

**Accommodation for near vision**
Figure 7.25

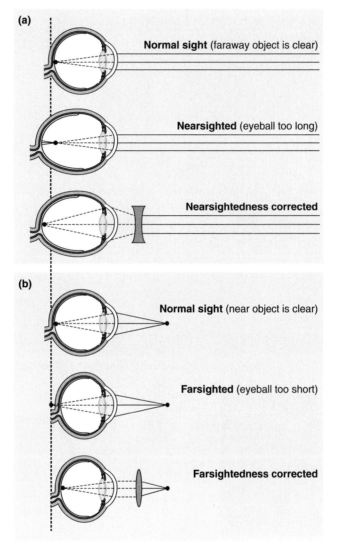

**Correction of vision defects**
Figure 7.26

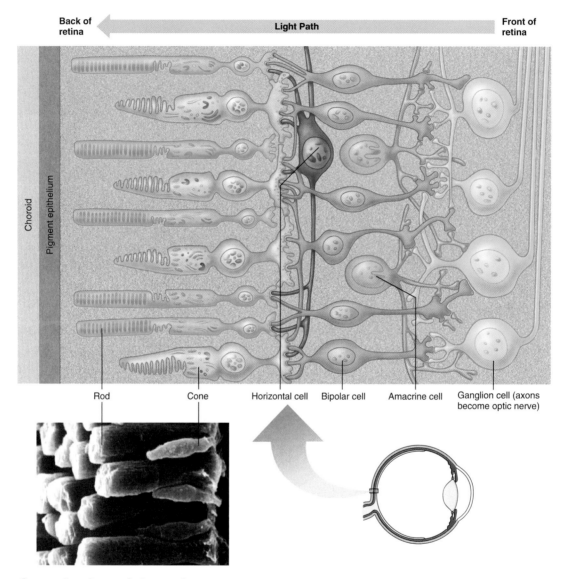

**Organization of the retina**
Figure 7.27

Courtesy of Beckman Vision Center @UCSF School of Medicine/D. Copenhagen, S. Miltman and M. Maglio

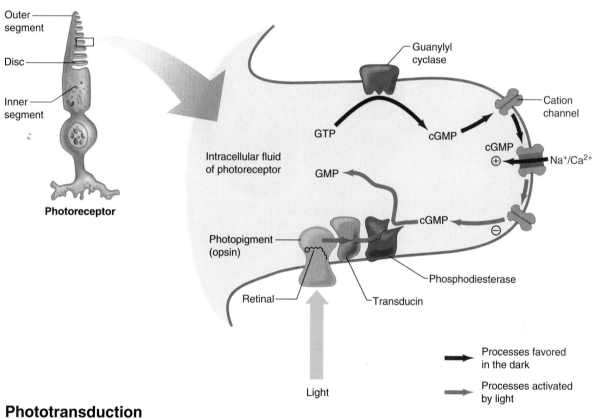

Outer segment

Disc

Inner segment

Photoreceptor

Guanylyl cyclase

Cation channel

GTP

cGMP

cGMP

$Na^+/Ca^{2+}$

⊕

Intracellular fluid of photoreceptor

GMP

cGMP

⊖

Photopigment (opsin)

Phosphodiesterase

Retinal

Transducin

Light

Processes favored in the dark

Processes activated by light

**Phototransduction**
Figure 7.28

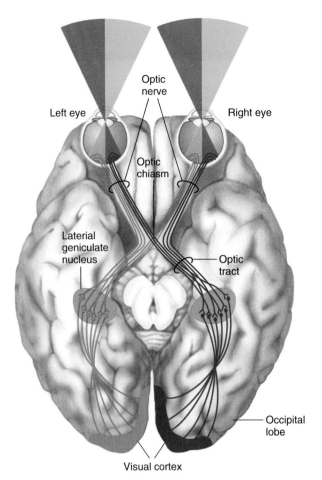

**Visual pathways viewed in cross section from above**

Figure 7.29

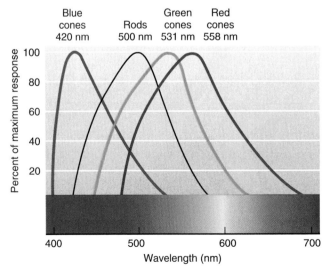

**The sensitivities of the photopigments in the normal human retina**

Figure 7.30

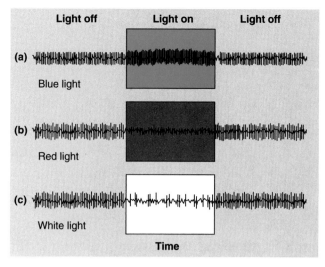

**Response of a single opponent color ganglion cell to blue, red, and white lights**
Figure 7.31

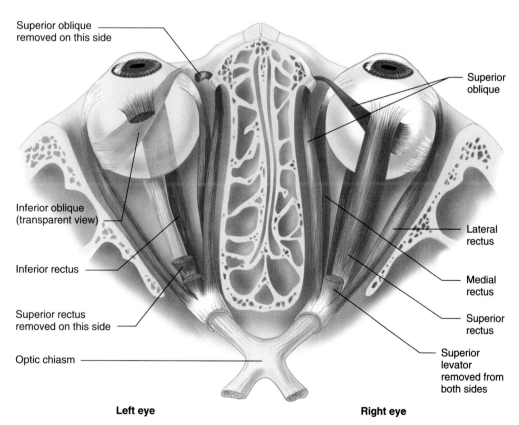

**A superior view of the eye muscles**
Figure 7.32

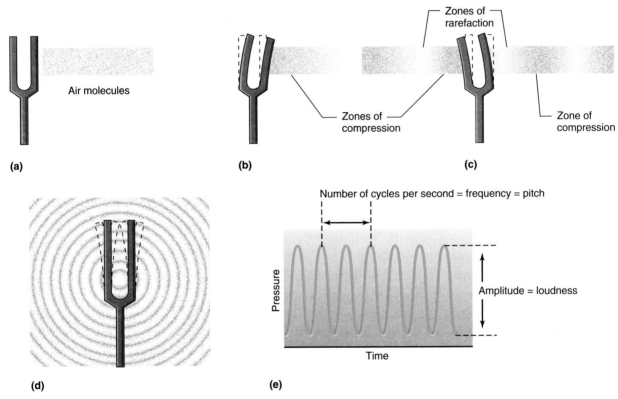

Air molecules

**(a)**

Zones of
rarefaction

Zones of
compression

**(b)**

Zone of
compression

**(c)**

Number of cycles per second = frequency = pitch

Pressure

Amplitude = loudness

Time

**(d)**

**(e)**

**Formation of sound waves from a vibrating tuning fork**
Figure 7.33

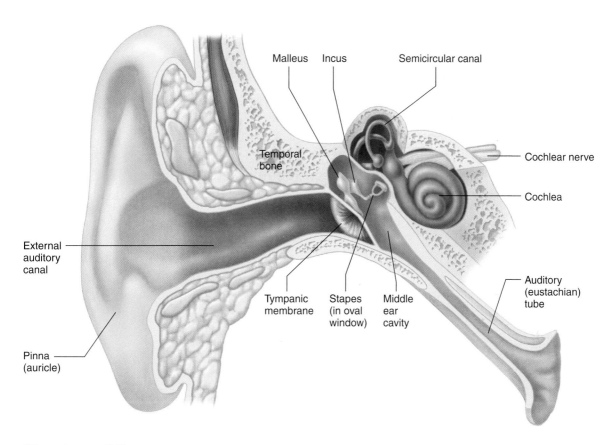

**Structure of the ear**
Figure 7.34

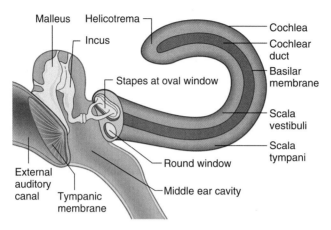

**Relationship between the middle ear bones and the cochlea**
Figure 7.35

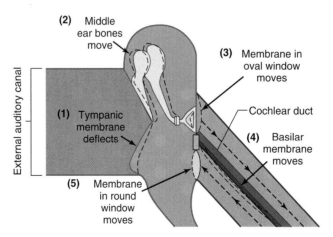

**Sound transmission pathway**
Figure 7.36

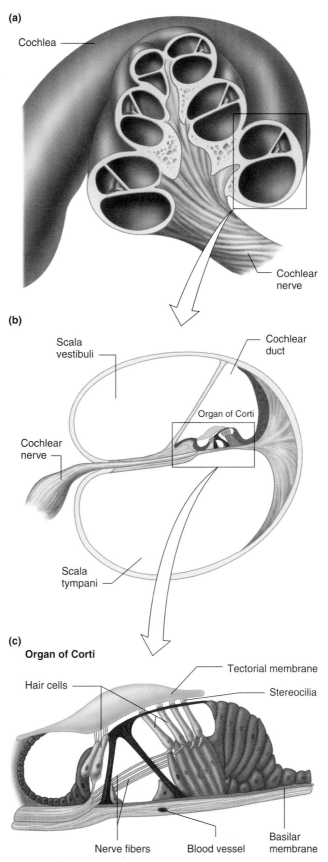

**(a)**

Cochlea

Cochlear nerve

**(b)**

Scala vestibuli

Cochlear duct

Organ of Corti

Cochlear nerve

Scala tympani

**(c)** **Organ of Corti**

Tectorial membrane

Hair cells

Stereocilia

Nerve fibers

Blood vessel

Basilar membrane

**Compartments of the inner ear**
Figure 7.37

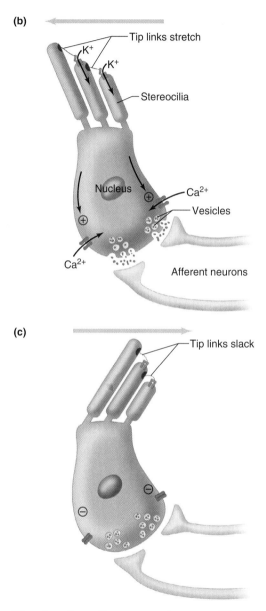

**Mechanism for neurotransmitter release in the hair cell of the auditory system**
Figure 7.38

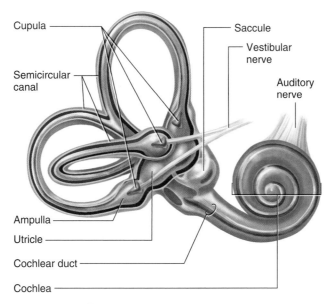

**The fluid-filled membranous duct system of the ear**
Figure 7.39

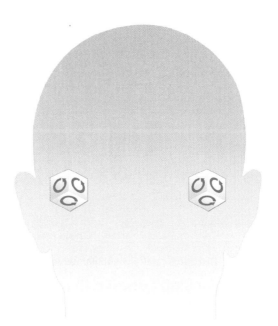

**Orientation of the semicircular canals within the labyrinth**
Figure 7.40

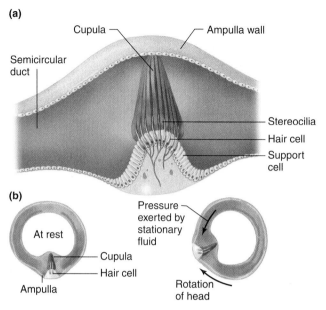

**(a)**

Cupula

Ampulla wall

Semicircular duct

Stereocilia

Hair cell

Support cell

**(b)**

At rest

Pressure exerted by stationary fluid

Cupula

Hair cell

Ampulla

Rotation of head

**Organization of the cupula and ampulla**
Figure 7.41

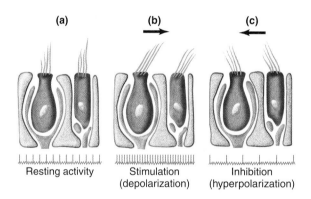

**(a)**          **(b)**          **(c)**

Resting activity

Stimulation (depolarization)

Inhibition (hyperpolarization)

**Discharge rate of vestibular nerve**

**The relationship between the position of hairs in the ampulla and action potential firing in afferent neurons**
Figure 7.42

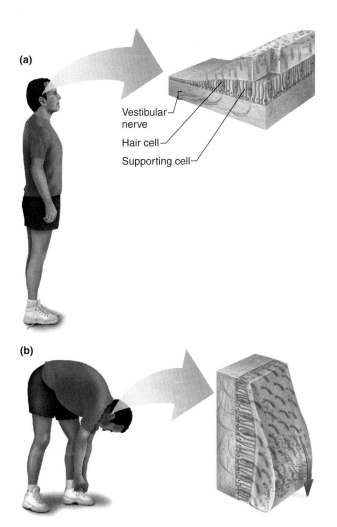

**(a)**

Vestibular nerve

Hair cell

Supporting cell

**(b)**

**Effect of head position on otolith organ
of the utricle**
Figure 7.43

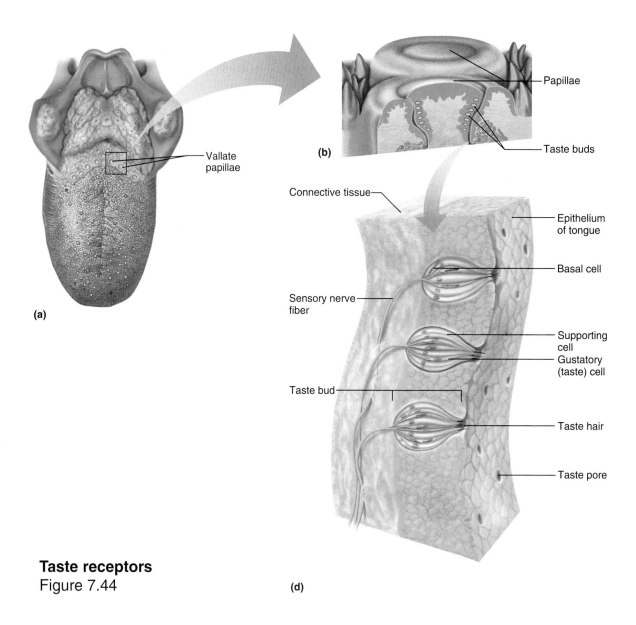

**(a)**

**(b)** Papillae

Taste buds

Connective tissue

Epithelium of tongue

Basal cell

Sensory nerve fiber

Supporting cell

Gustatory (taste) cell

Taste bud

Taste hair

Taste pore

Vallate papillae

**Taste receptors**
Figure 7.44

**(d)**

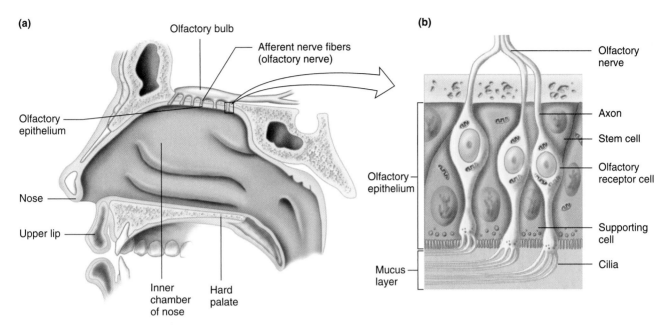

**(a)**

Olfactory bulb

Afferent nerve fibers
(olfactory nerve)

Olfactory
epithelium

Nose

Upper lip

Inner
chamber
of nose

Hard
palate

**(b)**

Olfactory
nerve

Axon

Stem cell

Olfactory
receptor cell

Olfactory
epithelium

Supporting
cell

Mucus
layer

Cilia

**Olfactory epithelium**
Figure 7.45

Time

**EEG patterns are wavelike**
Figure 8.1

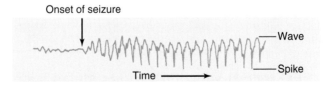

Onset of seizure

Wave

Spike

Time

**Spike and wave pattern in the EEG of a
patient during an epileptic seizure**
Figure 8.2

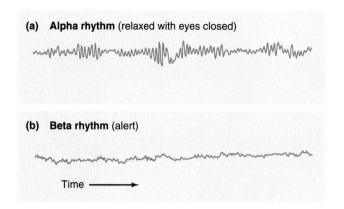

**The (a) alpha and (b) beta rhythms of the EEG**
Figure 8.3

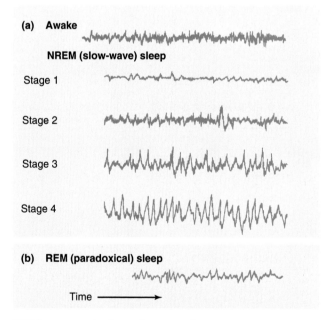

**EEG record showing various states from awake to deep sleep**
Figure 8.4

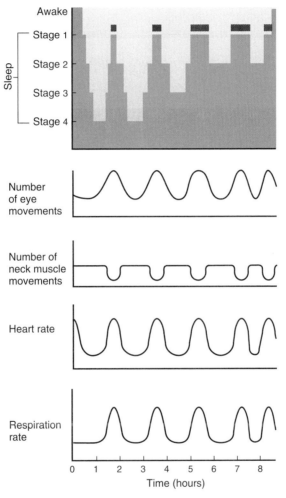

**EEG and other physiological changes associated with the stages of sleep**

Figure 8.5

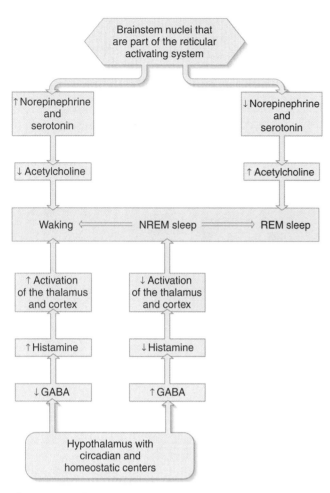

**Changes in aminergic and cholinergic influence the differing states of consciousness**
Figure 8.6

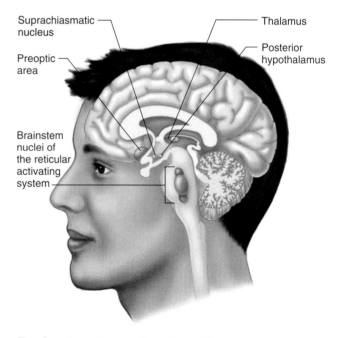

**Brain structures involved in sleep–wakefulness**
Figure 8.7

**Unilateral visual neglect**
Figure 8.8

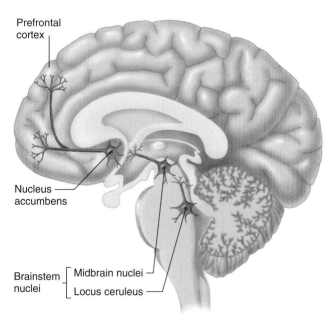

**Schematic drawing of the mesolimbic dopamine pathway**
Figure 8.9

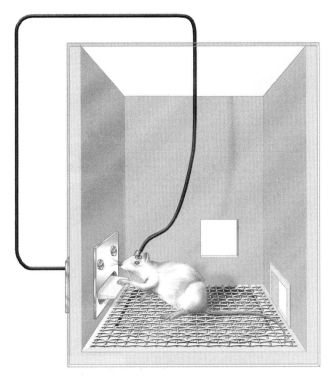

**Apparatus for self-stimulation experiments**
Figure 8.10

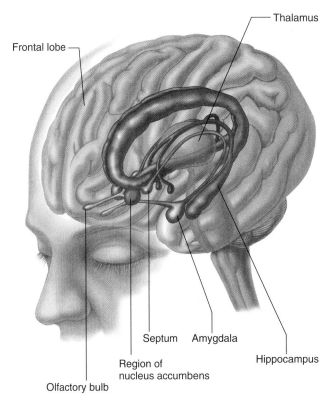

Thalamus

Frontal lobe

Septum    Amygdala

Region of
nucleus accumbens

Olfactory bulb

Hippocampus

**Brain structures involved in emotion**
Figure 8.11

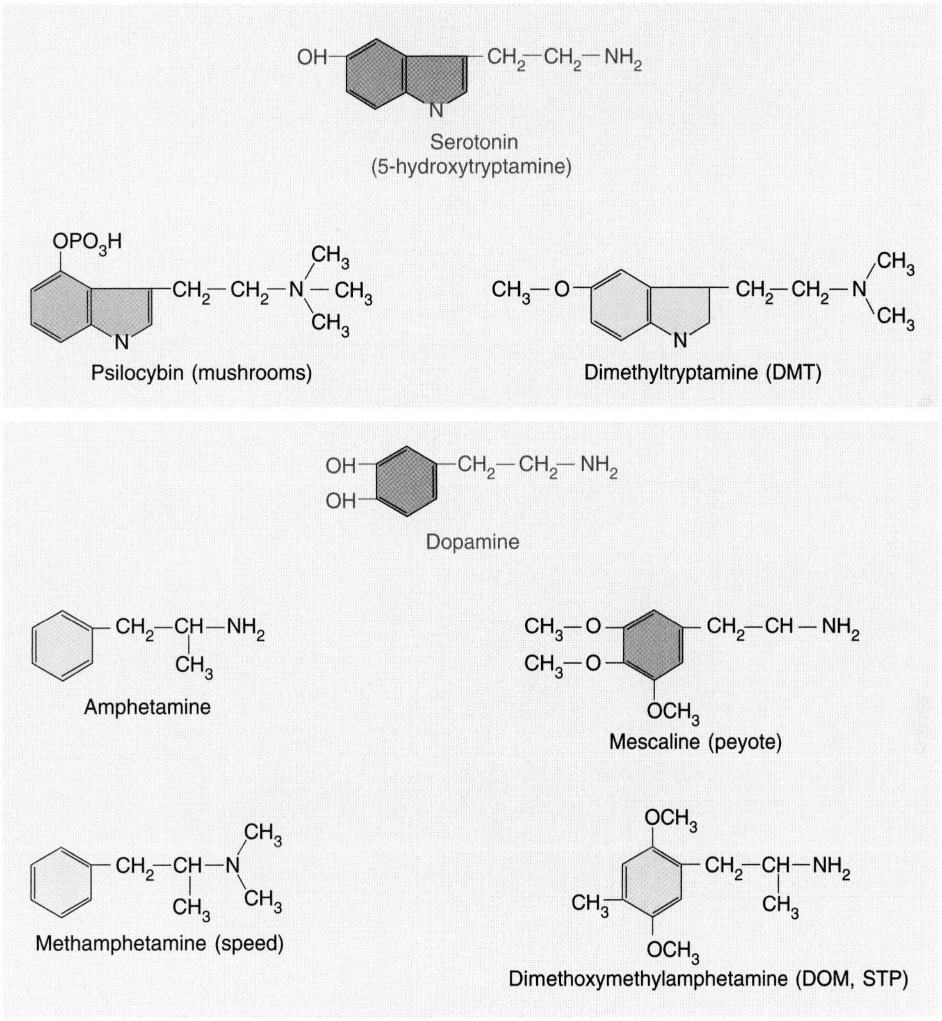

**Neurotransmitter and drug structures**
Figure 8.13

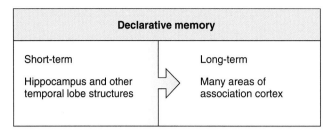

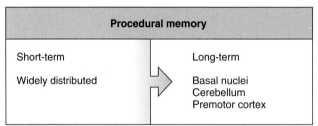

**Brain areas involved in encoding and storage of declarative and procedural memories**
Figure 8.14

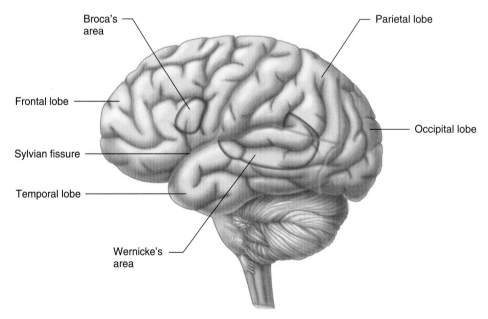

**Language areas of the brain**
Figure 8.17

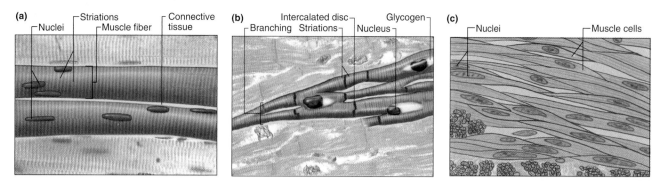

(a) Nuclei — Striations — Muscle fiber — Connective tissue

(b) Branching — Intercalated disc — Striations — Nucleus — Glycogen

(c) Nuclei — Muscle cells

## Comparison of skeletal muscle
Figure 9.1

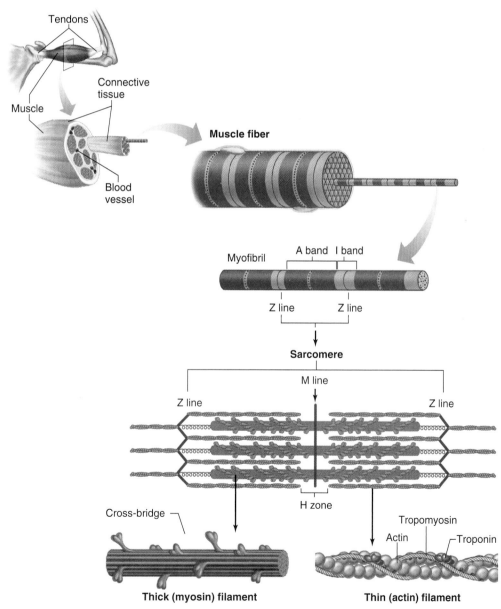

Tendons

Muscle

Connective tissue

Blood vessel

**Muscle fiber**

Myofibril — A band — I band

Z line — Z line

**Sarcomere**

M line

Z line — Z line

H zone

Cross-bridge

**Thick (myosin) filament**

Tropomyosin

Actin — Troponin

**Thin (actin) filament**

## Structure of skeletal muscle
Figure 9.2

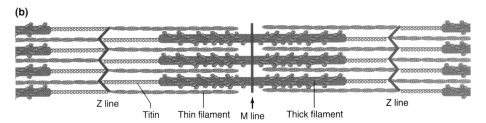

(b)

Z line  Titin  Thin filament  M line  Thick filament  Z line

**Arrangement of the thick and thin filaments in the sarcomere**
Figure 9.3

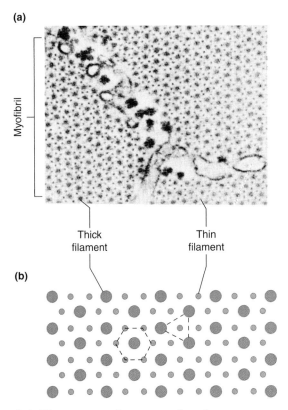

(a)

Myofibril

Thick filament

Thin filament

(b)

**(a) Electron micrograph of a cross section through three myofibrils in a single skeletal muscle fiber.**
**(b) Hexagonal arrangements of the thick and thin filaments**
Figure 9.4

**a:** From H. E. Huxley, *Journal of Molecular Biology,* 37-507-520 (1968)

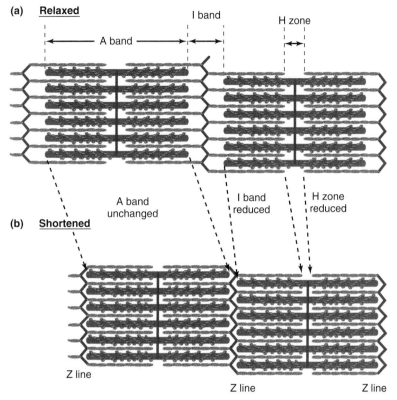

**(a)** <u>Relaxed</u>

I band

H zone

A band

A band
unchanged

I band
reduced

H zone
reduced

**(b)** <u>Shortened</u>

Z line

Z line

Z line

**Thick and thin filament sliding**
Figure 9.5

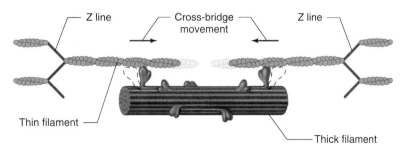

Z line

Cross-bridge
movement

Z line

Thin filament

Thick filament

**Cross-bridge movement**
Figure 9.6

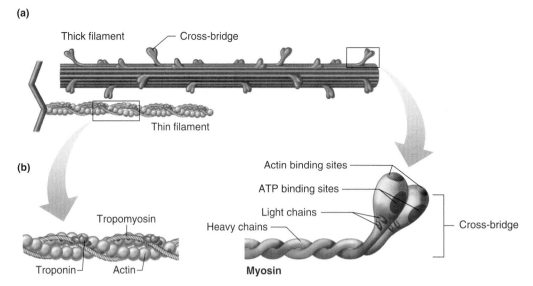

**(a) The heavy chains of myosin molecules form the core of a thick filament (b) Structure of thin filament and myosin molecule**
Figure 9.7

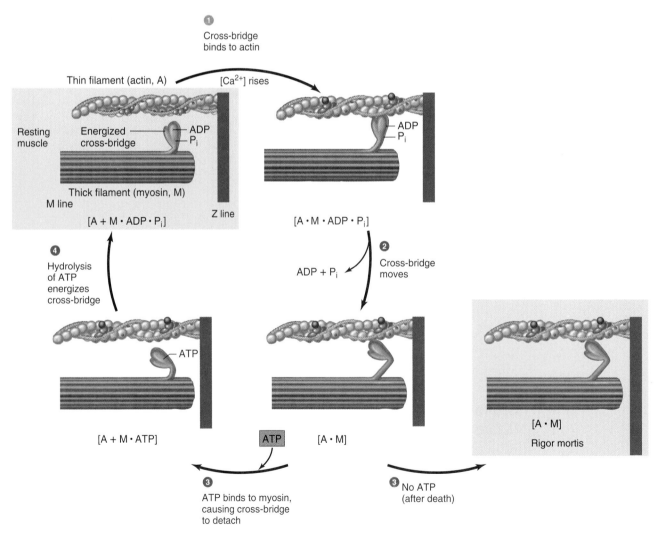

**Cross-bridge cycle**
Figure 9.8

**(a)** Low cytosolic calcium, relaxed muscle

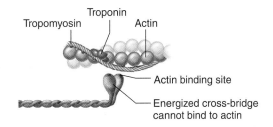

Tropomyosin
Troponin
Actin
Actin binding site
Energized cross-bridge cannot bind to actin

**(b)** High cytosolic calcium, Activated muscle

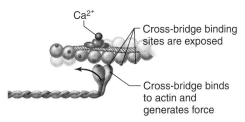

Ca²⁺
Cross-bridge binding sites are exposed
Cross-bridge binds to actin and generates force

## Activation of cross-bridge cycling by calcium
Figure 9.9

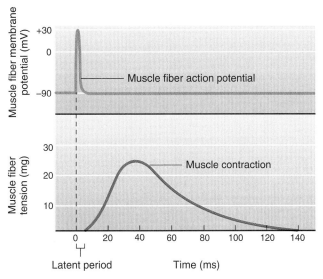

Muscle fiber action potential

Muscle contraction

Latent period

Time (ms)

## Time relations in skeletal muscle fiber
Figure 9.10

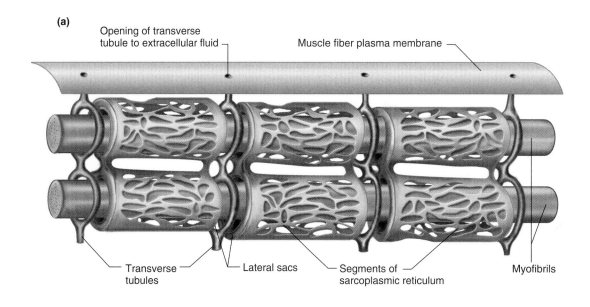

(a)

Opening of transverse tubule to extracellular fluid

Muscle fiber plasma membrane

Transverse tubules

Lateral sacs

Segments of sarcoplasmic reticulum

Myofibrils

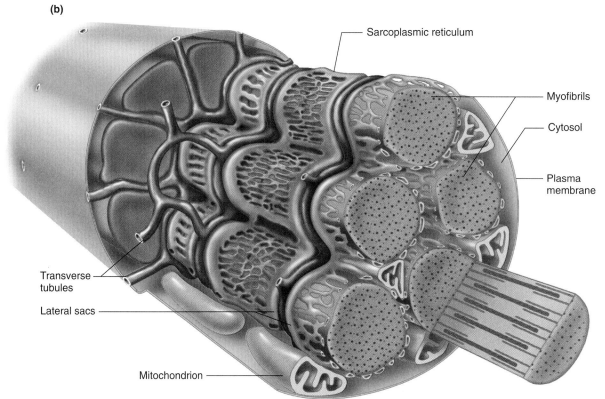

(b)

Sarcoplasmic reticulum

Myofibrils

Cytosol

Plasma membrane

Transverse tubules

Lateral sacs

Mitochondrion

**Myofibrils and associated structures**
Figure 9.11

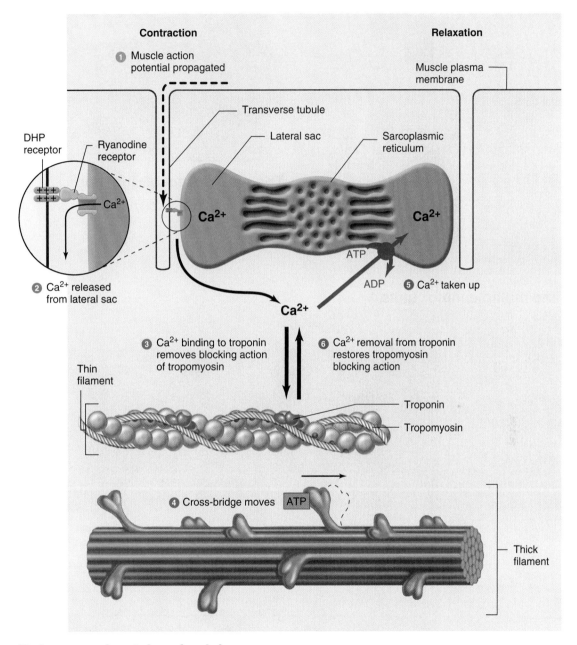

**Release and uptake of calcium**
Figure 9.12

**(a) Single motor unit**

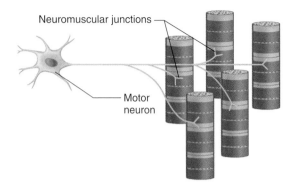

Neuromuscular junctions

Motor neuron

**(b) Two motor units**

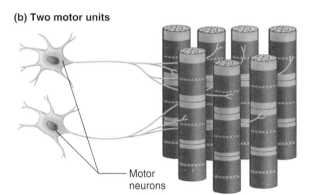

Motor neurons

**Single and multiple motor units**
Figure 9.13

**(b)**

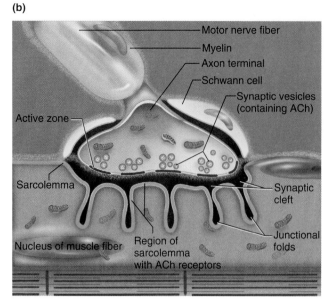

Motor nerve fiber
Myelin
Axon terminal
Schwann cell
Synaptic vesicles (containing ACh)

Active zone

Sarcolemma

Nucleus of muscle fiber

Region of sarcolemma with ACh receptors

Synaptic cleft

Junctional folds

**The neuromuscular junction**
Figure 9.14

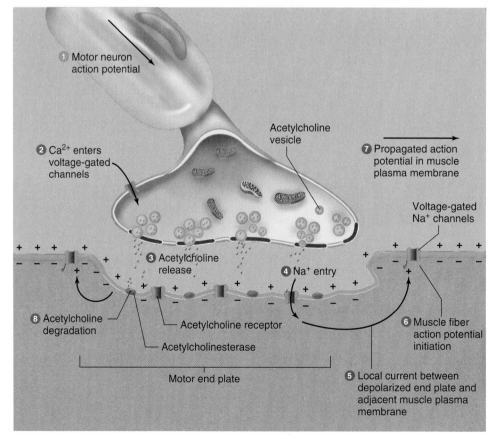

① Motor neuron action potential

② Ca²⁺ enters voltage-gated channels

Acetylcholine vesicle

⑦ Propagated action potential in muscle plasma membrane

③ Acetylcholine release

④ Na⁺ entry

Voltage-gated Na⁺ channels

⑧ Acetylcholine degradation

Acetylcholine receptor

Acetylcholinesterase

Motor end plate

⑥ Muscle fiber action potential initiation

⑤ Local current between depolarized end plate and adjacent muscle plasma membrane

**Simulation at neuromuscular junction**
Figure 9.15

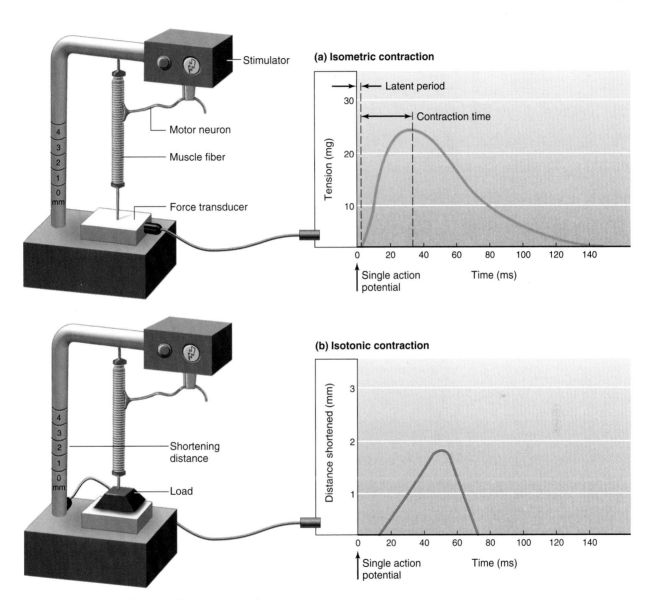

**(a) Isometric contraction**

Stimulator

Motor neuron

Muscle fiber

Force transducer

Latent period

Contraction time

Tension (mg)

Time (ms)

Single action potential

**(b) Isotonic contraction**

Shortening distance

Load

Distance shortened (mm)

Time (ms)

Single action potential

**Isometric and isotonic contractions**
Figure 9.16

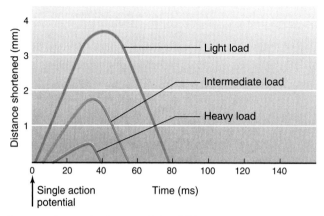

**Isotonic twitches with different loads**
Figure 9.17

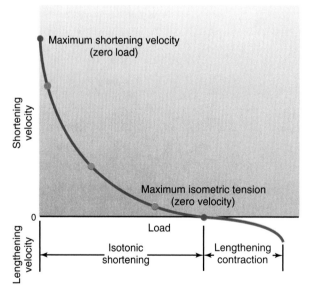

**Velocity of skeletal muscle fiber**
Figure 9.18

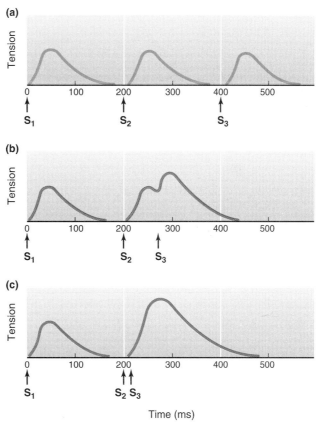

**Summation of isometric contractions**
Figure 9.19

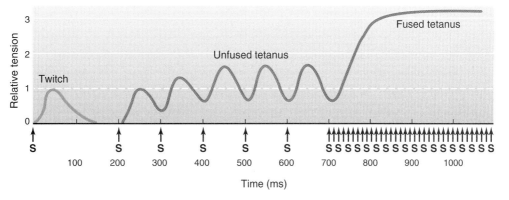

**Tetanus**
Figure 9.20

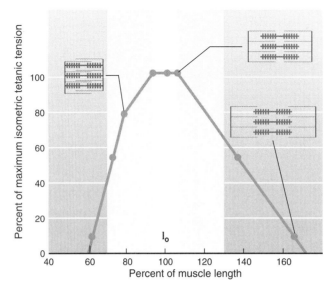

**Length vs. tension relationship**
Figure 9.21

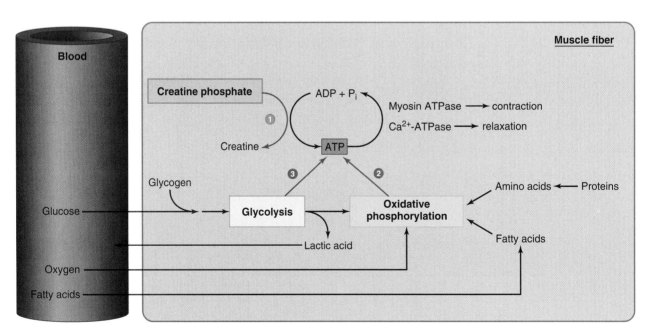

**The three sources of ATP production**
Figure 9.22

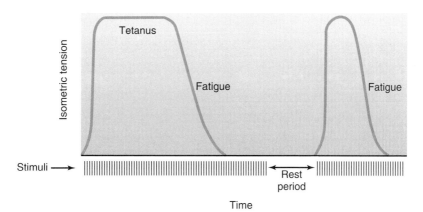

**Muscle fatigue**
Figure 9.23

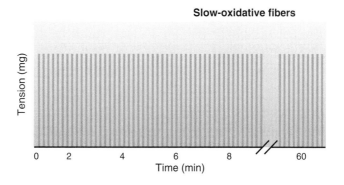

**Slow-oxidative fibers**

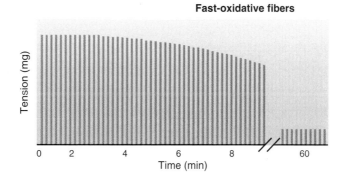

**Fast-oxidative fibers**

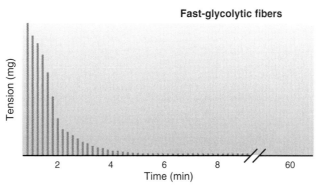

**Fast-glycolytic fibers**

**Rate of fatigue development**
Figure 9.25

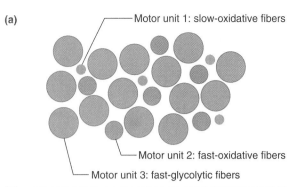

Motor unit 1: slow-oxidative fibers

Motor unit 2: fast-oxidative fibers

Motor unit 3: fast-glycolytic fibers

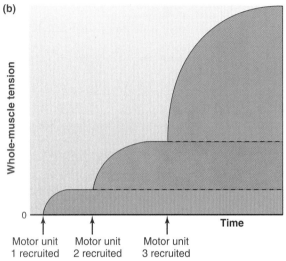

**Three types of motor units in muscle composition**
Figure 9.26

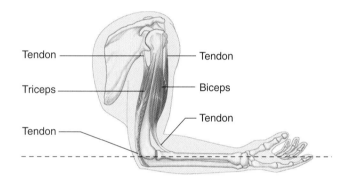

Tendon

Tendon

Triceps

Biceps

Tendon

Tendon

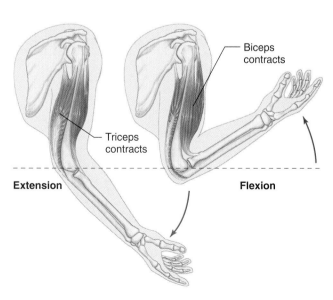

Biceps contracts

Triceps contracts

**Extension**

**Flexion**

**Antagonistic muscles of arm**
Figure 9.27

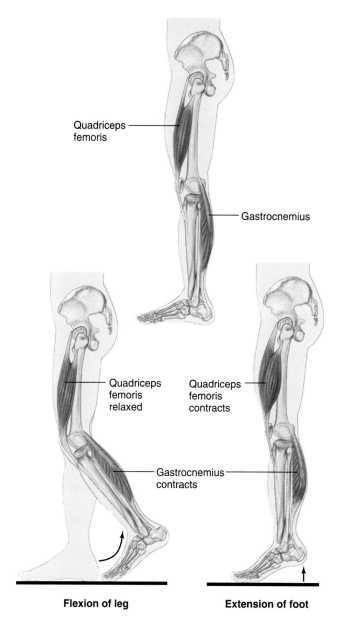

Quadriceps
femoris

Gastrocnemius

Quadriceps
femoris
relaxed

Quadriceps
femoris
contracts

Gastrocnemius
contracts

**Flexion of leg**

**Extension of foot**

## Flexion or extension of leg
Figure 9.28

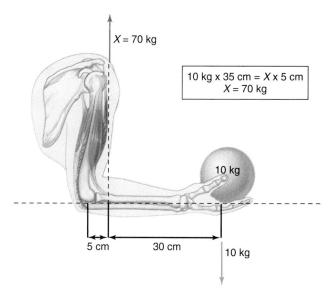

$X$ = 70 kg

10 kg x 35 cm = $X$ x 5 cm
$X$ = 70 kg

10 kg

5 cm    30 cm    10 kg

## Mechanical equilibrium of forces acting on the forearm
Figure 9.29

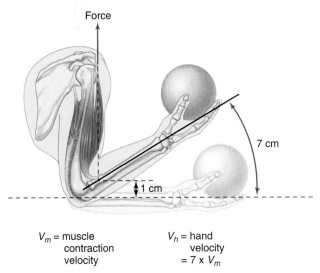

Force

7 cm

1 cm

$V_m$ = muscle contraction velocity

$V_h$ = hand velocity = 7 x $V_m$

**Amplificaton of bicep velocity**
Figure 9.30

1    2    3    4    5

**Boy with Duchenne muscular dystrophy**
Figure 9.31

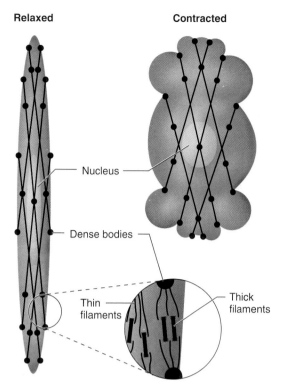

**Smooth muscle filaments**
Figure 9.33

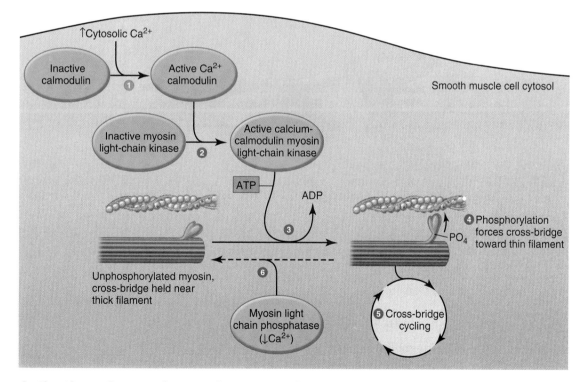

**Activation of smooth muscle contraction by calcium**
Figure 9.34

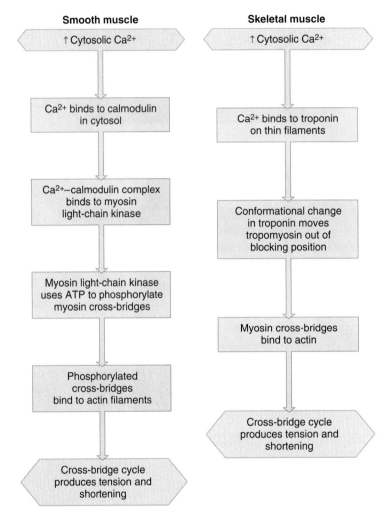

**Cross-bridge cycling in smooth and skeletal muscle**
Figure 9.35

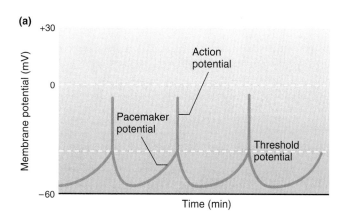

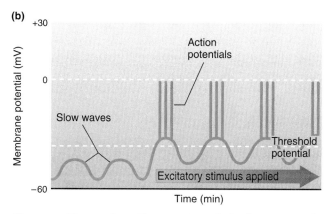

**Generation of action potentials in smooth muscle fibers**

Figure 9.36

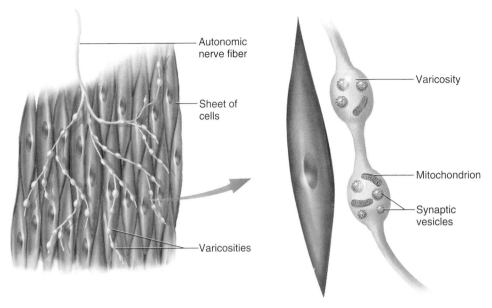

**Innervation of smooth muscle by a postganglionic autonomic neuron**
Figure 9.37

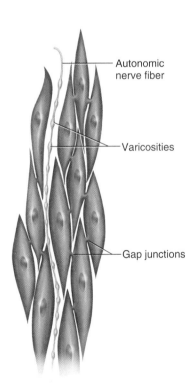

**Innervation of a single-unit smooth muscle is often restricted to only a few cells in the muscle**
Figure 9.38

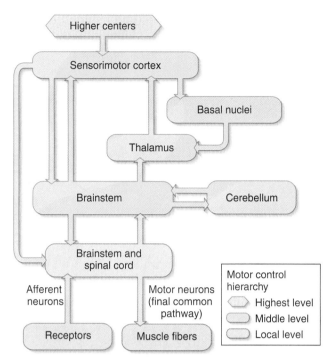

**Systems controlling body movement**
Figure 10.1

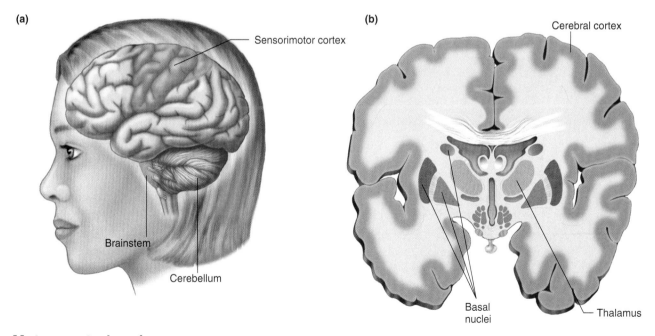

(a)
Sensorimotor cortex

Brainstem

Cerebellum

(b)
Cerebral cortex

Basal
nuclei

Thalamus

**Motor control regions**
Figure 10.2

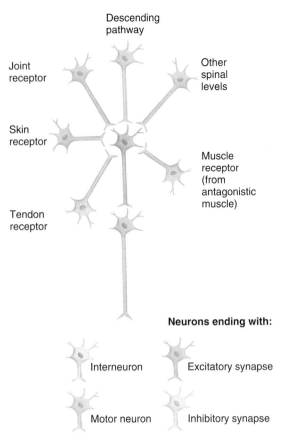

Joint receptor

Descending pathway

Other spinal levels

Skin receptor

Muscle receptor (from antagonistic muscle)

Tendon receptor

**Neurons ending with:**

Interneuron

Excitatory synapse

Motor neuron

Inhibitory synapse

**Convergence of axons onto a local interneuron**
Figure 10.3

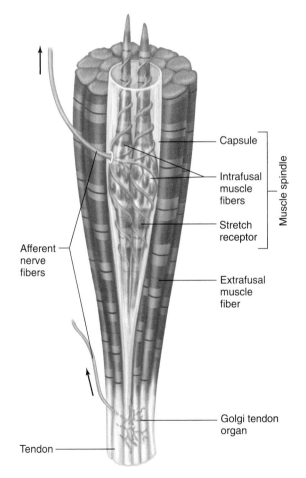

Capsule

Intrafusal muscle fibers

Stretch receptor

Muscle spindle

Afferent nerve fibers

Extrafusal muscle fiber

Golgi tendon organ

Tendon

**Muscle spindle and Golgi tendon organ**
Figure 10.4

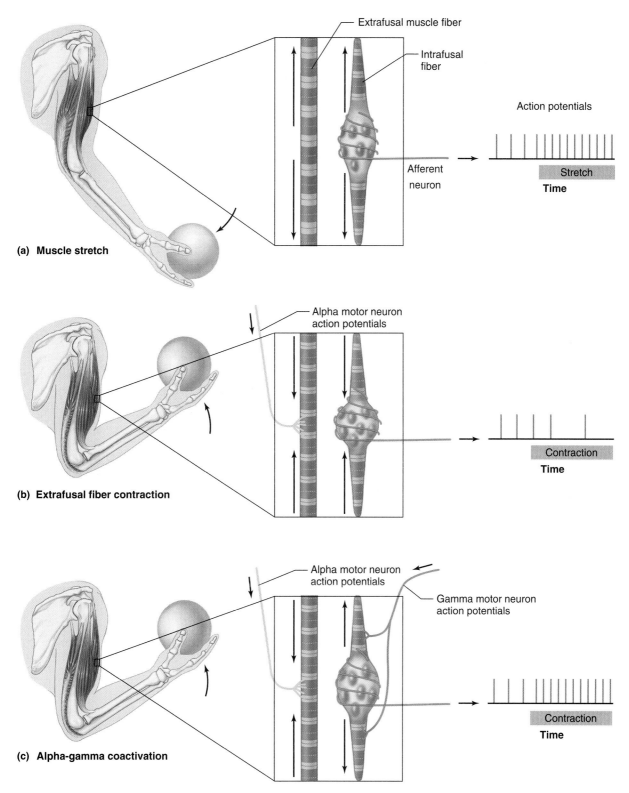

**Muscle spindles during stretching and contraction**
Figure 10.5

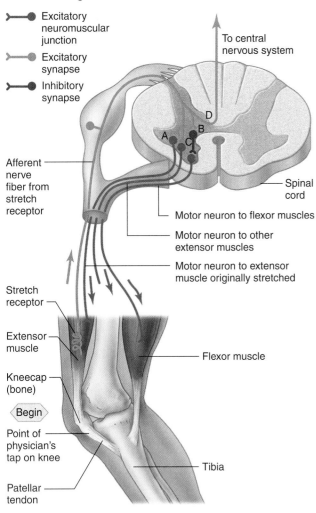

**Neurons ending with:**

- Excitatory neuromuscular junction
- Excitatory synapse
- Inhibitory synapse

To central nervous system

D

A B C

Afferent nerve fiber from stretch receptor

Spinal cord

Motor neuron to flexor muscles

Motor neuron to other extensor muscles

Motor neuron to extensor muscle originally stretched

Stretch receptor

Extensor muscle

Kneecap (bone)

Begin

Point of physician's tap on knee

Patellar tendon

Flexor muscle

Tibia

## Knee-jerk reflex
Figure 10.6

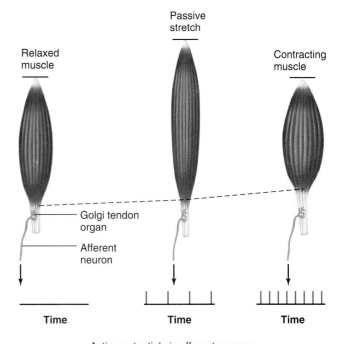

Relaxed muscle

Passive stretch

Contracting muscle

Golgi tendon organ

Afferent neuron

Time

Time

Time

Action potentials in afferent neurons

## Activation of Golgi tendon organs
Figure 10.7

**Neurons ending with:**

>—● Excitatory
neuromuscular
junction

>—◍ Excitatory
synapse

>—● Inhibitory
synapse

A B

Afferent
nerve
fiber from
Golgi tendon
organ

Spinal
cord

Motor neuron to
flexor muscles

Motor neuron to
extensor muscles

Extensor
muscle

⟨Begin⟩

Flexor muscle

Extensor
muscle
tendon with
Golgi
tendon
organ

Kneecap
(bone)

# Neural pathways underlying the Golgi tendon organ component
Figure 10.8

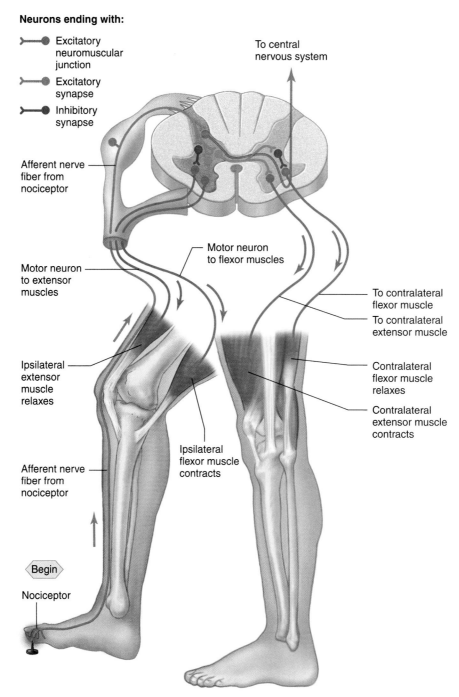

**Neurons ending with:**

- Excitatory neuromuscular junction
- Excitatory synapse
- Inhibitory synapse

To central nervous system

Afferent nerve fiber from nociceptor

Motor neuron to flexor muscles

Motor neuron to extensor muscles

To contralateral flexor muscle

To contralateral extensor muscle

Ipsilateral extensor muscle relaxes

Contralateral flexor muscle relaxes

Contralateral extensor muscle contracts

Ipsilateral flexor muscle contracts

Afferent nerve fiber from nociceptor

Begin

Nociceptor

**Pain-withdrawal reflex**
Figure 10.9

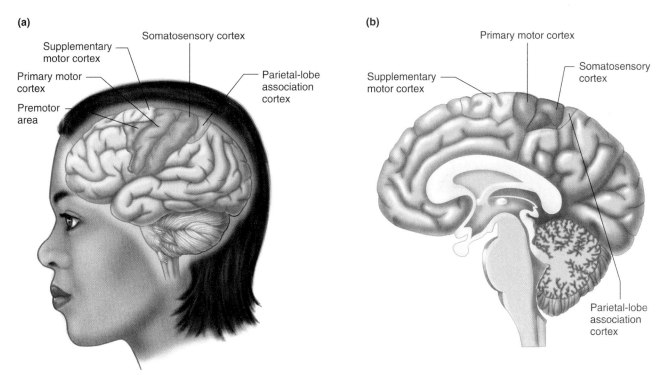

**(a)**

Supplementary
motor cortex

Primary motor
cortex

Premotor
area

Somatosensory cortex

Parietal-lobe
association
cortex

**(b)**

Primary motor cortex

Supplementary
motor cortex

Somatosensory
cortex

Parietal-lobe
association
cortex

**The major motor areas of cerebral cortex (with midline view)**
Figure 10.10

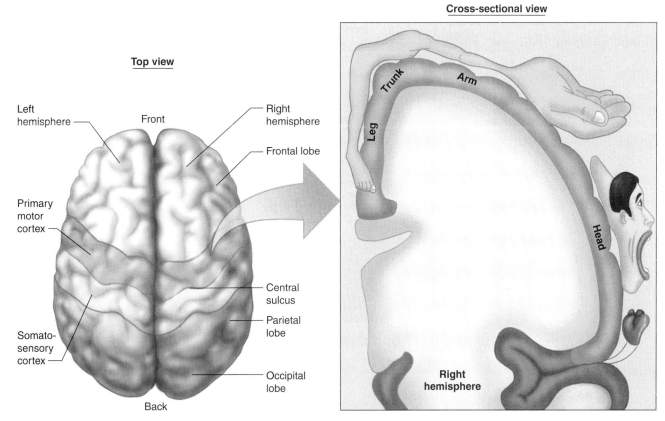

**Cross-sectional view**

**Top view**

Left
hemisphere

Front

Right
hemisphere

Frontal lobe

Primary
motor
cortex

Central
sulcus

Parietal
lobe

Somato-
sensory
cortex

Occipital
lobe

Back

Leg

Trunk

Arm

Head

**Right
hemisphere**

**Major body areas mapped to motor cortex**
Figure 10.11

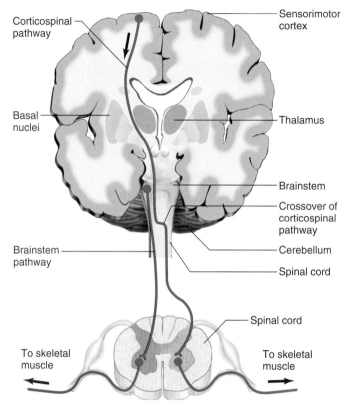

**Corticospinal and brainstem pathways**
Figure 10.12

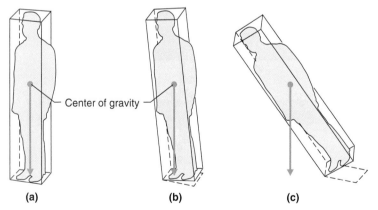

(a)          (b)          (c)

Center of gravity

**The center of gravity during stable and unstable conditions**
Figure 10.13

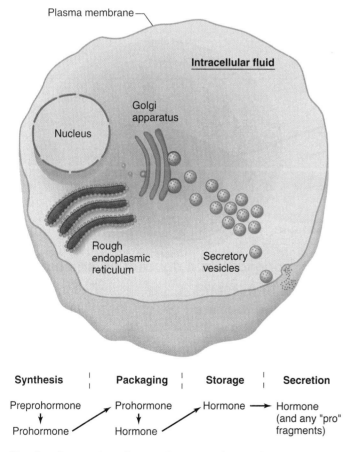

3, 5, 3', 5'– Tetraiodothyronine (thyroxine, $T_4$)

3, 5, 3'– Triiodothyronine ($T_3$)

Norepinephrine

Epinephrine

Dopamine

## Chemical structures of the amine hormones
Figure 11.1

| Synthesis | Packaging | Storage | Secretion |
|-----------|-----------|---------|-----------|
| Preprohormone | Prohormone | Hormone | Hormone (and any "pro" fragments) |
| Prohormone | Hormone | | |

## Typical synthesis and secretion of peptide hormones
Figure 11.2

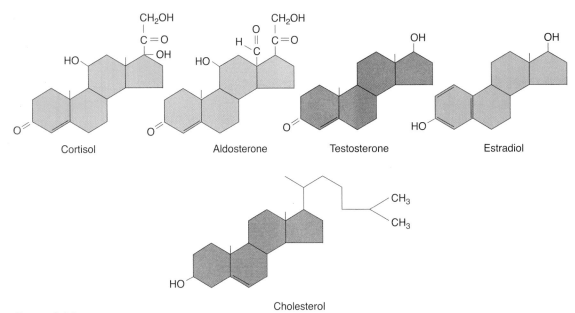

**Steroid hormones**
Figure 11.3

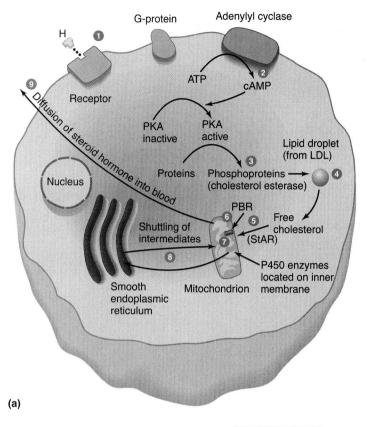

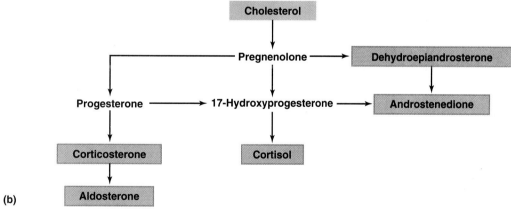

**(a) Schematic overview of steps involved in steroid synthesis**
**(b) Simplified flow sheet**
Figure 11.4

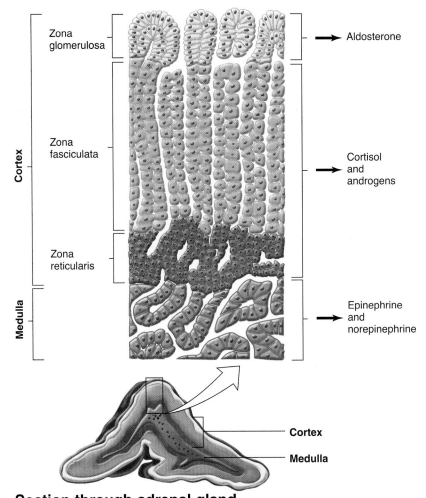

**Section through adrenal gland**
Figure 11.5

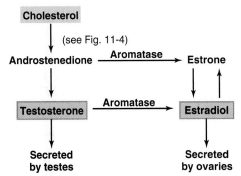

**Gonadal production of steroids**
Figure 11.6

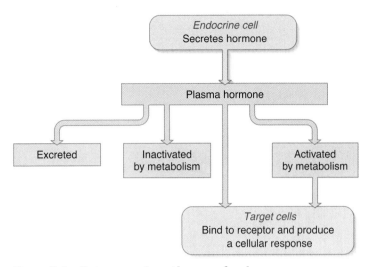

**Possible fates and actions of a hormone**
Figure 11.7

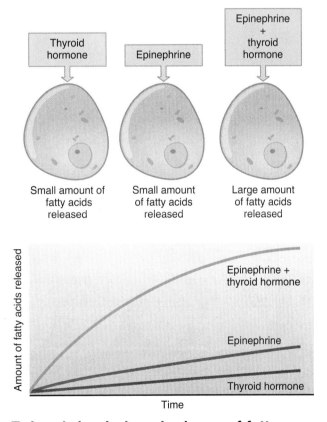

**Epinephrine-induced release of fatty acids**
Figure 11.8

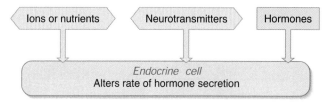

**Inputs on endocrine gland cells**
Figure 11.9

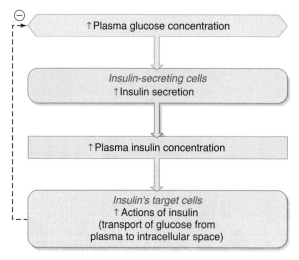

**Direct control of hormone secretion**
Figure 11.10

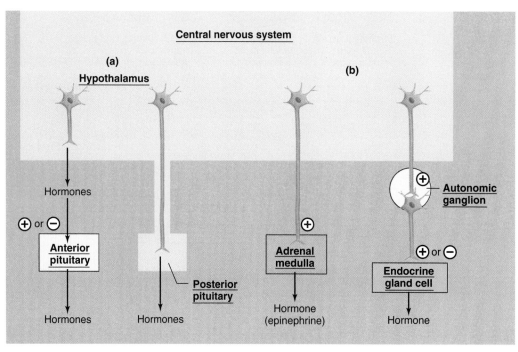

**The nervous system influences hormone secretion**
Figure 11.11

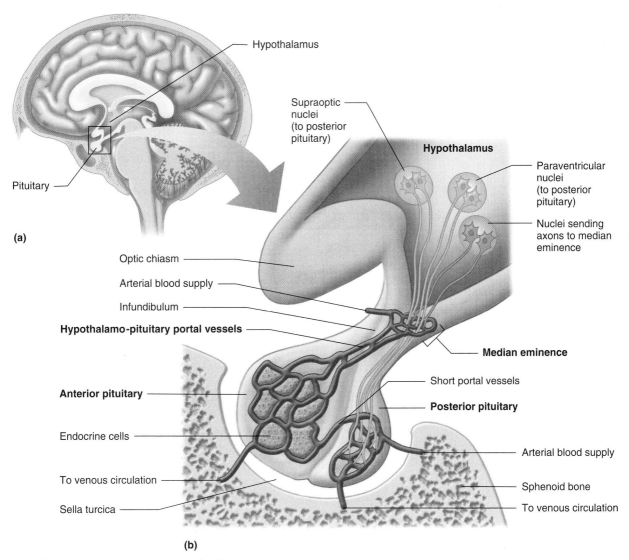

Labels for part (a):
- Hypothalamus
- Pituitary
- (a)

Labels for part (b):
- Supraoptic nuclei (to posterior pituitary)
- Hypothalamus
- Paraventricular nuclei (to posterior pituitary)
- Nuclei sending axons to median eminence
- Optic chiasm
- Arterial blood supply
- Infundibulum
- **Hypothalamo-pituitary portal vessels**
- **Median eminence**
- **Anterior pituitary**
- Short portal vessels
- **Posterior pituitary**
- Endocrine cells
- Arterial blood supply
- To venous circulation
- Sphenoid bone
- Sella turcica
- To venous circulation
- (b)

**Pituitary gland and hypothalamus**
Figure 11.12

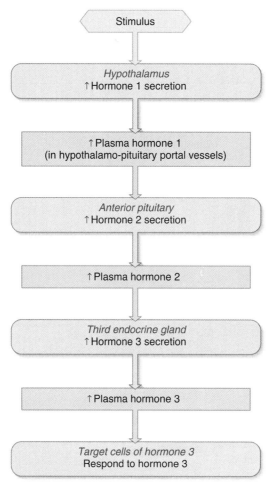

**Typical sequential pattern**
Figure 11.13

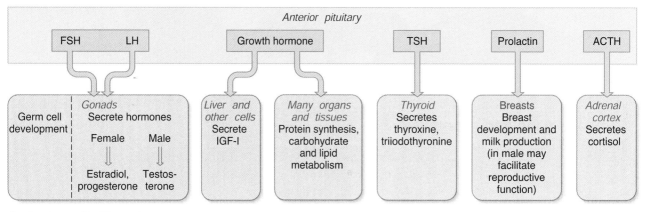

**Anterior pituitary hormones**
Figure 11.14

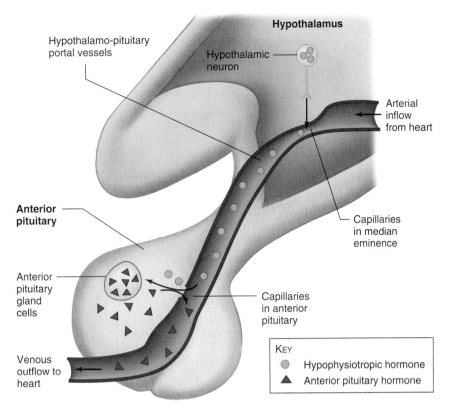

**Hormone secretion by the anterior pituitary**
Figure 11.15

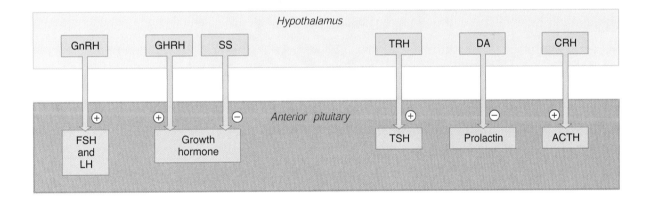

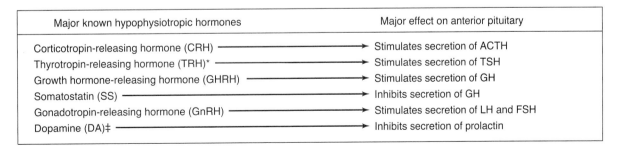

| Major known hypophysiotropic hormones | Major effect on anterior pituitary |
| --- | --- |
| Corticotropin-releasing hormone (CRH) | Stimulates secretion of ACTH |
| Thyrotropin-releasing hormone (TRH)* | Stimulates secretion of TSH |
| Growth hormone-releasing hormone (GHRH) | Stimulates secretion of GH |
| Somatostatin (SS) | Inhibits secretion of GH |
| Gonadotropin-releasing hormone (GnRH) | Stimulates secretion of LH and FSH |
| Dopamine (DA)‡ | Inhibits secretion of prolactin |

*TRH can also stimulate the release of prolactin, but whether this occurs physiologically is unclear.

‡Dopamine is a catecholamine; all the other hypophysiotropic hormones are peptides.

**Definitely established hypophysiotropic hormones**
Figure 11.16

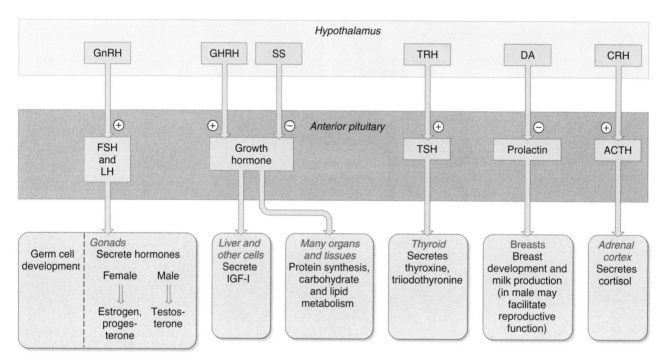

**Summary of hypothalamic-anterior pituitary system**
Figure 11.17

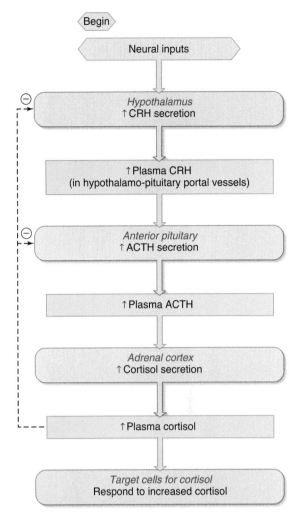

**CRH-ACTH-cortisol sequence**
Figure 11.18

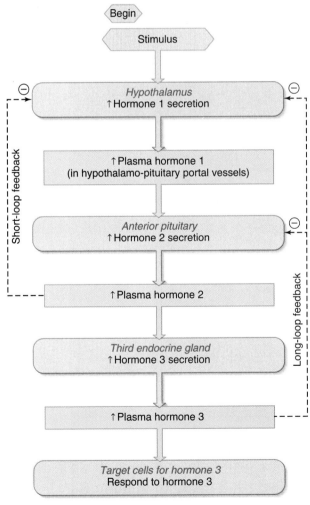

**Types of negative feedback**
Figure 11.19

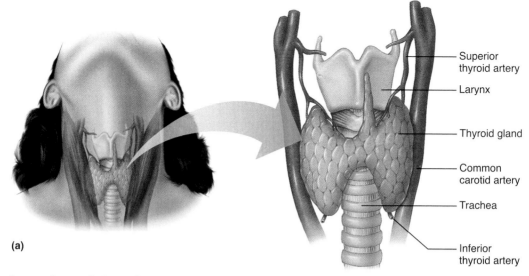

(a)

**Location of thyroid**
Figure 11.20

Superior thyroid artery
Larynx
Thyroid gland
Common carotid artery
Trachea
Inferior thyroid artery

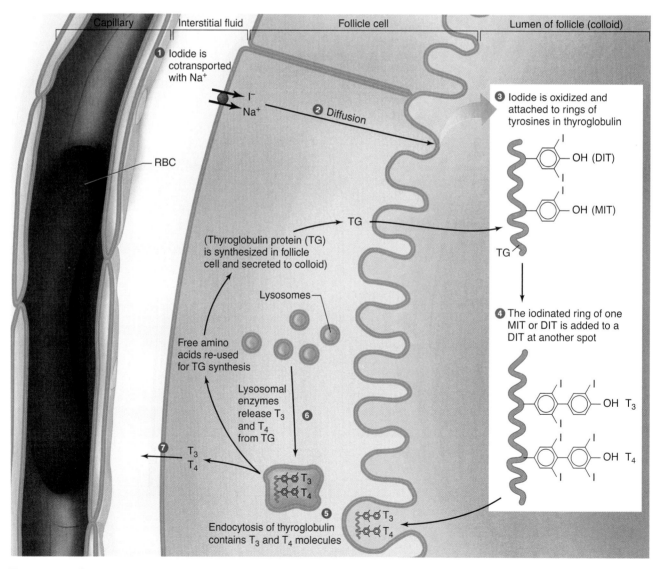

Capillary | Interstitial fluid | Follicle cell | Lumen of follicle (colloid)

❶ Iodide is cotransported with $Na^+$

$I^-$
$Na^+$
❷ Diffusion

RBC

❸ Iodide is oxidized and attached to rings of tyrosines in thyroglobulin

OH (DIT)
OH (MIT)

TG

(Thyroglobulin protein (TG) is synthesized in follicle cell and secreted to colloid)

Lysosomes

Free amino acids re-used for TG synthesis

Lysosomal enzymes release $T_3$ and $T_4$ from TG

❻

❹ The iodinated ring of one MIT or DIT is added to a DIT at another spot

OH $T_3$
OH $T_4$

❼ $T_3$ $T_4$

$T_3$
$T_4$

$T_3$
$T_4$

❺

Endocytosis of thyroglobulin contains $T_3$ and $T_4$ molecules

**$T_3$ and $T_4$ formation**
Figure 11.21

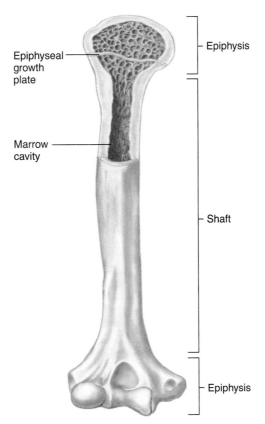

**Anatomy of long bone**
Figure 11.25

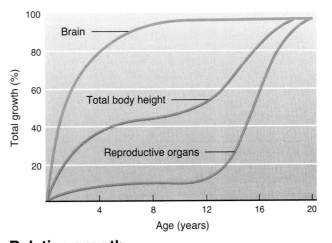

**Relative growth**
Figure 11.26

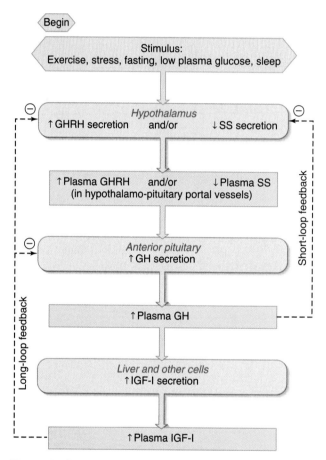

**Regulation of GH and IGF-1**
Figure 11.27

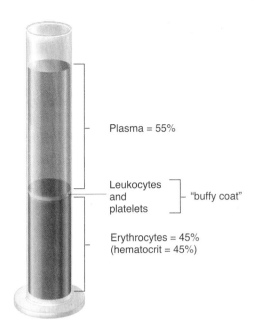

**Measurement of the hematocrit by centrifugation**
Figure 12.1

Plasma = 55%

Leukocytes and platelets — "buffy coat"

Erythrocytes = 45% (hematocrit = 45%)

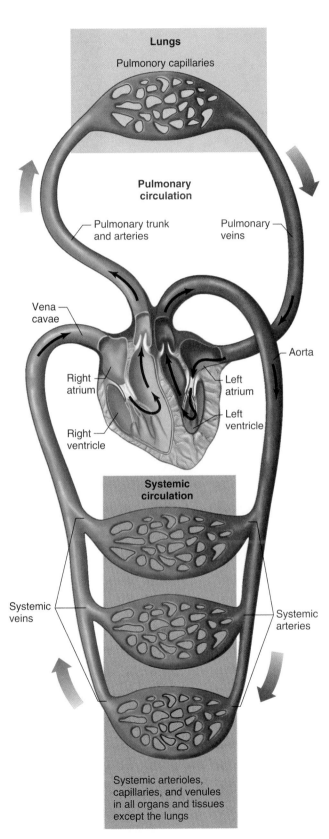

**Lungs**
Pulmonory capillaries

**Pulmonary circulation**

Pulmonary trunk and arteries

Pulmonary veins

Vena cavae

Right atrium

Right ventricle

Aorta

Left atrium

Left ventricle

**Systemic circulation**

Systemic veins

Systemic arteries

Systemic arterioles, capillaries, and venules in all organs and tissues except the lungs

**Overview of circulation**
Figure 12.2

| Organ | Flow at rest ml/min |
|---|---|
| Brain | 650 (13%) |
| Heart | 215 (4%) |
| Skeletal muscle | 1030 (20%) |
| Skin | 430 (9%) |
| Kidney | 950 (20%) |
| Abdominal organs | 1200 (24%) |
| Other | 525 (10%) |
| Total | 5000 (100%) |

**Distribution of systemic blood flow**
Figure 12.3

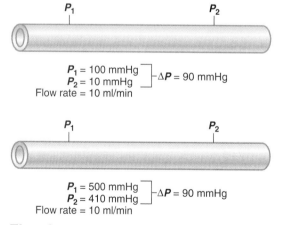

$P_1$       $P_2$

$P_1$ = 100 mmHg
$P_2$ = 10 mmHg    $\Delta P$ = 90 mmHg
Flow rate = 10 ml/min

$P_1$       $P_2$

$P_1$ = 500 mmHg
$P_2$ = 410 mmHg    $\Delta P$ = 90 mmHg
Flow rate = 10 ml/min

**Flow between two points within a tube**
Figure 12.4

**(a)**

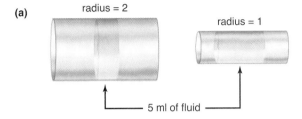

radius = 2

radius = 1

5 ml of fluid

**(b)**

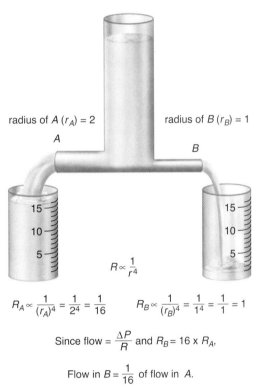

radius of $A$ $(r_A) = 2$

$A$

radius of $B$ $(r_B) = 1$

$B$

$R \propto \dfrac{1}{r^4}$

$R_A \propto \dfrac{1}{(r_A)^4} = \dfrac{1}{2^4} = \dfrac{1}{16}$   $R_B \propto \dfrac{1}{(r_B)^4} = \dfrac{1}{1^4} = \dfrac{1}{1} = 1$

Since flow $= \dfrac{\Delta P}{R}$ and $R_B = 16 \times R_A$,

Flow in $B = \dfrac{1}{16}$ of flow in $A$.

## Effect of tube radius ($r$) on resistance ($R$) and flow
Figure 12.5

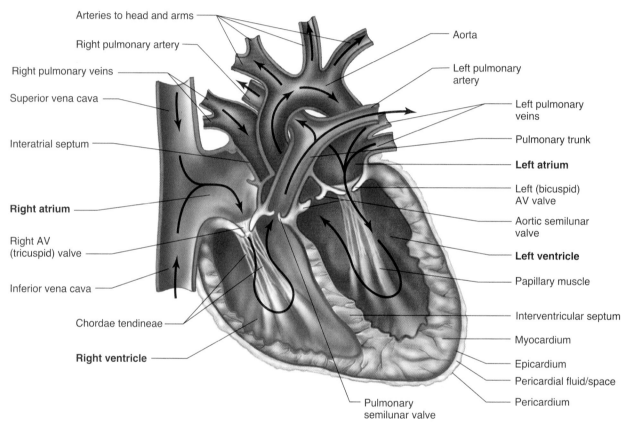

Arteries to head and arms

Right pulmonary artery

Right pulmonary veins

Superior vena cava

Interatrial septum

**Right atrium**

Right AV (tricuspid) valve

Inferior vena cava

Chordae tendineae

**Right ventricle**

Aorta

Left pulmonary artery

Left pulmonary veins

Pulmonary trunk

**Left atrium**

Left (bicuspid) AV valve

Aortic semilunar valve

**Left ventricle**

Papillary muscle

Interventricular septum

Myocardium

Epicardium

Pericardial fluid/space

Pericardium

Pulmonary semilunar valve

**Section through the heart**
Figure 12.6

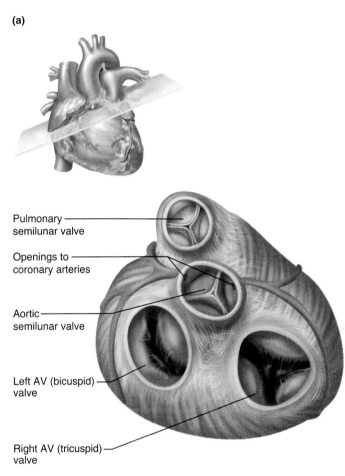

**(a)**

Pulmonary semilunar valve

Openings to coronary arteries

Aortic semilunar valve

Left AV (bicuspid) valve

Right AV (tricuspid) valve

**Valves of the heart**
Figure 12.7

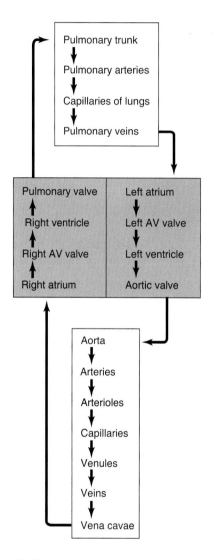

**Path of blood flow**
Figure 12.8

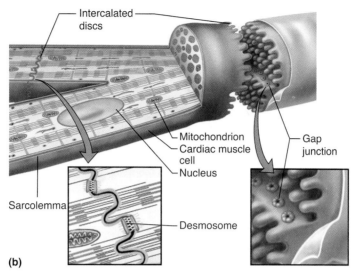

Intercalated
discs

Mitochondrion
Cardiac muscle
cell
Nucleus

Gap
junction

Sarcolemma

Desmosome

(b)

**Diagram of cardiac muscle**
Figure 12.9

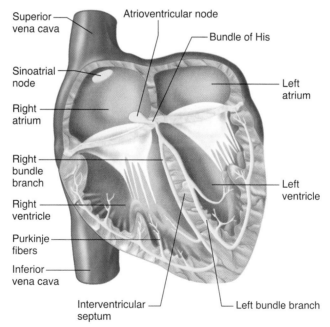

Superior
vena cava

Atrioventricular node

Bundle of His

Sinoatrial
node

Left
atrium

Right
atrium

Right
bundle
branch

Left
ventricle

Right
ventricle

Purkinje
fibers

Inferior
vena cava

Interventricular
septum

Left bundle branch

**Conducting system of the heart**
Figure 12.10

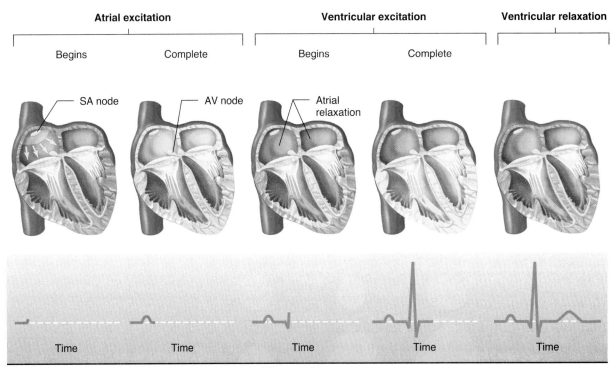

**Atrial excitation**

Begins      Complete

**Ventricular excitation**

Begins      Complete

**Ventricular relaxation**

SA node    AV node    Atrial relaxation

Time    Time    Time    Time    Time

Electrocardiogram

**Sequence of cardiac excitation**
Figure 12.11

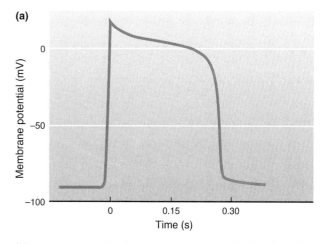

(a)

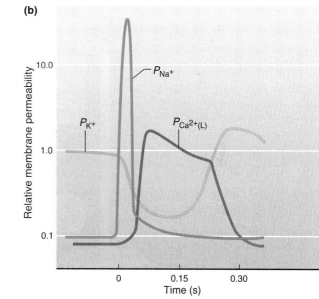

(b)

**Potential and permeability changes in heart muscle**
Figure 12.12

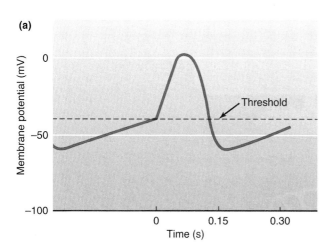

(a)

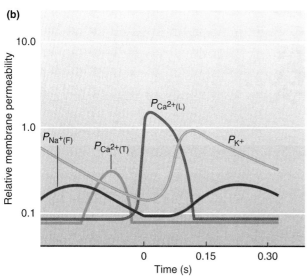

(b)

**Potential and permeability changes in heart muscle (cont'd.)**
Figure 12.13

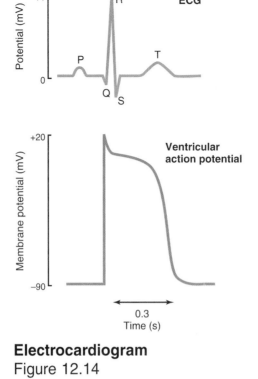

**Electrocardiogram**
Figure 12.14

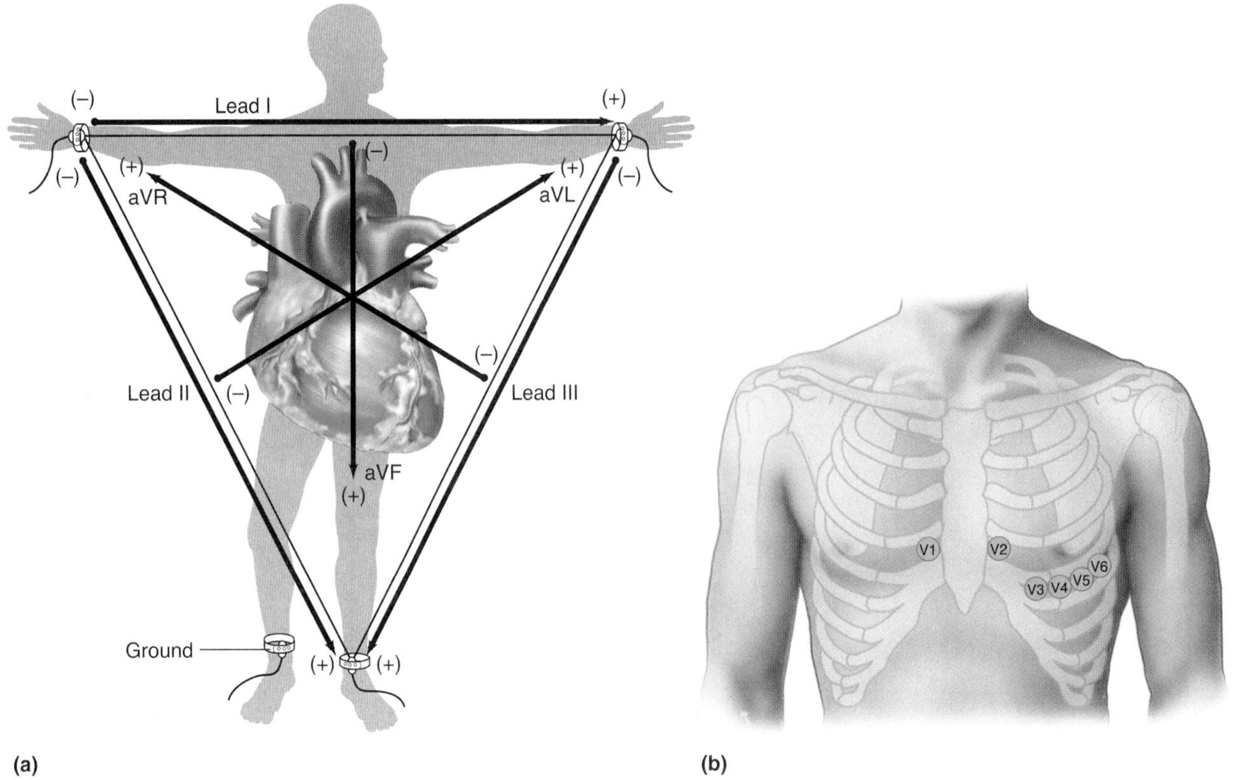

**Placement of electrodes in electrocardiography**
Figure 12.15

(a)

(b)

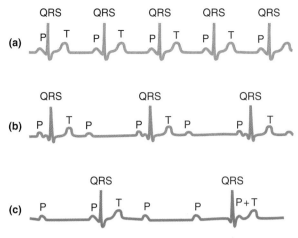

**Electrocardiogram results**

Figure 12.16

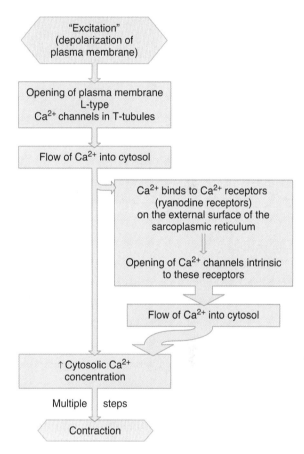

**Excitation-contraction coupling in cardiac muscle**

Figure 12.17

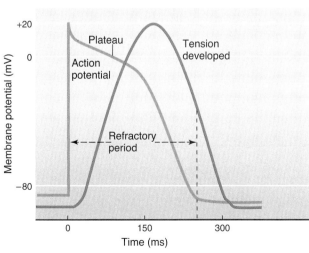

**Relationship between membrane potential changes and contraction**

Figure 12.18

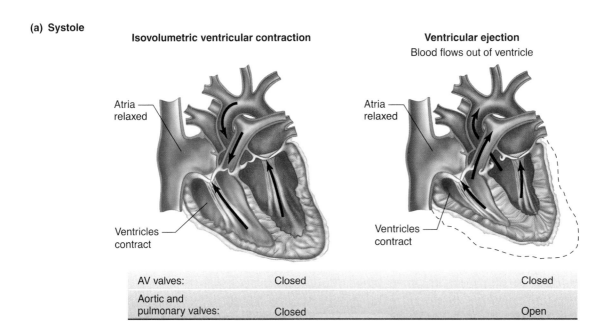

**(a) Systole**

**Isovolumetric ventricular contraction**

**Ventricular ejection**
Blood flows out of ventricle

Atria relaxed

Atria relaxed

Ventricles contract

Ventricles contract

| AV valves: | Closed | Closed |
|---|---|---|
| Aortic and pulmonary valves: | Closed | Open |

**(b) Diastole**

**Isovolumetric ventricular relaxation**

**Ventricular filling**
Blood flows into ventricles

Atrial contraction

Atria relaxed

Atria relaxed

Atria contract

Ventricles relaxed

Ventricles relaxed

Ventricles relaxed

| AV valves: | Closed | Open | Open |
|---|---|---|---|
| Aortic and pulmonary valves: | Closed | Closed | Closed |

**Cardiac cycle**
Figure 12.19

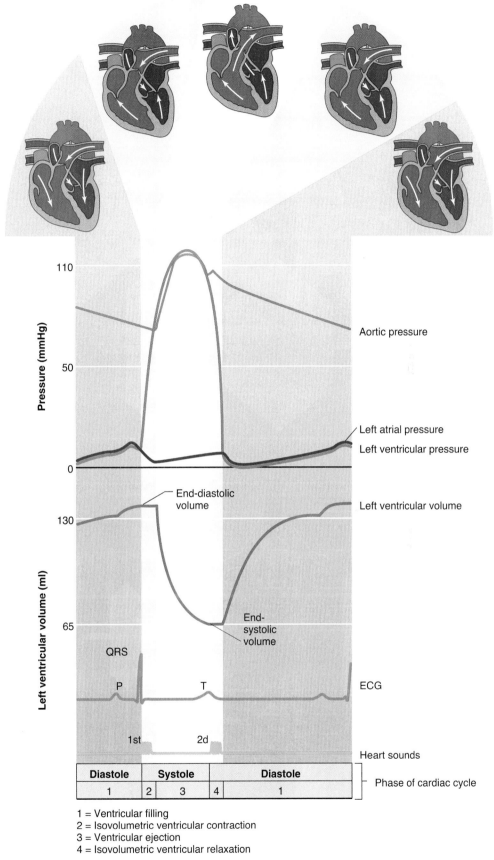

**Summary of events in cardiac cycle**
Figure 12.20

1 = Ventricular filling
2 = Isovolumetric ventricular contraction
3 = Ventricular ejection
4 = Isovolumetric ventricular relaxation

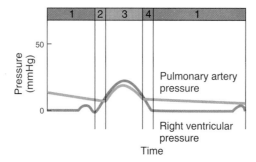

1 = Ventricular filling
2 = Isovolumetric ventricular contraction
3 = Ventricular ejection
4 = Isovolumetric ventricular relaxation

**Pressures during the cardiac cycle**
Figure 12.21

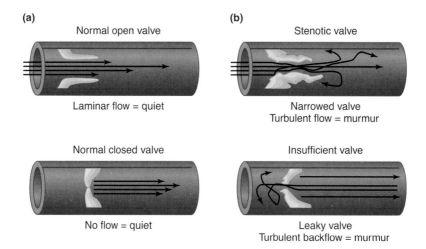

**(a)**

Normal open valve

Laminar flow = quiet

Normal closed valve

No flow = quiet

**(b)**

Stenotic valve

Narrowed valve
Turbulent flow = murmur

Insufficient valve

Leaky valve
Turbulent backflow = murmur

**Heart valve defects causing turbulent blood flow and murmurs**
Figure 12.22

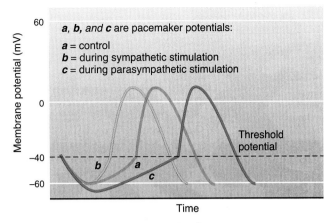

**Effects of nerve stimulation**
Figure 12.23

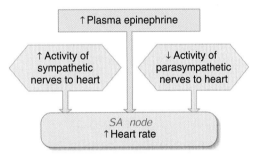

**Major factors that influence heart rate**
Figure 12.24

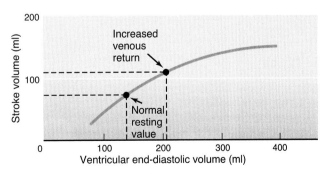

**A ventricular function curve**
Figure 12.25

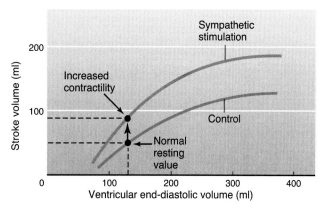

**Effects on stroke volume**
Figure 12.26

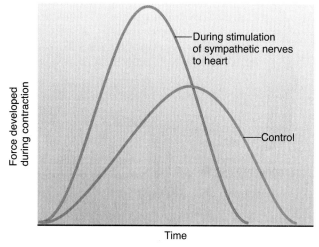

**Effects of sympathetic stimulation**
Figure 12.27

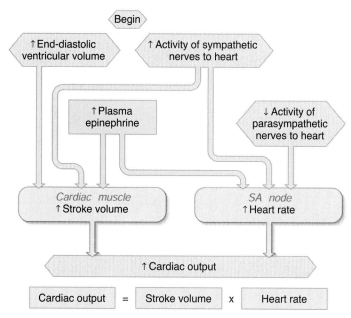

**Major factors determining cardiac output**
Figure 12.28

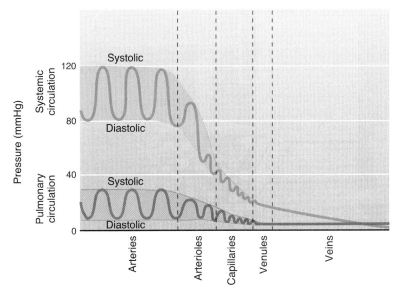

**Pressures in the systemic vessels**
Figure 12.29

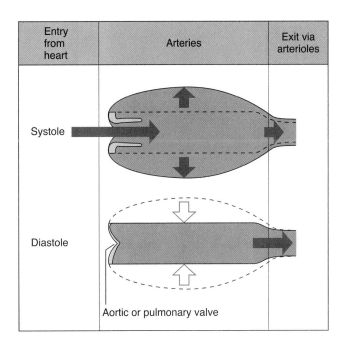

**Movement of blood**
Figure 12.30

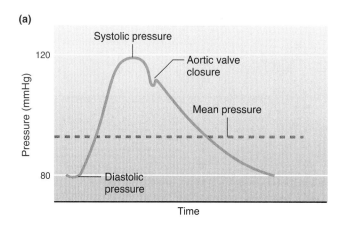

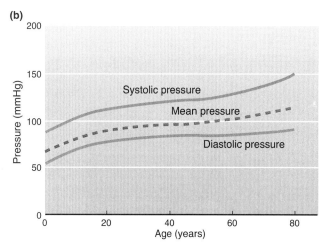

**Fluctuations during the cardiac cycle**
Figure 12.31

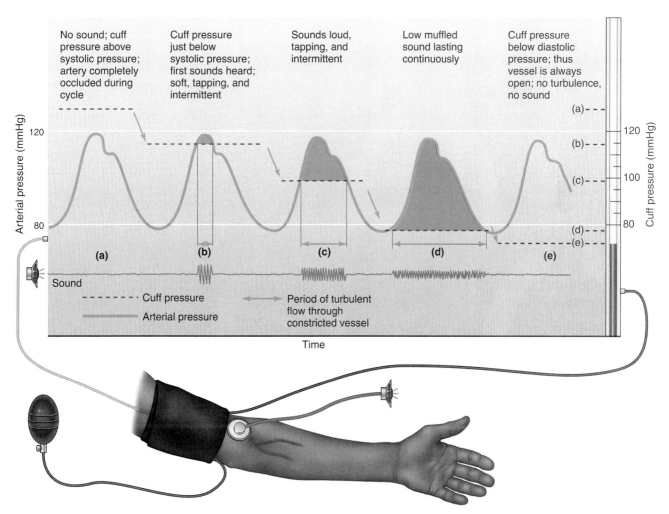

**Sounds heard through a stethoscope**
Figure 12.32

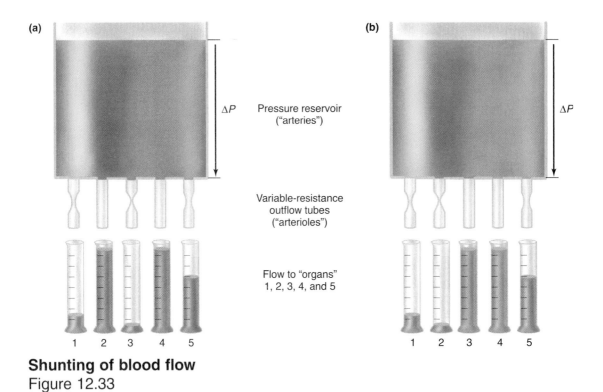

**(a)**

$\Delta P$    Pressure reservoir ("arteries")

Variable-resistance outflow tubes ("arterioles")

Flow to "organs" 1, 2, 3, 4, and 5

**(b)**

$\Delta P$

1 2 3 4 5

1 2 3 4 5

**Shunting of blood flow**
Figure 12.33

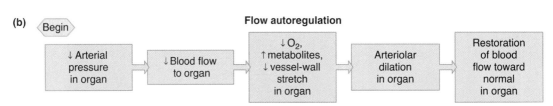

**(a)** Begin    **Active hyperemia**

↑ Metabolic activity of organ → ↓ $O_2$, ↑ metabolites in organ interstitial fluid → Arteriolar dilation in organ → ↑ Blood flow to organ

**(b)** Begin    **Flow autoregulation**

↓ Arterial pressure in organ → ↓ Blood flow to organ → ↓ $O_2$, ↑ metabolites, ↓ vessel-wall stretch in organ → Arteriolar dilation in organ → Restoration of blood flow toward normal in organ

**Local control of organ blood flow**
Figure 12.34

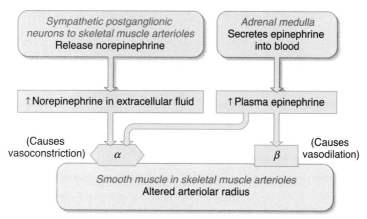

**Effects on the arterioles in skeletal muscle**
Figure 12.35

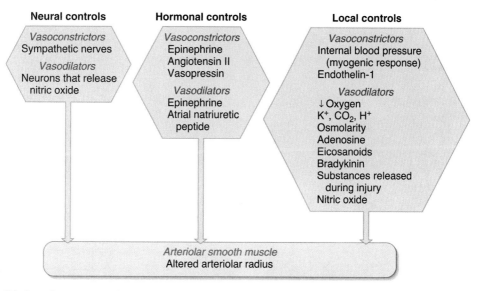

**Major factors affecting arteriolar radius**
Figure 12.36

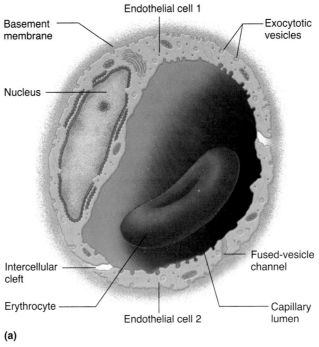

**Capillary cross section**
Figure 12.37

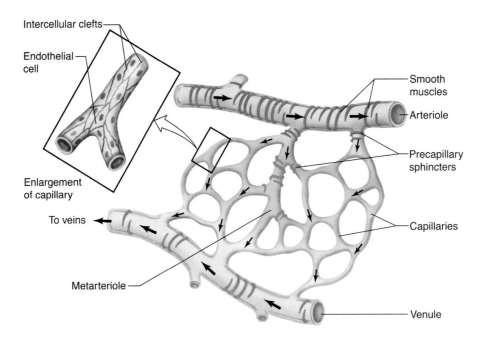

**Microcirculation**
Figure 12.38

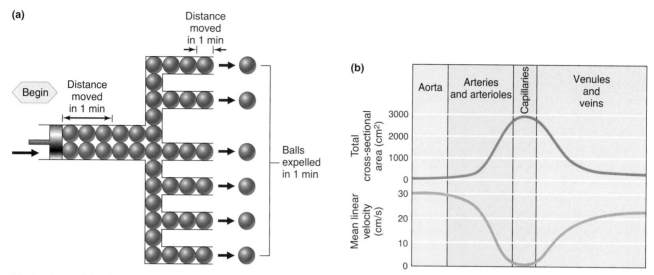

**Relationship between total cross-sectional area and flow velocity**
Figure 12.39

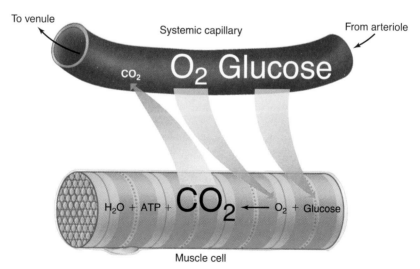

**Diffusion gradients at a systemic capillary**
Figure 12.40

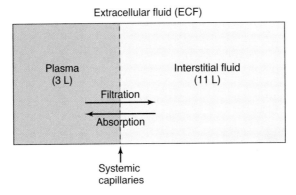

**Distribution of the extracellular fluid by bulk flow**
Figure 12.41

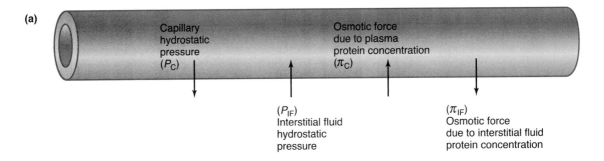

Net filtration pressure = $P_C + \pi_{IF} - P_{IF} - \pi_C$

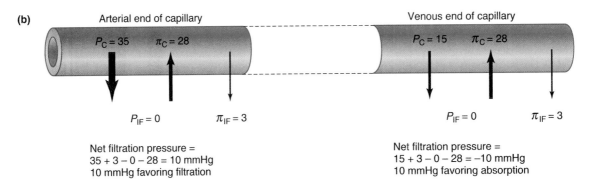

(b)

Arterial end of capillary

$P_C = 35$    $\pi_C = 28$

$P_{IF} = 0$    $\pi_{IF} = 3$

Net filtration pressure =
35 + 3 − 0 − 28 = 10 mmHg
10 mmHg favoring filtration

Venous end of capillary

$P_C = 15$    $\pi_C = 28$

$P_{IF} = 0$    $\pi_{IF} = 3$

Net filtration pressure =
15 + 3 − 0 − 28 = −10 mmHg
10 mmHg favoring absorption

**Fluid movement across capillaries**
Figure 12.42

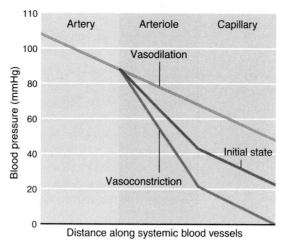

**Effects on capillary blood pressure**
Figure 12.43

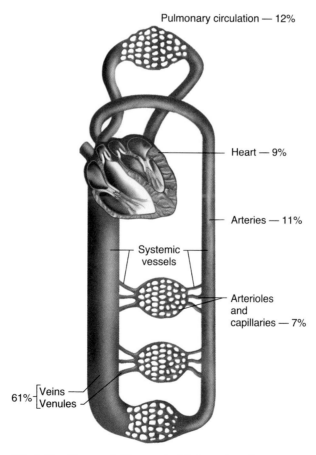

**Distribution of the total blood volume**
Figure 12.44

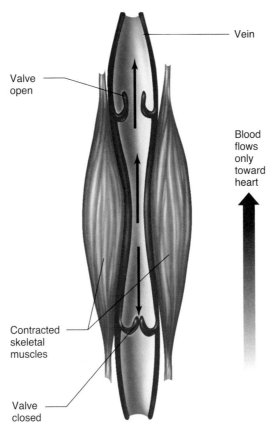

Vein

Valve
open

Blood
flows
only
toward
heart

Contracted
skeletal
muscles

Valve
closed

**Skeletal muscle pump**
Figure 12.45

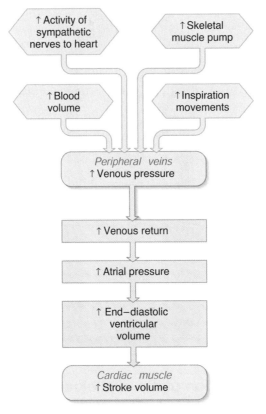

↑ Activity of
sympathetic
nerves to heart

↑ Skeletal
muscle pump

↑ Blood
volume

↑ Inspiration
movements

*Peripheral veins*
↑ Venous pressure

↑ Venous return

↑ Atrial pressure

↑ End–diastolic
ventricular
volume

*Cardiac muscle*
↑ Stroke volume

**Stroke volume and venous return**
Figure 12.46

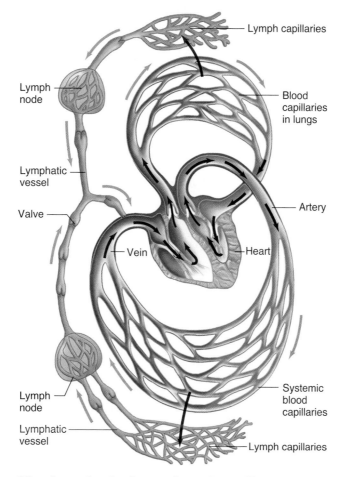

Lymph capillaries

Lymph
node

Lymphatic
vessel

Valve

Vein

Blood
capillaries
in lungs

Artery

Heart

Lymph
node

Systemic
blood
capillaries

Lymphatic
vessel

Lymph capillaries

**The lymphatic (green) and cardiovascular
(blue and red) systems**
Figure 12.47

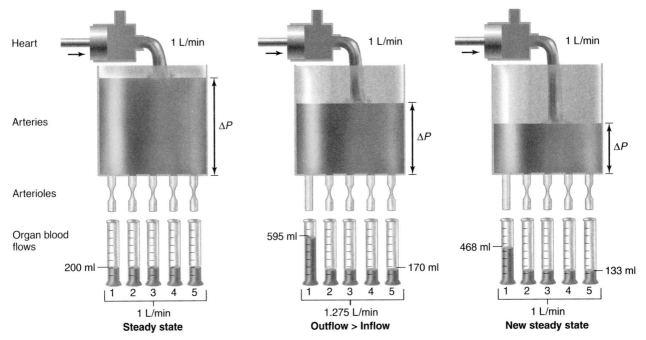

**Dependence of arterial blood pressure**
Figure 12.49

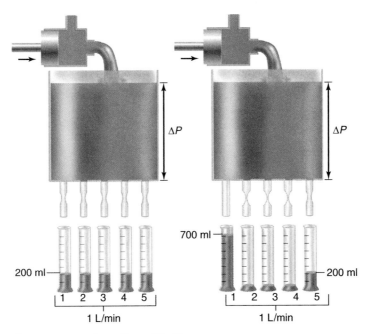

**Compensation for dilation**
Figure 12.50

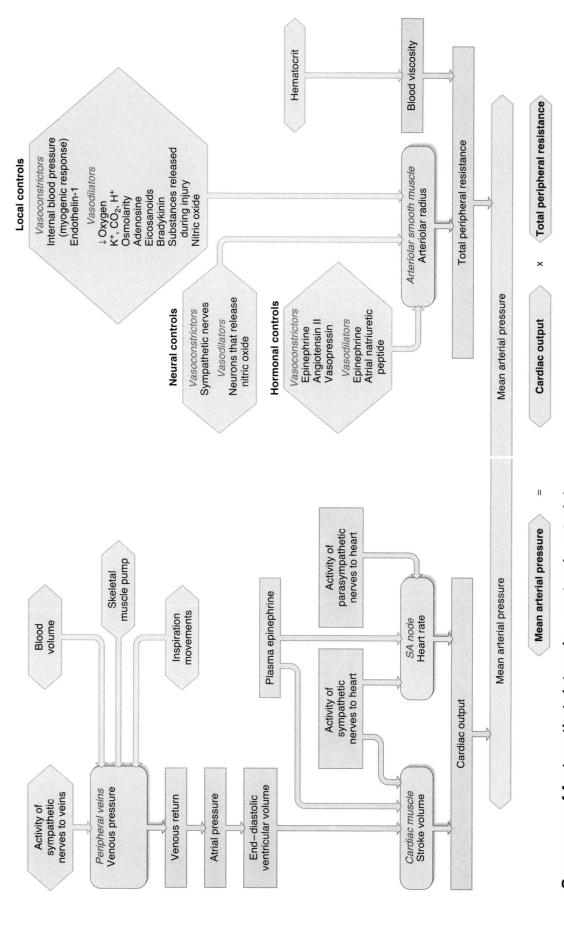

**Summary of factors that determine systemic arterial pressure**
Figure 12.51

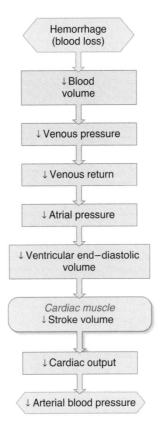

**Sequence of events to decrease arterial pressure**
Figure 12.52

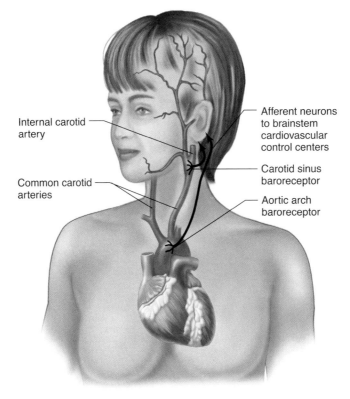

Internal carotid artery

Common carotid arteries

Afferent neurons to brainstem cardiovascular control centers

Carotid sinus baroreceptor

Aortic arch baroreceptor

**Locations of arterial baroreceptors**
Figure 12.53

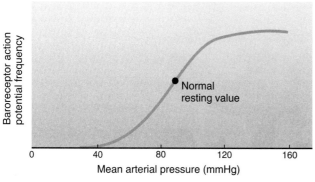

**Effect of changing mean arterial pressure (MAP)**
Figure 12.54

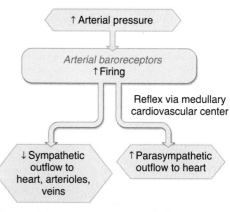

**Neural components of the arterial baroreceptor reflex**
Figure 12.55

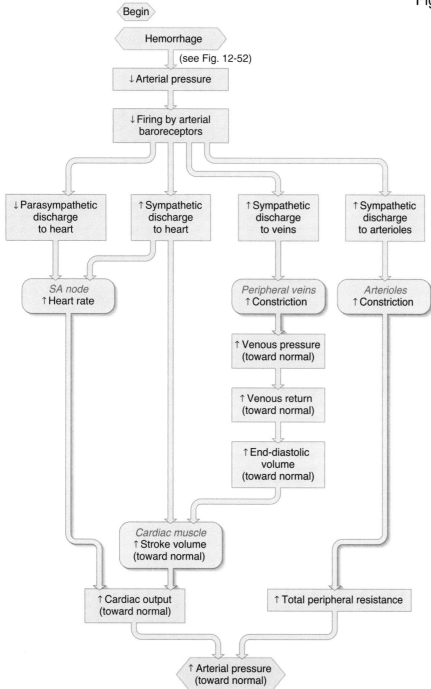

**Baroreceptor reflex after hemorrhage**
Figure 12.56

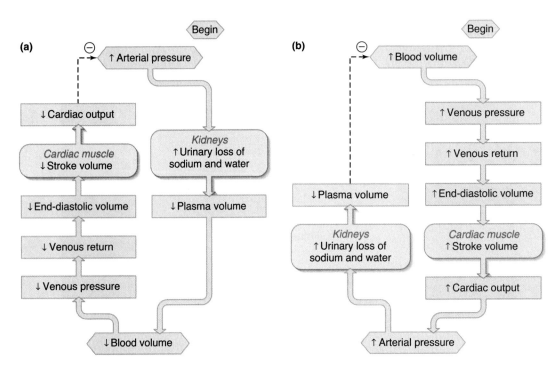

**Reciprocal relationships between arterial pressure and blood volume**
Figure 12.57

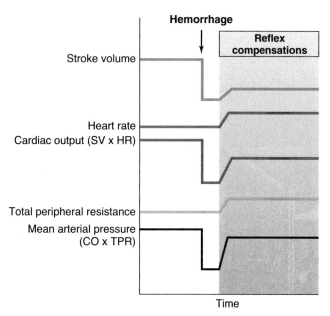

**Cardiovascular effects of hemorrhage**
Figure 12.58

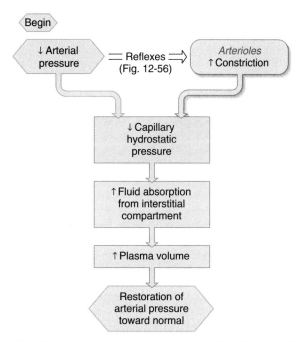

**Mechanisms compensating for blood loss**
Figure 12.59

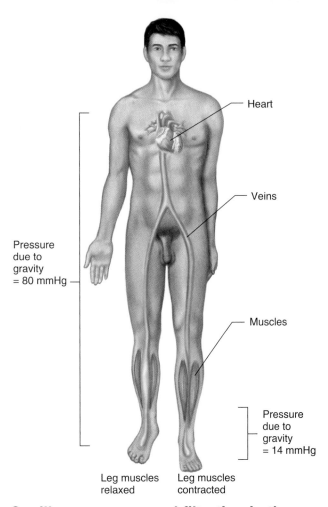

**Capillary pressure and filtration in the upright position**
Figure 12.60

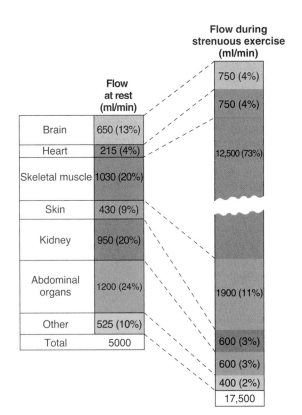

| | Flow at rest (ml/min) | Flow during strenuous exercise (ml/min) |
|---|---|---|
| Brain | 650 (13%) | 750 (4%) |
| Heart | 215 (4%) | 750 (4%) |
| Skeletal muscle | 1030 (20%) | 12,500 (73%) |
| Skin | 430 (9%) | |
| Kidney | 950 (20%) | 1900 (11%) |
| Abdominal organs | 1200 (24%) | 600 (3%) |
| Other | 525 (10%) | 600 (3%) |
| | | 400 (2%) |
| Total | 5000 | 17,500 |

**Distribution of the systemic cardiac output**
Figure 12.61

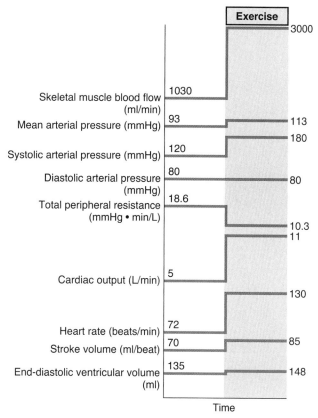

**Cardiovascular changes during mild upright exercise**

Figure 12.62

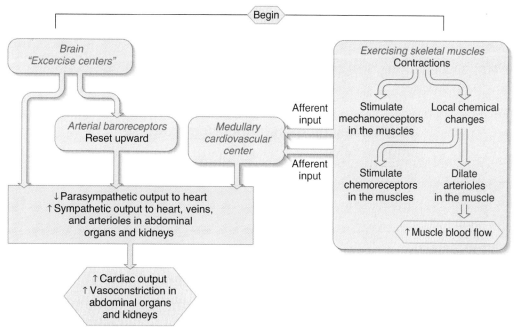

**Response to exercise**

Figure 12.63

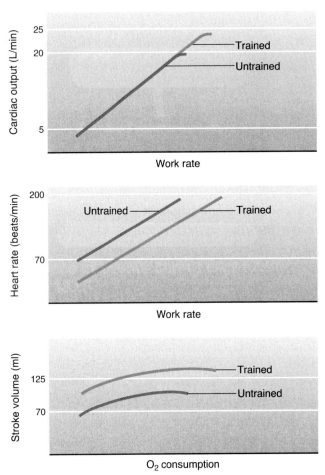

**Cardiovascular system during exercise**
Figure 12.64

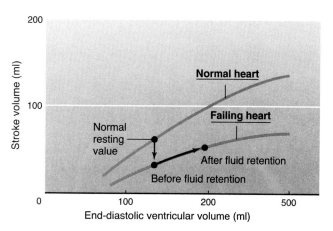

## Changes with increasing workload
Figure 12.65

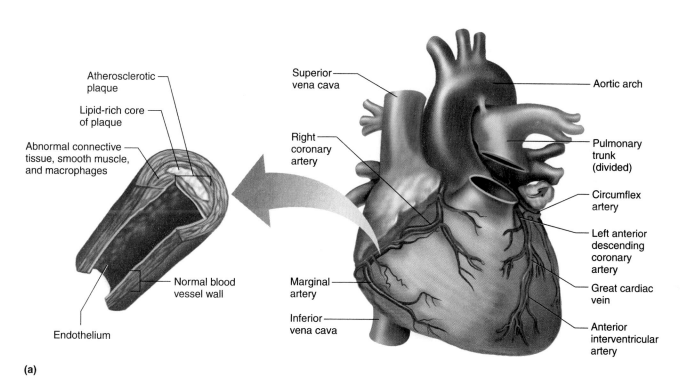

Atherosclerotic plaque

Lipid-rich core of plaque

Abnormal connective tissue, smooth muscle, and macrophages

Endothelium

Normal blood vessel wall

(a)

Superior vena cava

Right coronary artery

Marginal artery

Inferior vena cava

Aortic arch

Pulmonary trunk (divided)

Circumflex artery

Left anterior descending coronary artery

Great cardiac vein

Anterior interventricular artery

## Coronary artery disease and its treatment
Figure 12.66

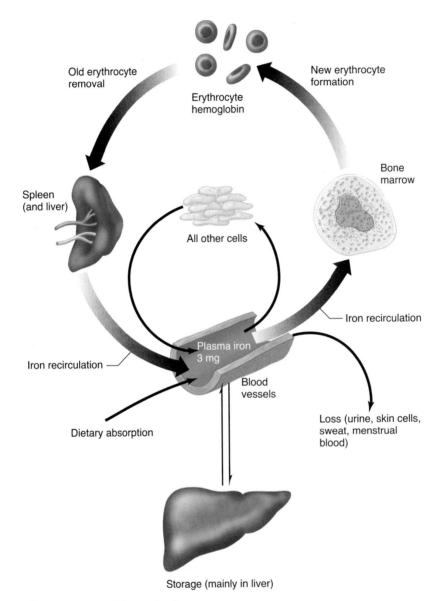

Old erythrocyte removal

Erythrocyte hemoglobin

New erythrocyte formation

Bone marrow

Spleen (and liver)

All other cells

Iron recirculation

Iron recirculation

Plasma iron 3 mg

Blood vessels

Dietary absorption

Loss (urine, skin cells, sweat, menstrual blood)

Storage (mainly in liver)

**Summary of iron balance**
Figure 12.68

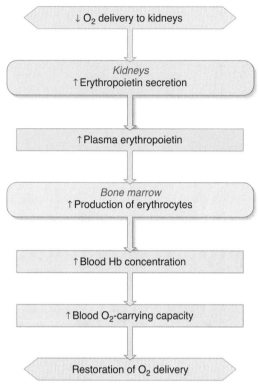

**Oxygen delivery to the kidneys**
Figure 12.69

| Erythrocytes | Leukocytes | | | | | Platelets |
| --- | --- | --- | --- | --- | --- | --- |
| | Polymorphonuclear granulocytes | | | Monocytes | Lymphocytes | |
| | Neutrophils | Eosinophils | Basophils | | | |

**Classes of blood cells**
Figure 12.70

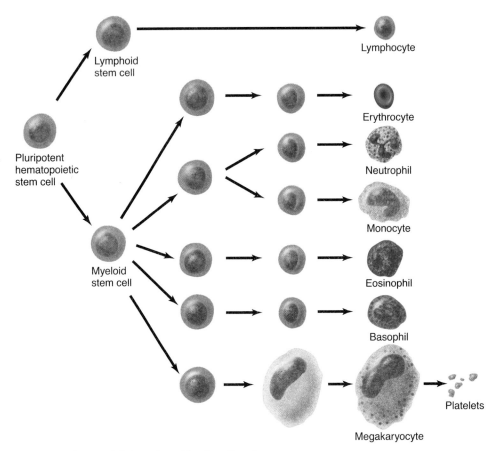

Lymphoid
stem cell

Lymphocyte

Pluripotent
hematopoietic
stem cell

Myeloid
stem cell

Erythrocyte

Neutrophil

Monocyte

Eosinophil

Basophil

Megakaryocyte

Platelets

**Production of blood cells by the bone marrow**
Figure 12.71

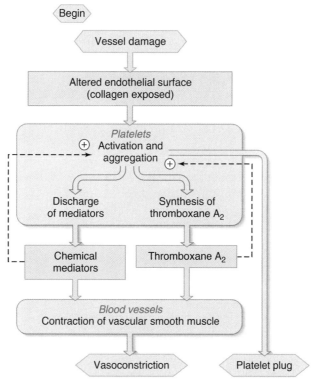

**Events following blood vessel damage**
Figure 12.72

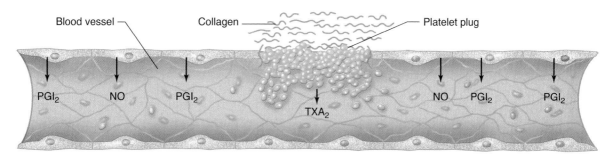

**Prostacyclin (PGI₂) and nitric oxide (NO) inhibit platelet aggregation**
Figure 12.73

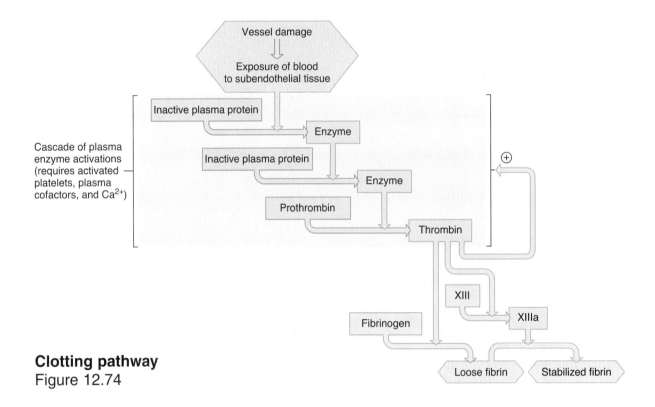

**Clotting pathway**
Figure 12.74

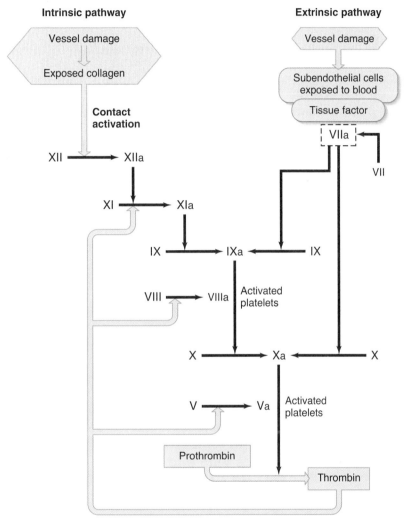

**Two clotting pathways**
Figure 12.76

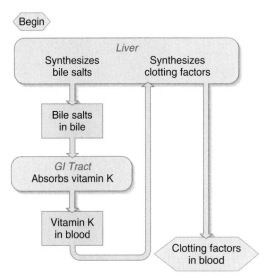

**Roles of the liver in clotting**
Figure 12.77

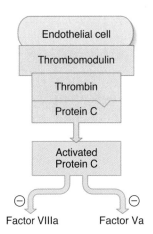

**Thrombin inactivates factors VIIIa and Va**
Figure 12.78

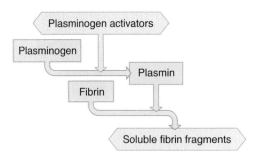

**Basic fibrinolytic system**
Figure 12.79

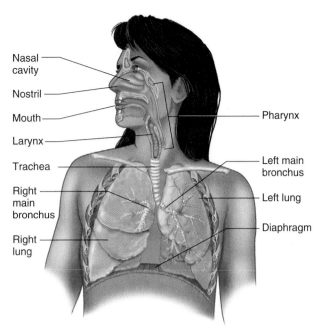

**Organization of respiratory system**
Figure 13.1

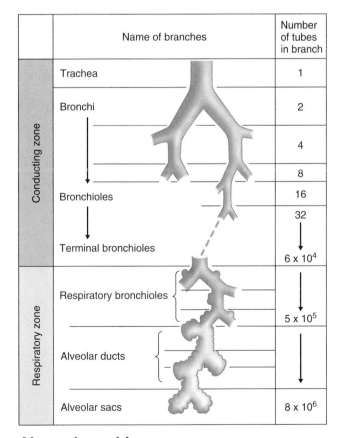

| | Name of branches | | Number of tubes in branch |
|---|---|---|---|
| Conducting zone | Trachea | | 1 |
| | Bronchi | | 2 |
| | | | 4 |
| | | | 8 |
| | Bronchioles | | 16 |
| | | | 32 |
| | Terminal bronchioles | | $6 \times 10^4$ |
| Respiratory zone | Respiratory bronchioles | | |
| | | | $5 \times 10^5$ |
| | Alveolar ducts | | |
| | Alveolar sacs | | $8 \times 10^6$ |

**Airway branching**
Figure 13.2

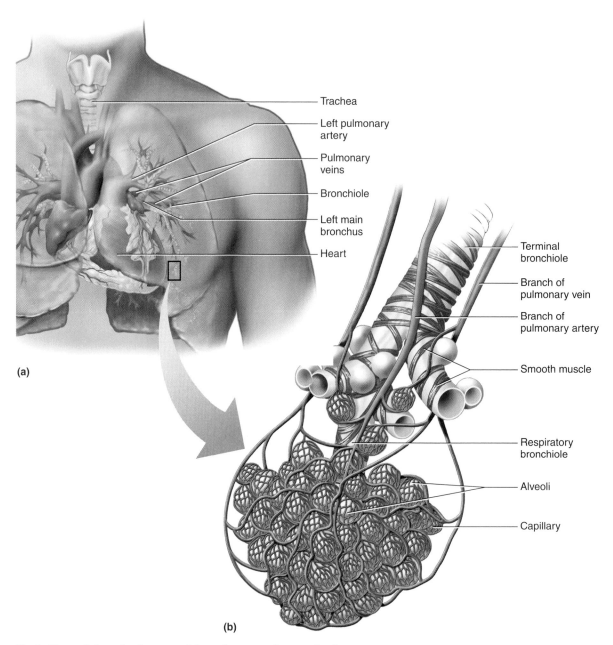

(a)

(b)

Trachea

Left pulmonary artery

Pulmonary veins

Bronchiole

Left main bronchus

Heart

Terminal bronchiole

Branch of pulmonary vein

Branch of pulmonary artery

Smooth muscle

Respiratory bronchiole

Alveoli

Capillary

**Relationships between blood vessels and airways**
Figure 13.3

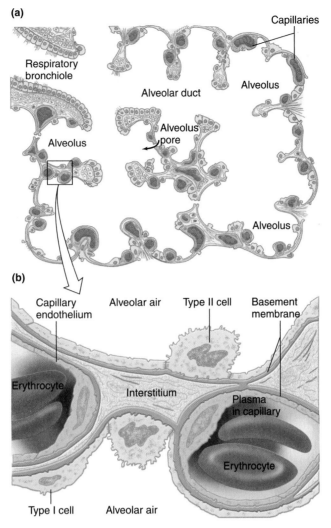

**(a)**

Respiratory bronchiole

Capillaries

Alveolar duct

Alveolus

Alveolus

Alveolus pore

Alveolus

**(b)**

Capillary endothelium

Alveolar air

Type II cell

Basement membrane

Erythrocyte

Interstitium

Plasma in capillary

Erythrocyte

Type I cell

Alveolar air

**Alveoli**

Figure 13.4

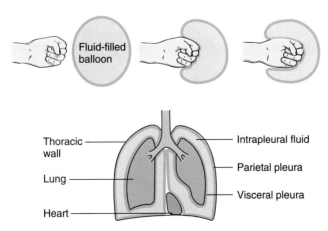

Fluid-filled balloon

Thoracic wall

Intrapleural fluid

Lung

Parietal pleura

Heart

Visceral pleura

**Relationship of lungs, pleura, and thoracic wall**

Figure 13.5

① Ventilation: Exchange of air between atmosphere and alveoli by *bulk flow*
② Exchange of $O_2$ and $CO_2$ between alveolar air and blood in lung capillaries by *diffusion*
③ Transport of $O_2$ and $CO_2$ through pulmonary and systemic circulation by *bulk flow*
④ Exchange of $O_2$ and $CO_2$ between blood in tissue capillaries and cells in tissues by *diffusion*
⑤ Cellular utilization of $O_2$ and production of $CO_2$

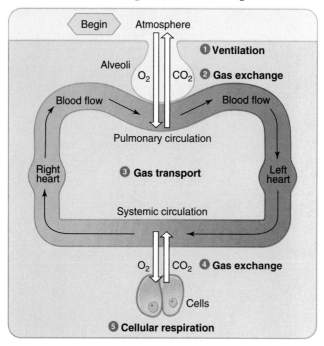

**Steps of respiration**
Figure 13.6

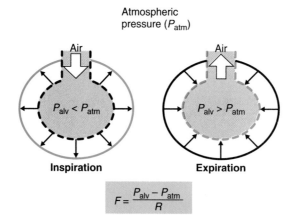

$$F = \frac{P_{alv} - P_{atm}}{R}$$

**Relationships required for ventilation**
Figure 13.7

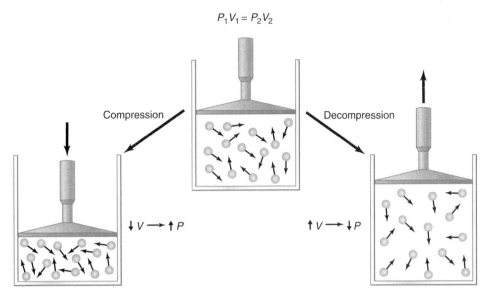

$$P_1V_1 = P_2V_2$$

Compression

Decompression

$\downarrow V \longrightarrow \uparrow P$

$\uparrow V \longrightarrow \downarrow P$

**Boyle's law**
Figure 13.8

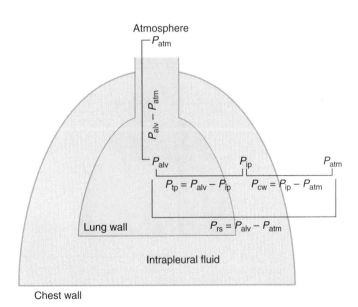

Atmosphere

$P_{atm}$

$P_{alv} - P_{atm}$

$P_{alv}$

$P_{ip}$

$P_{atm}$

$P_{tp} = P_{alv} - P_{ip}$

$P_{cw} = P_{ip} - P_{atm}$

Lung wall

$P_{rs} = P_{alv} - P_{atm}$

Intrapleural fluid

Chest wall

**Pressure differences involved in ventilation**
Figure 13.9

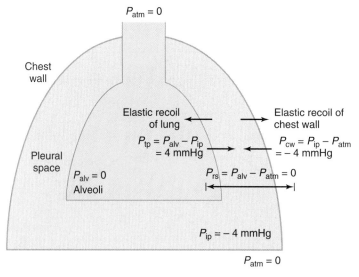

**Pressures between breaths (no air flow)**
Figure 13.10

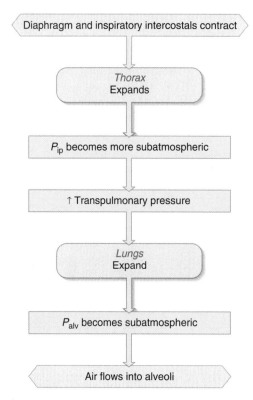

**Sequence of events during inspiration**
Figure 13.12

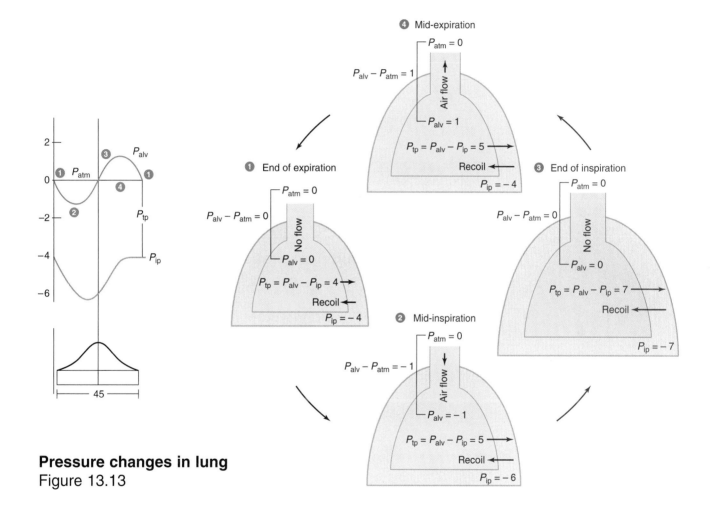

**Pressure changes in lung**

Figure 13.13

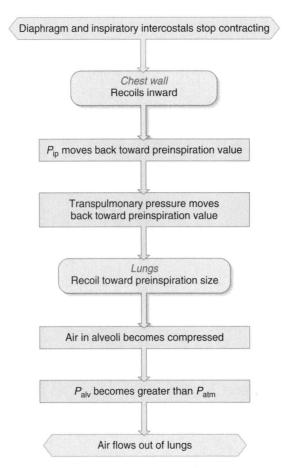

## Sequence of events during expiration
Figure 13.15

$$\text{Compliance} = \frac{\Delta \text{ Lung volume}}{\Delta (P_{alv} - P_{ip})} = \frac{\Delta V}{\Delta P_{tp}}$$

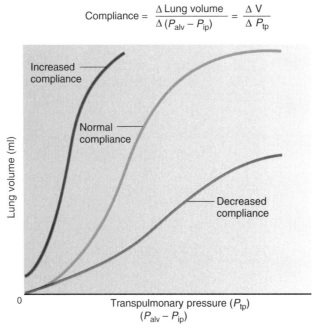

## Representation of lung compliance
Figure 13.16

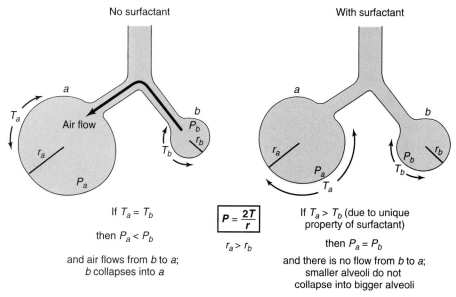

No surfactant

With surfactant

If $T_a = T_b$

then $P_a < P_b$

and air flows from $b$ to $a$;
$b$ collapses into $a$

$$P = \frac{2T}{r}$$

$r_a > r_b$

If $T_a > T_b$ (due to unique property of surfactant)

then $P_a = P_b$

and there is no flow from $b$ to $a$;
smaller alveoli do not
collapse into bigger alveoli

### Stabilizing effect of surfactant
Figure 13.17

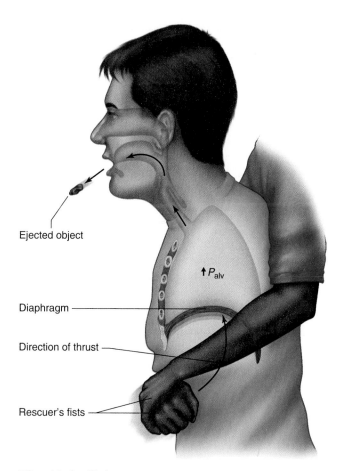

Ejected object

$\uparrow P_{alv}$

Diaphragm

Direction of thrust

Rescuer's fists

### The Heimlich maneuver
Figure 13.18

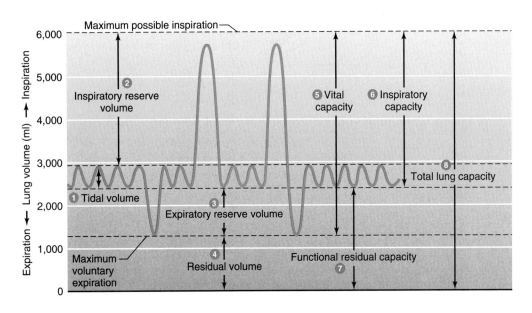

| Respiratory Volumes and Capacities for an Average Young Adult Male | | |
|---|---|---|
| Measurement | Typical Value | Definition |
| **Respiratory Volumes** | | |
| ❶ Tidal volume (TV) | 500 ml | Amount of air inhaled or exhaled in one breath during relaxed, quiet breathing |
| ❷ Inspiratory reserve volume (IRV) | 3,000 ml | Amount of air in excess of tidal inspiration that can be inhaled with maximum effort |
| ❸ Expiratory reserve volume (ERV) | 1,200 ml | Amount of air in excess of tidal expiration that can be exhaled with maximum effort |
| ❹ Residual volume (RV) | 1,200 ml | Amount of air remaining in the lungs after maximum expiration; keeps alveoli inflated between breaths and mixes with fresh air on next inspiration |
| **Respiratory Capacities** | | |
| ❺ Vital capacity (VC) | 4,700 ml | Amount of air that can be exhaled with maximum effort after maximum inspiration (ERV + TV + IRV); used to assess strength of thoracic muscles as well as pulmonary function |
| ❻ Inspiratory capacity (IC) | 3,500 ml | Maximum amount of air that can be inhaled after a normal tidal expiration (TV + IRV) |
| ❼ Functional residual capacity (FRC) | 2,400 ml | Amount of air remaining in the lungs after a normal tidal expiration (RV + ERV) |
| ❽ Total lung capacity (TLC) | 5,900 ml | Maximum amount of air the lungs can contain (RV + VC) |

## Lung volumes and capacities

Figure 13.19

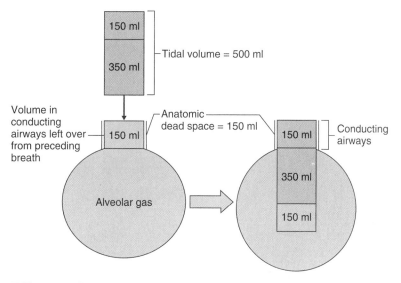

**Effects of anatomic dead space**
Figure 13.20

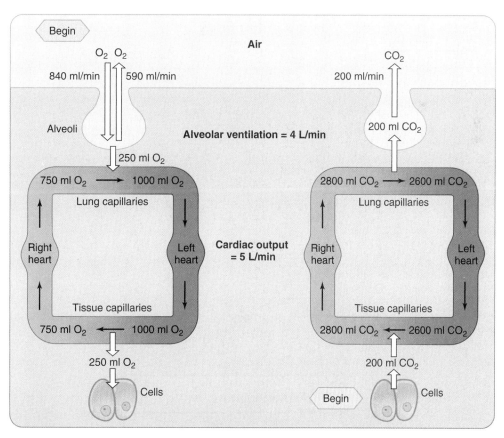

**Oxygen and carbon dioxide exchanges**
Figure 13.21

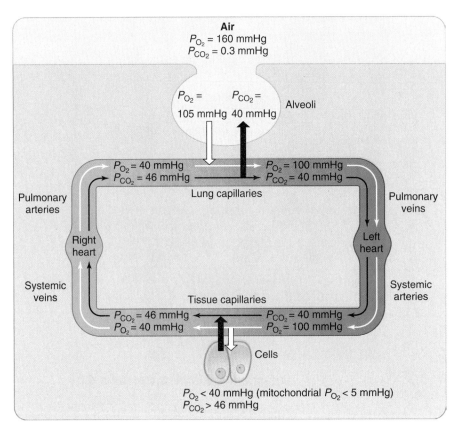

**Partial pressures of gases in the body**
Figure 13.22

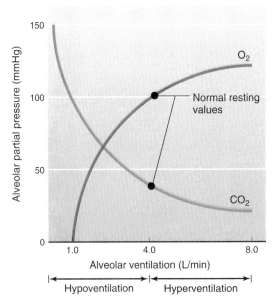

**Effects of increasing or decreasing alveolar ventilation**
Figure 13.23

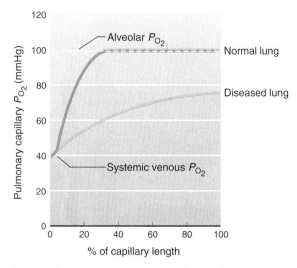

**Equilibration of blood $P_{O_2}$ with alveolar $P_{O_2}$**
Figure 13.24

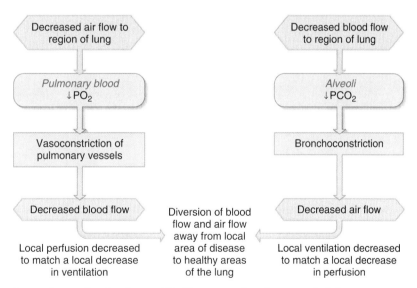

**Local control of ventilation-perfusion matching**
Figure 13.25

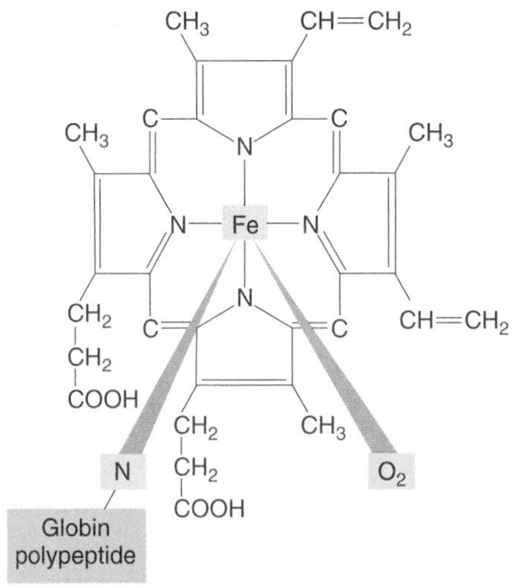

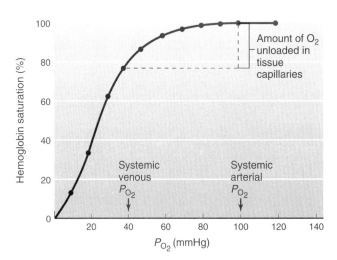

**Heme**

Figure 13.26

**Oxygen-hemoglobin dissociation curve**

Figure 13.27

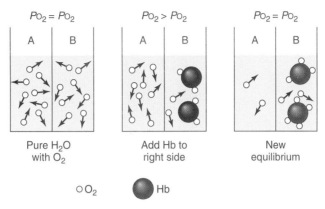

**Effect of added hemoglobin on oxygen**
Figure 13.28

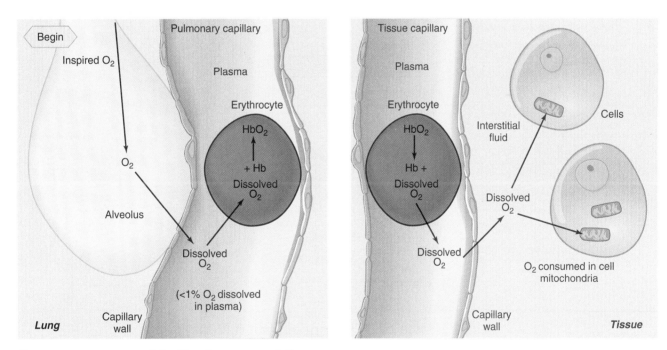

**Oxygen movement in the lungs and tissues**
Figure 13.29

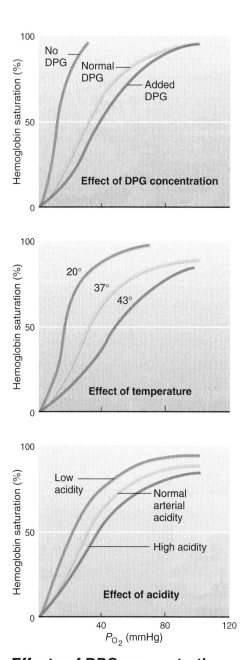

**Effects of DPG concentration, temperature, and acidity**
Figure 13.30

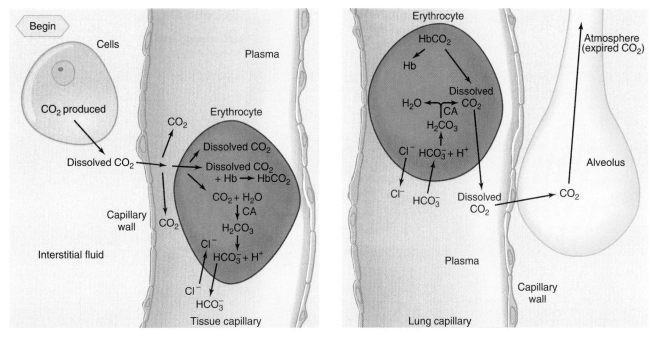

**CO₂ movement**
Figure 13.31

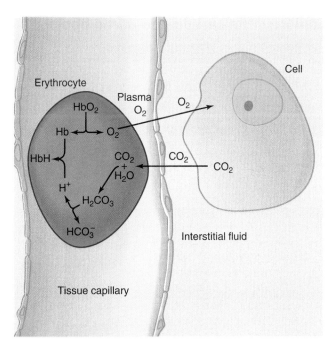

**Binding of hydrogen ions**
Figure 13.32

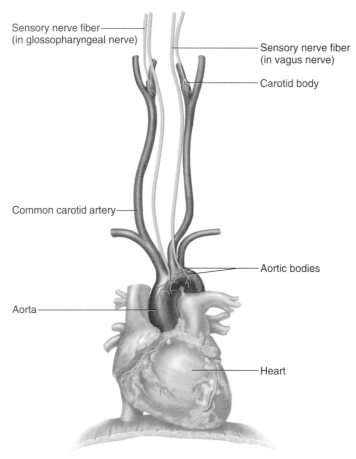

Sensory nerve fiber
(in glossopharyngeal nerve)

Sensory nerve fiber
(in vagus nerve)

Carotid body

Common carotid artery

Aortic bodies

Aorta

Heart

**Location of the carotid and aortic bodies**
Figure 13.33

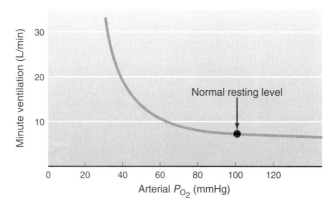

**The effect of low-oxygen mixtures**
Figure 13.34

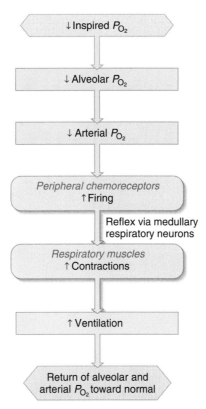

**Sequence of events causing hyperventilation**
Figure 13.35

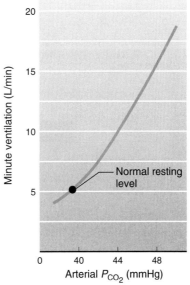

**Effects of adding carbon dioxide to inspired air**
Figure 13.36

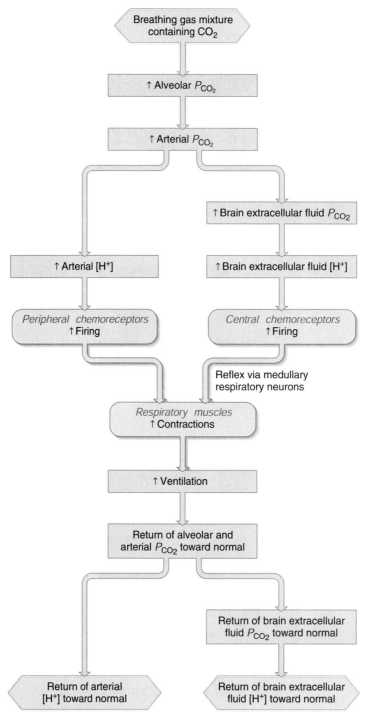

**Effect of CO<sub>2</sub> on ventilation**
Figure 13.37

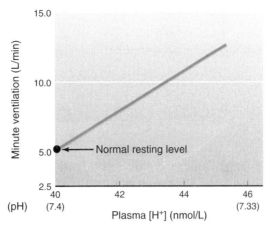

**Changes produced by lactic acid**
Figure 13.38

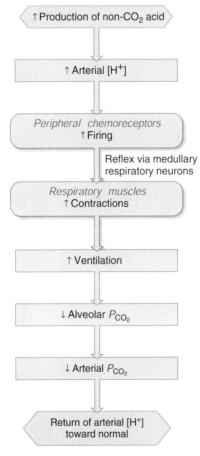

**Reflexly induced hyperventilation**
Figure 13.39

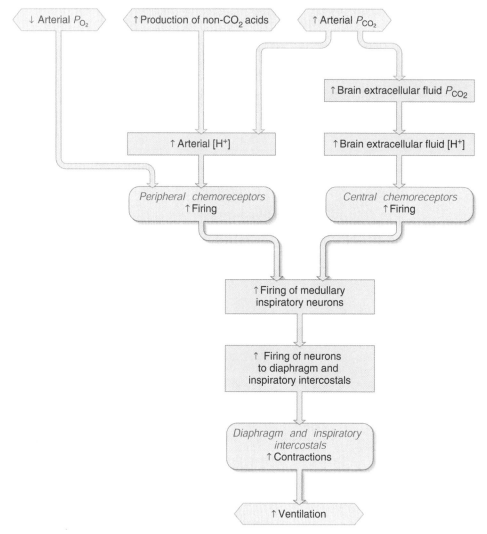

**Summary of control of ventilation**
Figure 13.40

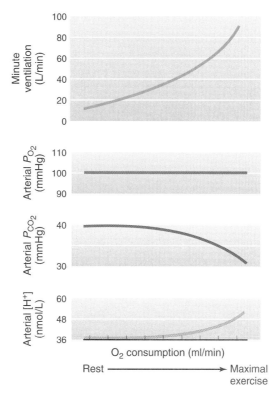

**The effects of exercise**
Figure 13.41

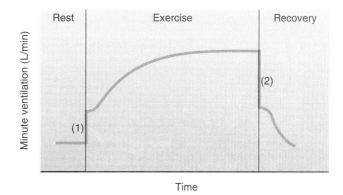

**Ventilation changes during exercise**
Figure 13.42

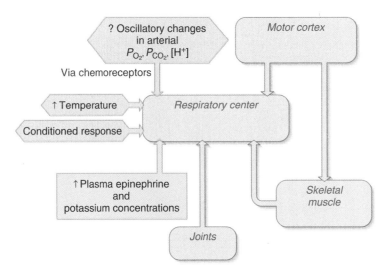

**Factors that stimulate ventilation during exercise**
Figure 13.43

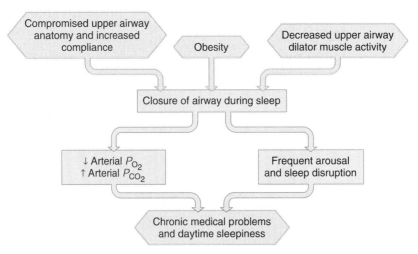

**Pathogenesis of obstructive sleep apnea**
Figure 13.44

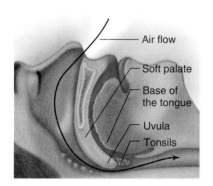 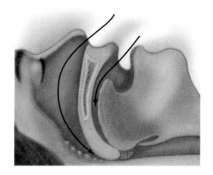 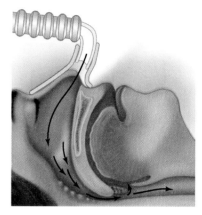

| Air flow |
|---|
| Soft palate |
| Base of the tongue |
| Uvula |
| Tonsils |

During normal sleep, air flows freely past the structures in the throat.

During sleep apnea, air flow is completely blocked.

With CPAP, a mask over the nose gently directs air into the throat to keep the air passage open.

**The pathophysiology and a standard treatment of obstructive sleep apnea**
Figure 13.45

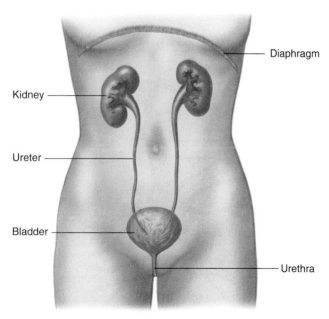

Diaphragm

Kidney

Ureter

Bladder

Urethra

**Urinary system in a woman**
Figure 14.1

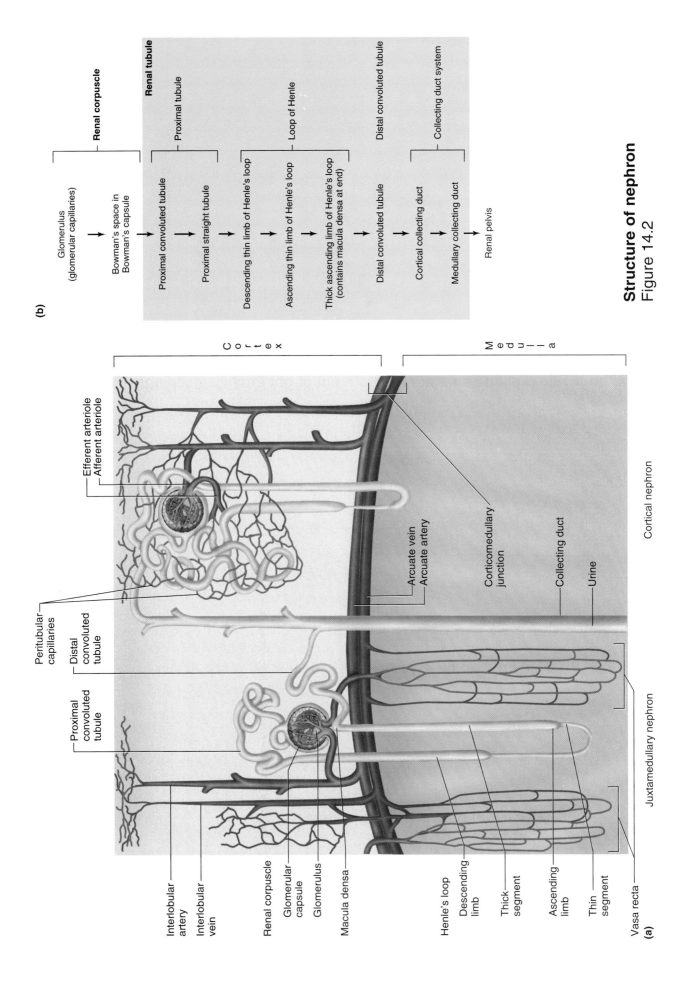

**Structure of nephron**
Figure 14.2

244

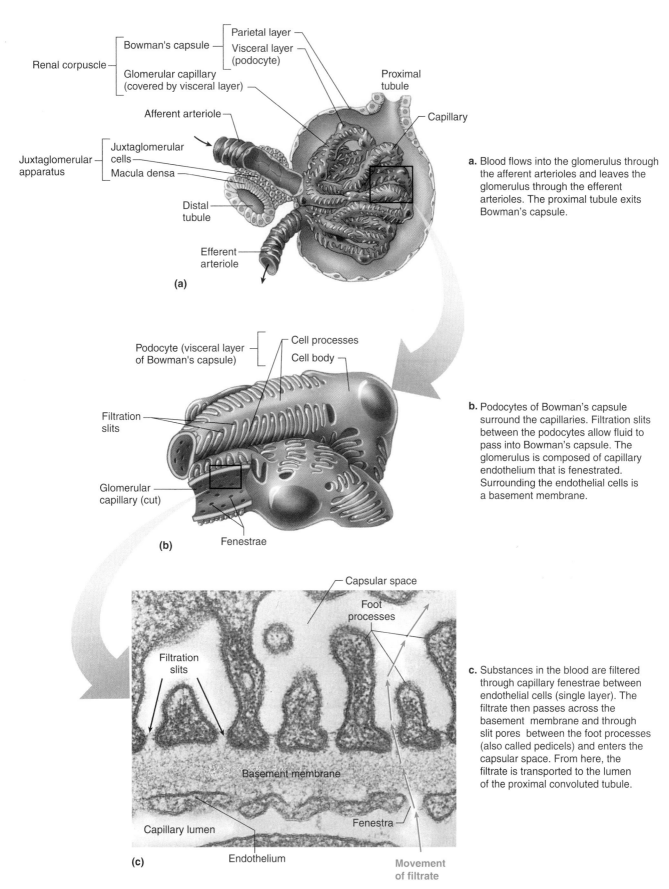

**a.** Blood flows into the glomerulus through the afferent arterioles and leaves the glomerulus through the efferent arterioles. The proximal tubule exits Bowman's capsule.

**b.** Podocytes of Bowman's capsule surround the capillaries. Filtration slits between the podocytes allow fluid to pass into Bowman's capsule. The glomerulus is composed of capillary endothelium that is fenestrated. Surrounding the endothelial cells is a basement membrane.

**c.** Substances in the blood are filtered through capillary fenestrae between endothelial cells (single layer). The filtrate then passes across the basement membrane and through slit pores between the foot processes (also called pedicels) and enters the capsular space. From here, the filtrate is transported to the lumen of the proximal convoluted tubule.

**(a) Renal corpuscle, (b) Podocytes and capillaries, (c) EM of filtration slits**
Figure 14.3

© Daniel Friend from W. Bloom and D. W. Fawcett, *Textbook of Histology,* 10/ed., W. B. Saunders Co. (Reproduced by permission of Edward Arnold)

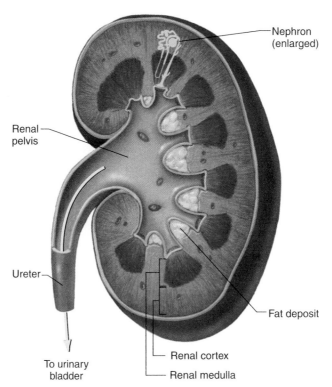

**Section of a kidney**
Figure 14.4

- Nephron (enlarged)
- Renal pelvis
- Ureter
- To urinary bladder
- Fat deposit
- Renal cortex
- Renal medulla

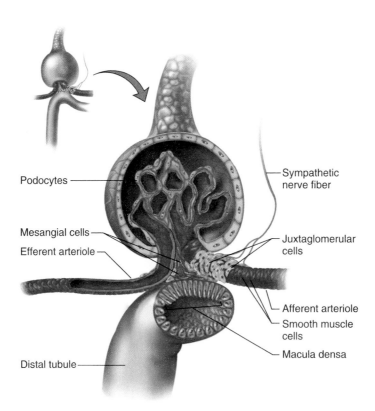

**The juxtaglomerular apparatus**
Figure 14.5

- Podocytes
- Mesangial cells
- Efferent arteriole
- Distal tubule
- Sympathetic nerve fiber
- Juxtaglomerular cells
- Afferent arteriole
- Smooth muscle cells
- Macula densa

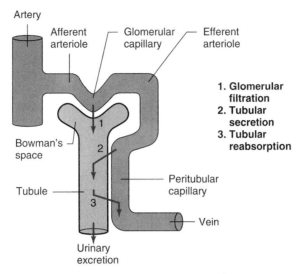

1. **Glomerular filtration**
2. **Tubular secretion**
3. **Tubular reabsorption**

**The three basic components of renal function**
Figure 14.6

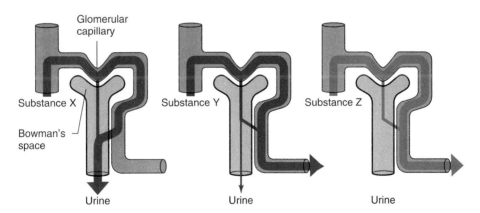

**Renal handling of filtered substances**
Figure 14.7

247

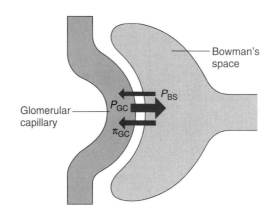

| Forces | mmHg |
|---|---|
| **Favoring filtration:** | |
| Glomerular capillary blood pressure ($P_{GC}$) | 60 |
| **Opposing filtration:** | |
| Fluid pressure in Bowman's space ($P_{BS}$) | 15 |
| Osmotic force due to protein in plasma ($\pi_{GC}$) | 29 |
| **Net glomerular filtration pressure = $P_{GC} - P_{BS} - \pi_{GC}$** | 16 |

## Forces involved in glomerular filtration
Figure 14.8

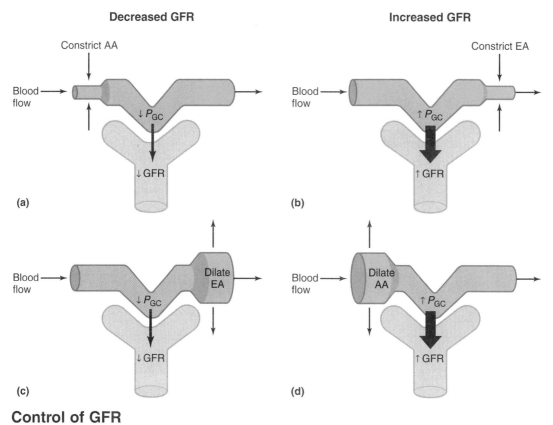

## Control of GFR
Figure 14.9

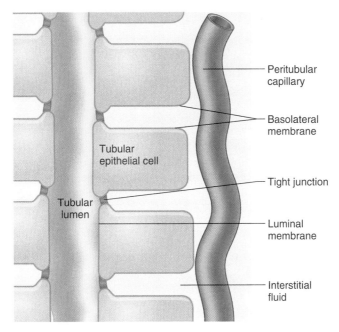

**Tubular epithelium**
Figure 14.10

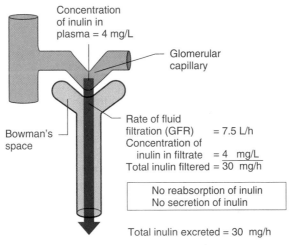

Concentration
of inulin in
plasma = 4 mg/L

Glomerular
capillary

Bowman's
space

Rate of fluid
filtration (GFR) = 7.5 L/h
Concentration of
inulin in filtrate = 4 mg/L
Total inulin filtered = 30 mg/h

No reabsorption of inulin
No secretion of inulin

Total inulin excreted = 30 mg/h

**Example of renal handling of inulin**
Figure 14.11

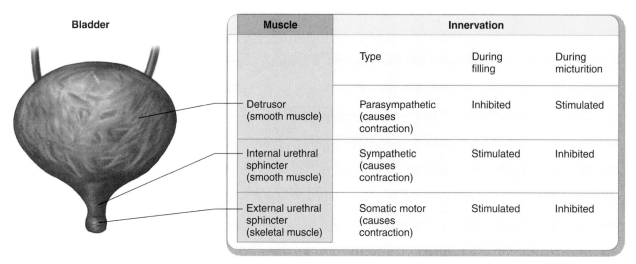

| Muscle | Innervation | | |
|---|---|---|---|
| | Type | During filling | During micturition |
| Detrusor (smooth muscle) | Parasympathetic (causes contraction) | Inhibited | Stimulated |
| Internal urethral sphincter (smooth muscle) | Sympathetic (causes contraction) | Stimulated | Inhibited |
| External urethral sphincter (skeletal muscle) | Somatic motor (causes contraction) | Stimulated | Inhibited |

**Control of the bladder**
Figure 14.12

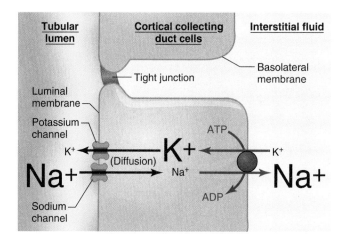

**Sodium reabsorption**
Figure 14.13

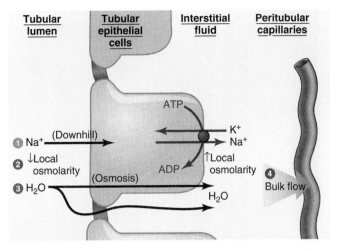

**Coupling of water and sodium reabsorption**
Figure 14.14

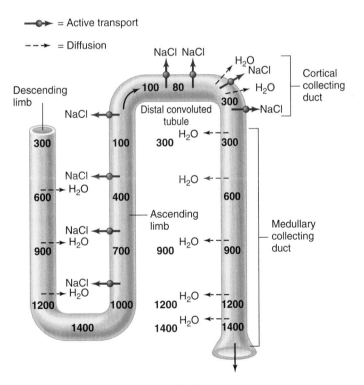

**Countercurrent multiplier**
Figure 14.15

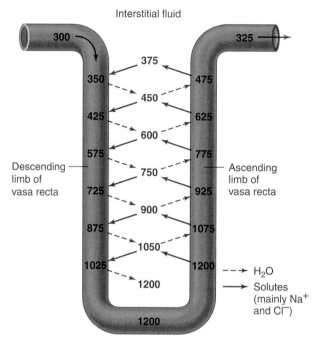

**Function of the vasa recta**
Figure 14.16

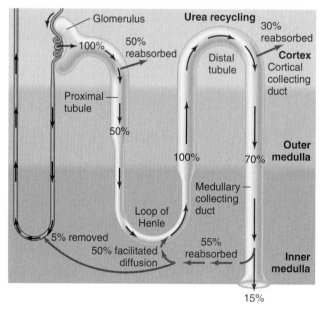

**Urea recycling**
Figure 14.17

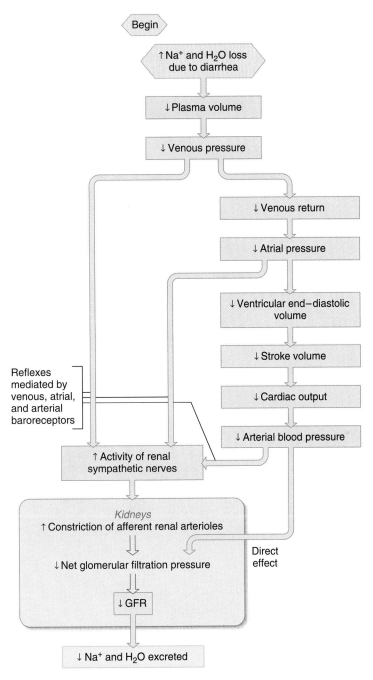

**Control of GFR**

Figure 14.18

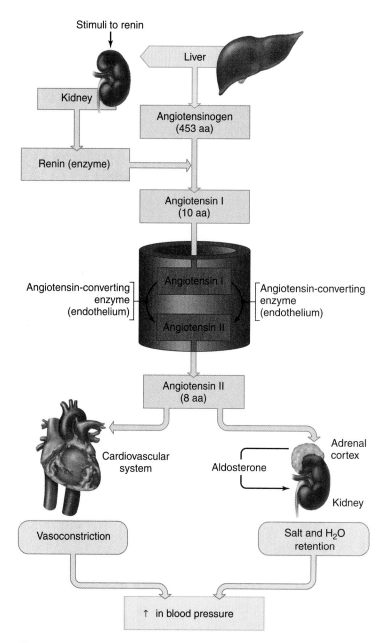

**Summary of the renin-angiotensin system and the stimulation of aldosterone secretion by angiotensin II**
Figure 14.19

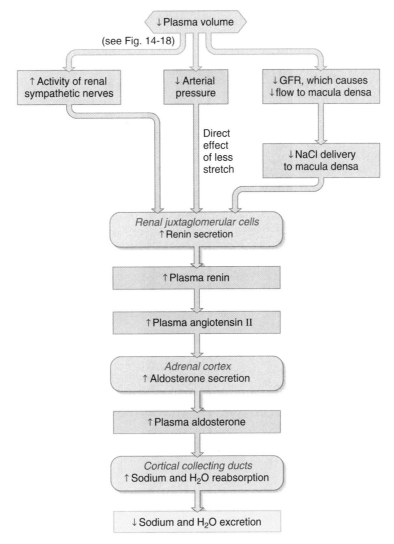

**Pathways to increased sodium reabsorption**
Figure 14.20

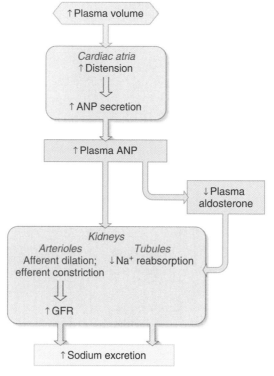

**Atrial natriuretic peptide (ANP)**
Figure 14.21

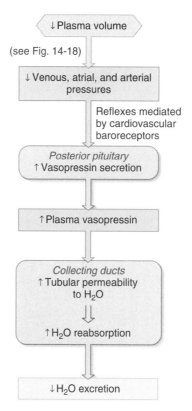

**Baroreceptor pathway**
Figure 14.22

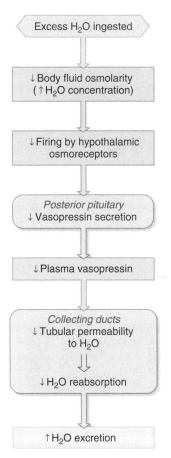

**Osmoreceptor pathway**
Figure 14.23

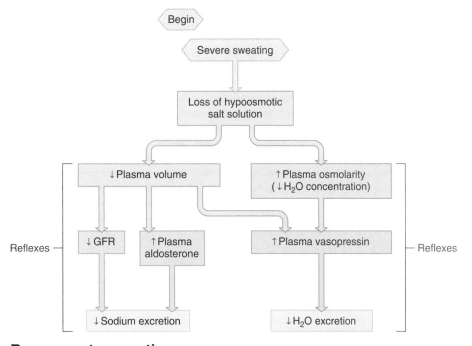

**Response to sweating**
Figure 14.24

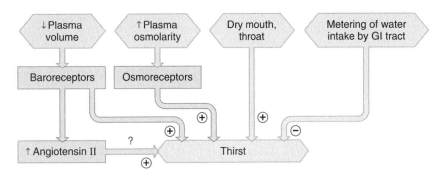

**Inputs controlling thirst**

Figure 14.25

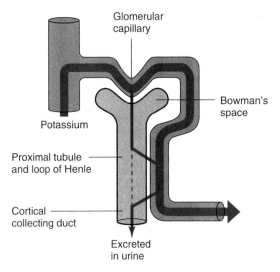

**Simplified model of the basic renal processing of potassium**

Figure 14.26

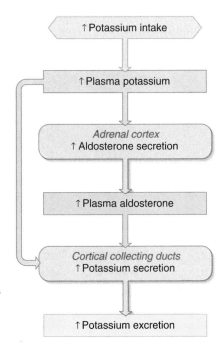

**Basic renal processing of greater potassium excretion**

Figure 14.27

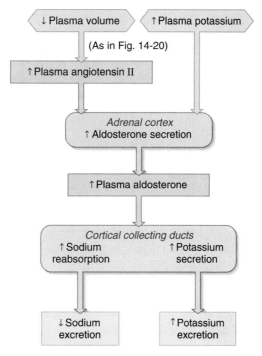

**Control of aldosterone**
Figure 14.28

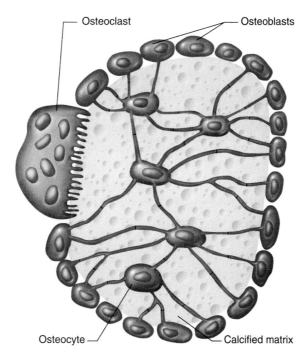

**Cross-section through bone**
Figure 14.29

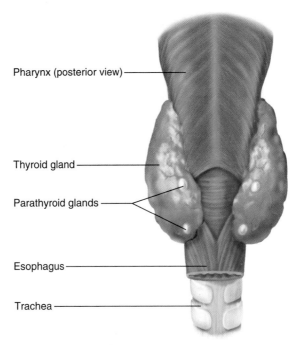

Pharynx (posterior view)

Thyroid gland

Parathyroid glands

Esophagus

Trachea

**The parathyroid glands**
Figure 14.30

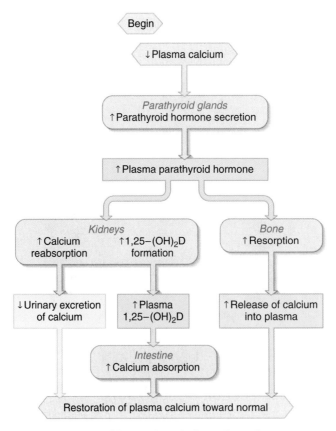

Begin

↓ Plasma calcium

*Parathyroid glands*
↑ Parathyroid hormone secretion

↑ Plasma parathyroid hormone

*Kidneys*
↑ Calcium     ↑ 1,25–$(OH)_2$D
reabsorption     formation

*Bone*
↑ Resorption

↓ Urinary excretion
of calcium

↑ Plasma
1,25–$(OH)_2$D

↑ Release of calcium
into plasma

*Intestine*
↑ Calcium absorption

Restoration of plasma calcium toward normal

**Regulation of blood calcium level**
Figure 14.31

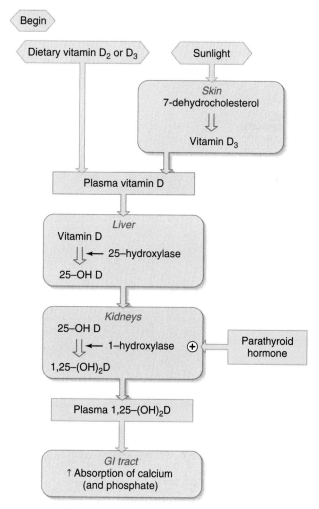

**Metabolism of vitamin D**
Figure 14.32

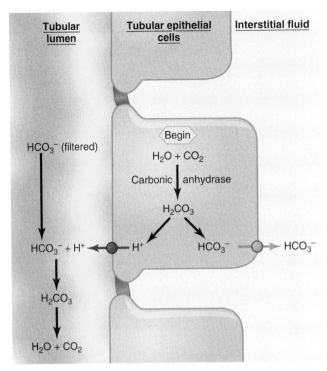

**Reabsorption of bicarbonate**
Figure 14.33

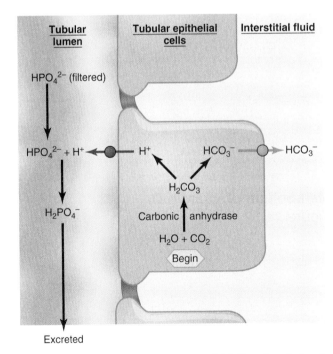

**Renal contribution of new HCO$_3^-$ by tubular secretion of H$^+$**
Figure 14.34

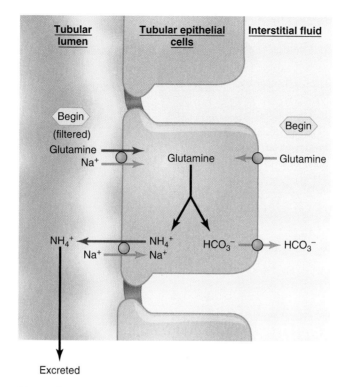

**Renal contribution of new HCO₃⁻ by renal metabolism**

Figure 14.35

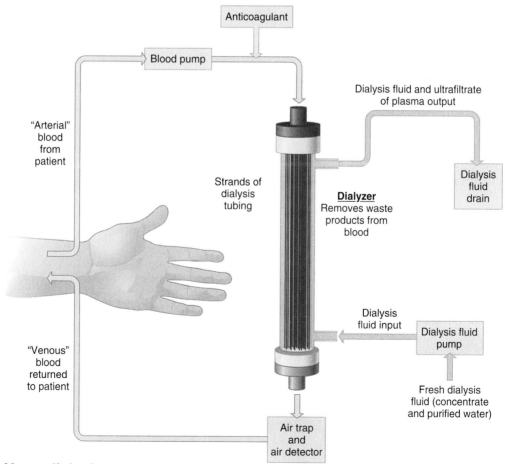

**Hemodialysis**

Figure 14.36

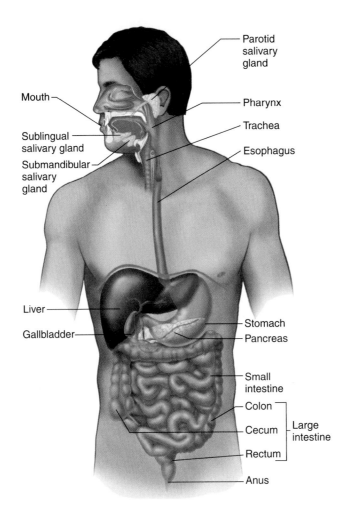

**Anatomy of GI system**
Figure 15.1

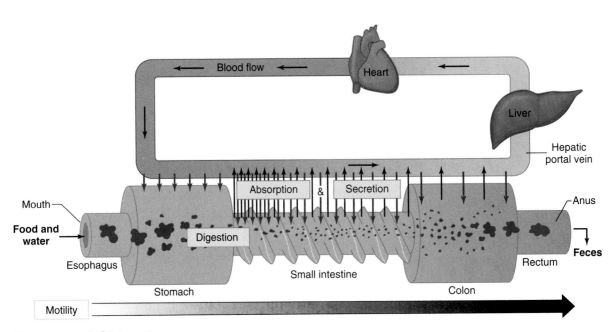

**Process of GI tract**
Figure 15.2

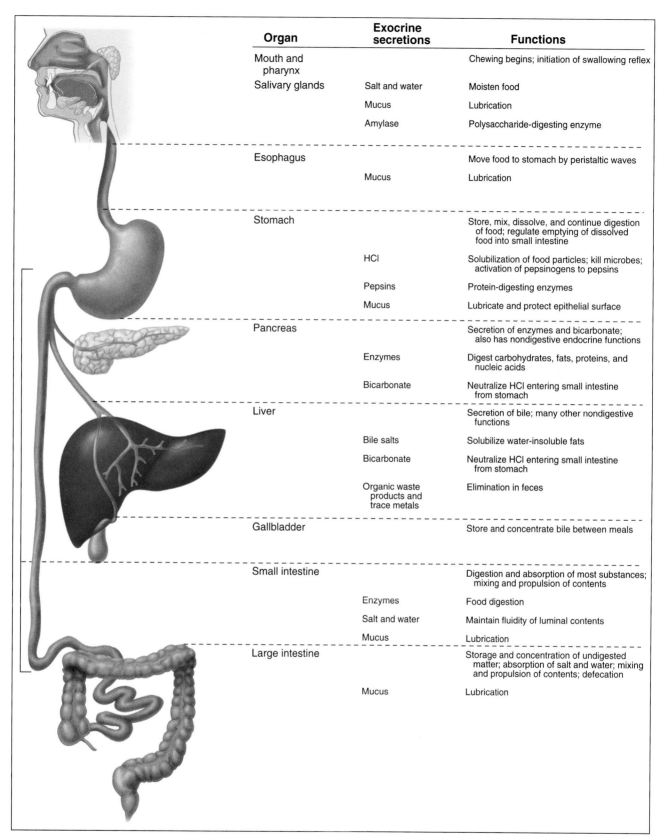

| Organ | Exocrine secretions | Functions |
|---|---|---|
| Mouth and pharynx | | Chewing begins; initiation of swallowing reflex |
| Salivary glands | Salt and water | Moisten food |
| | Mucus | Lubrication |
| | Amylase | Polysaccharide-digesting enzyme |
| Esophagus | | Move food to stomach by peristaltic waves |
| | Mucus | Lubrication |
| Stomach | | Store, mix, dissolve, and continue digestion of food; regulate emptying of dissolved food into small intestine |
| | HCl | Solubilization of food particles; kill microbes; activation of pepsinogens to pepsins |
| | Pepsins | Protein-digesting enzymes |
| | Mucus | Lubricate and protect epithelial surface |
| Pancreas | | Secretion of enzymes and bicarbonate; also has nondigestive endocrine functions |
| | Enzymes | Digest carbohydrates, fats, proteins, and nucleic acids |
| | Bicarbonate | Neutralize HCl entering small intestine from stomach |
| Liver | | Secretion of bile; many other nondigestive functions |
| | Bile salts | Solubilize water-insoluble fats |
| | Bicarbonate | Neutralize HCl entering small intestine from stomach |
| | Organic waste products and trace metals | Elimination in feces |
| Gallbladder | | Store and concentrate bile between meals |
| Small intestine | | Digestion and absorption of most substances; mixing and propulsion of contents |
| | Enzymes | Food digestion |
| | Salt and water | Maintain fluidity of luminal contents |
| | Mucus | Lubrication |
| Large intestine | | Storage and concentration of undigested matter; absorption of salt and water; mixing and propulsion of contents; defecation |
| | Mucus | Lubrication |

**Functions of the gastrointestinal organs**
Figure 15.3

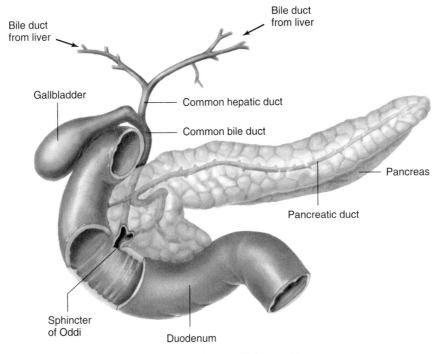

**Pancreas, gall bladder, and small intestine**
Figure 15.4

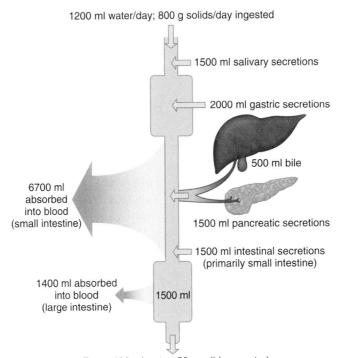

1200 ml water/day; 800 g solids/day ingested

1500 ml salivary secretions

2000 ml gastric secretions

500 ml bile

6700 ml
absorbed
into blood
(small intestine)

1500 ml pancreatic secretions

1500 ml intestinal secretions
(primarily small intestine)

1400 ml absorbed
into blood
(large intestine)

1500 ml

Feces 100 ml water; 50 g solids excreted

**Average amounts of solids and fluid
ingested, secreted, absorbed, and excreted
from the gastrointestinal tract daily**
Figure 15.5

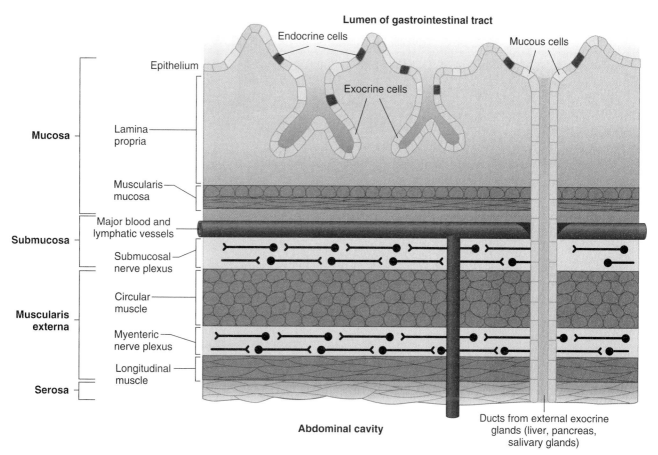

**Structure of GI wall**

Figure 15.6

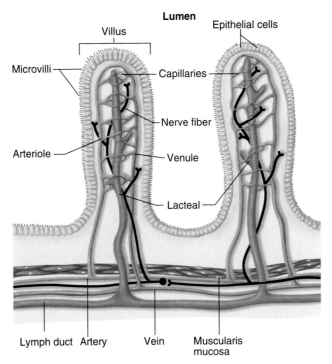

**Structure of small intestine villi**
Figure 15.7

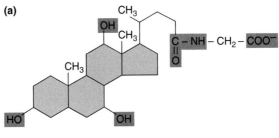

Bile salt (glycocholic acid)

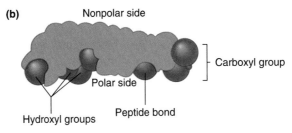

**Structure of bile salts**
Figure 15.9

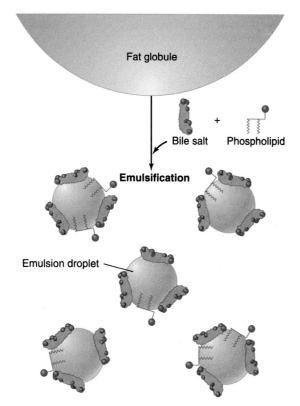

Fat globule

Bile salt + Phospholipid

Emulsification

Emulsion droplet

**Emulsification of fats**
Figure 15.10

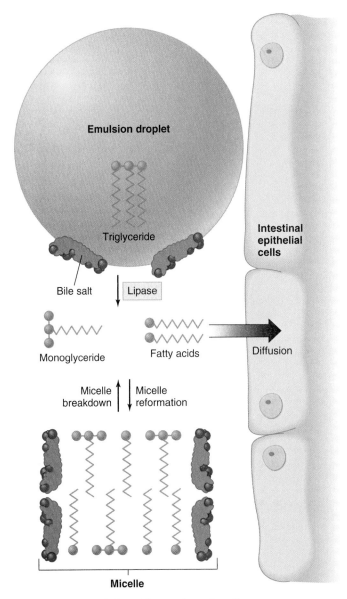

**Products of fat digestion by lipase**
Figure 15.11

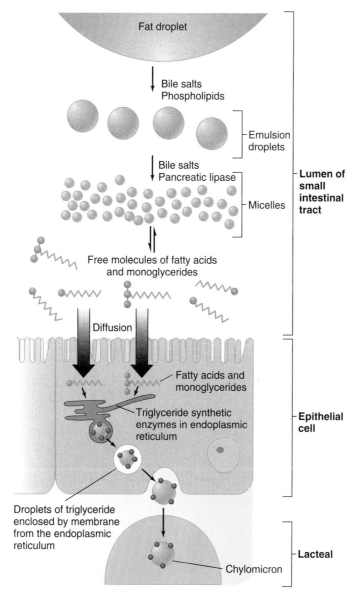

**Fat absorption**
Figure 15.12

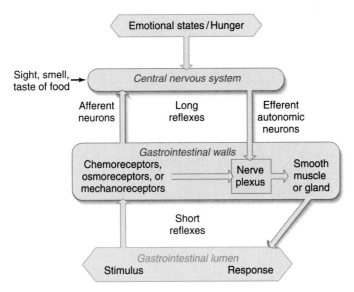

**Long and short neural reflex pathways**
Figure 15.13

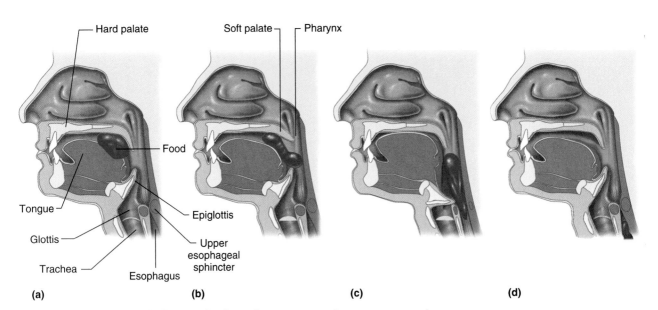

(a)      (b)      (c)      (d)

**Movements of food through the pharynx and upper esophagus**
Figure 15.14

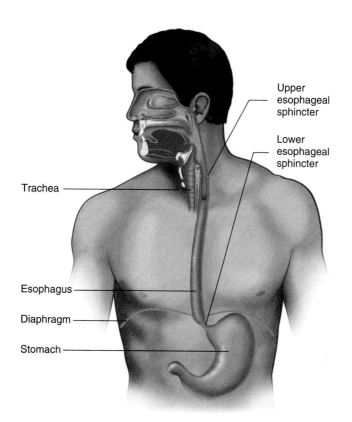

## Location of upper and lower esophageal sphincters
Figure 15.15

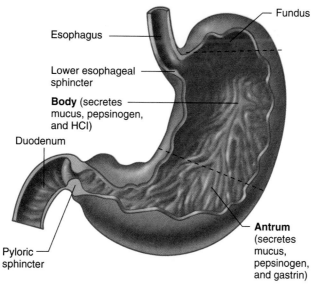

## Regions of the stomach
Figure 15.16

273

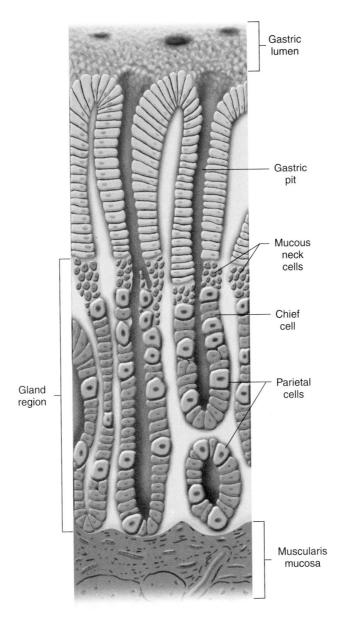

Gastric
lumen

Gastric
pit

Mucous
neck
cells

Chief
cell

Parietal
cells

Gland
region

Muscularis
mucosa

**Gastric glands in the body of stomach**
Figure 15.17

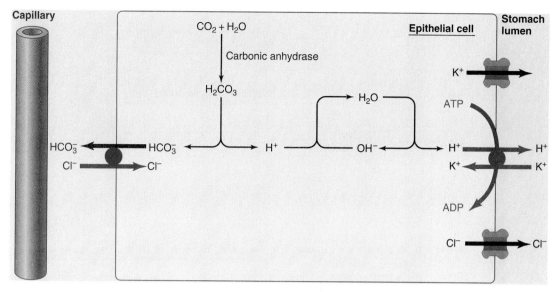

**Secretion of hydrochloric acid by parietal cells**
Figure 15.18

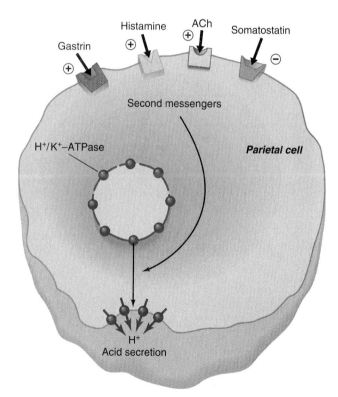

**The four inputs to parietal cells**
Figure 15.19

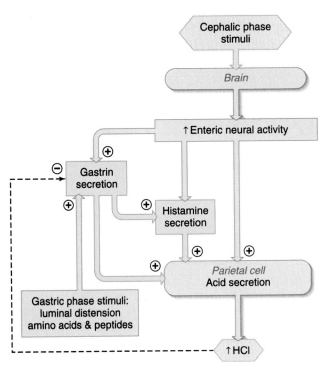

**Cephalic and gastric phases**
Figure 15.20

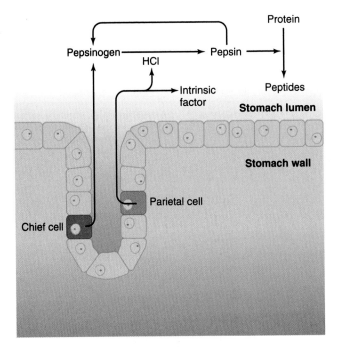

**Conversion of pepsinogen to pepsin in the lumen of the stomach**
Figure 15.21

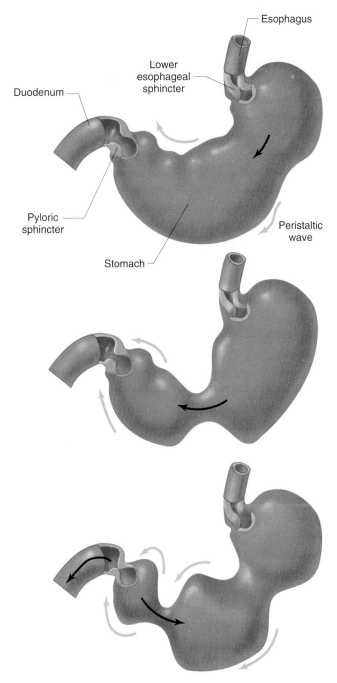

**Peristaltic in stomach**
Figure 15.22

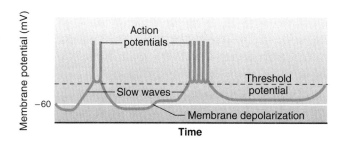
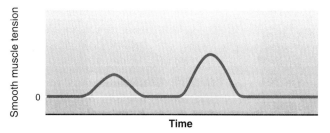

**Slow wave oscillations in gastric smooth muscle fibers**

Figure 15.23

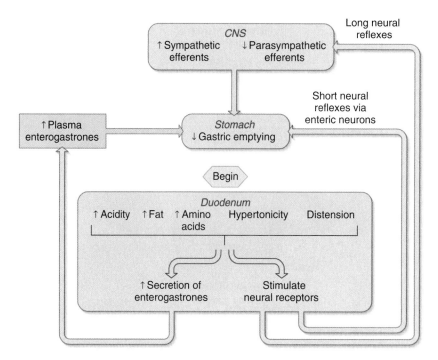

**Intestinal-phase pathways inhibiting gastric emptying**

Figure 15.24

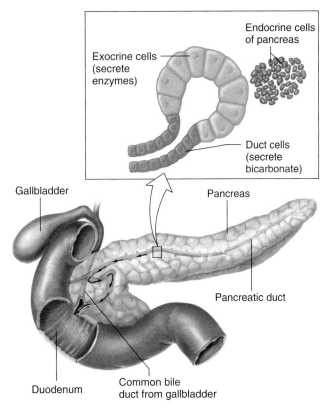

**Structure of the pancreas**
Figure 15.25

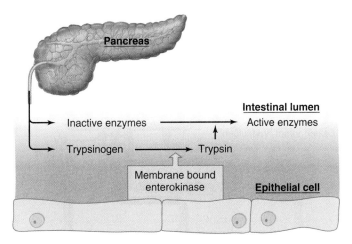

**Activation of pancreatic enzyme precursors in the small intestine**
Figure 15.26

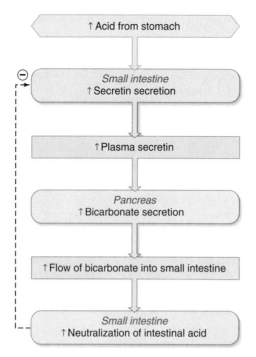

**Hormonal regulation of pancreatic bicarbonate secretion**
Figure 15.27

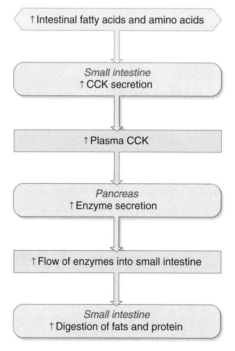

**Hormonal regulation of pancreatic enzyme secretion**
Figure 15.28

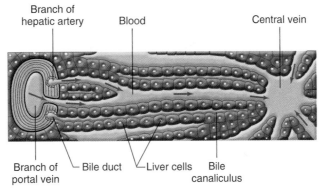

**A small section of the liver**
Figure 15.29

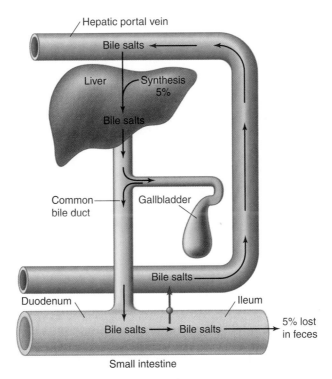

**Enterohepatic circulation**
Figure 15.30

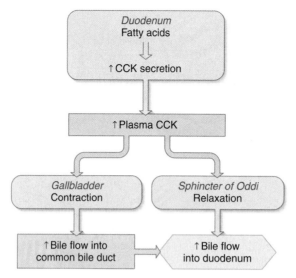

**Regulation of bile entry into the small intestine**

Figure 15.31

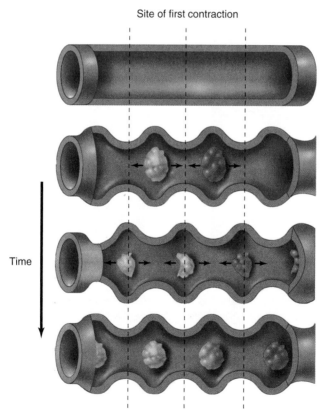

**Segmentation contractions in a portion of the small intestine**

Figure 15.32

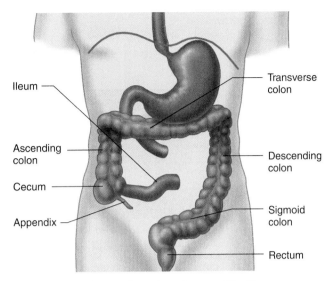

**The large intestine begins with the cecum**
Figure 15.33

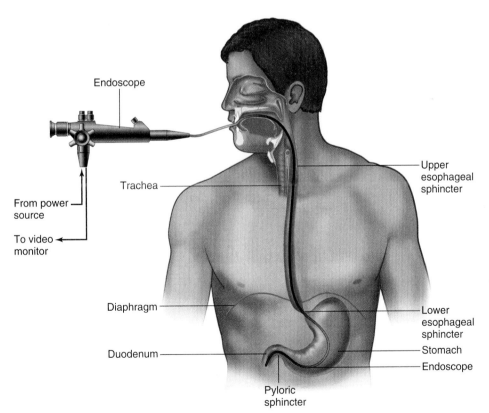

**Video endoscopy of the upper GI tract**
Figure 15.34

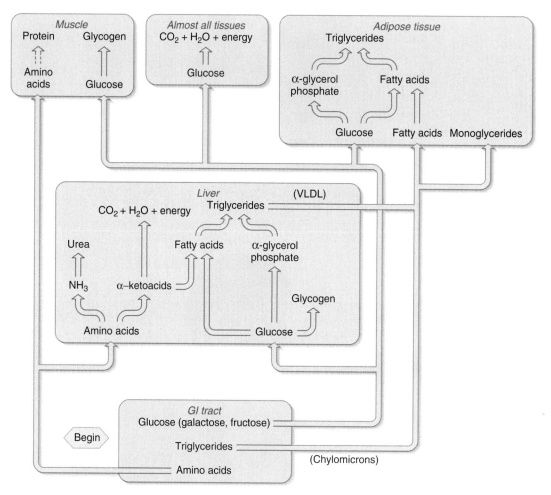

**Major metabolic pathways of the absorptive state**
Figure 16.1

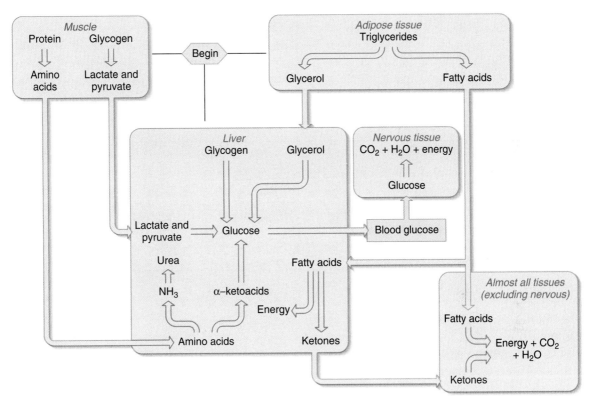

**Major metabolic pathways of the postabsorptive state**
Figure 16.2

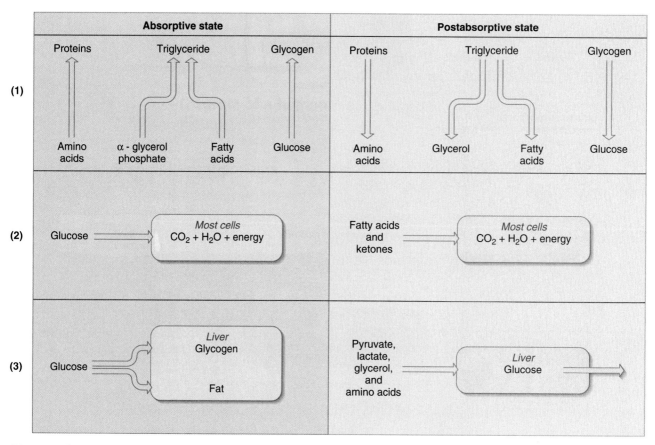

**Absorptive and postabsorptive states**
Figure 16.3

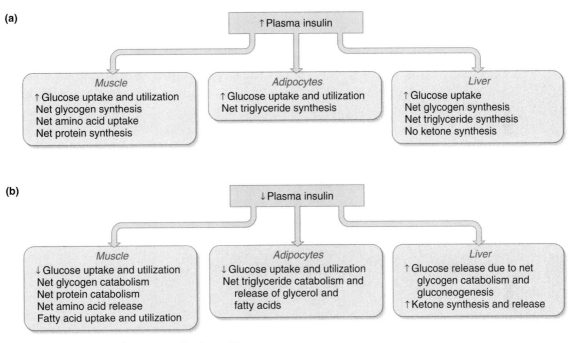

**Responses to changes in insulin**
Figure 16.4

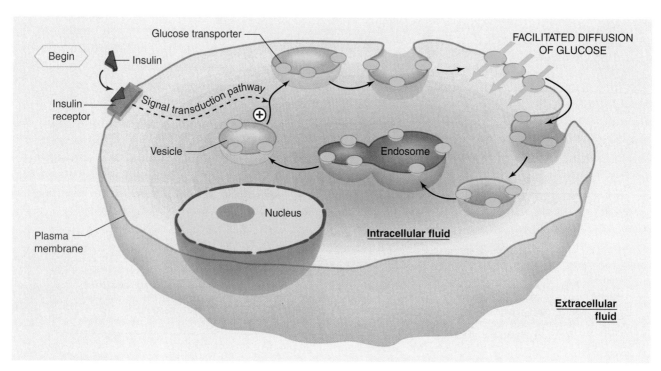

**Insulin action**
Figure 16.5

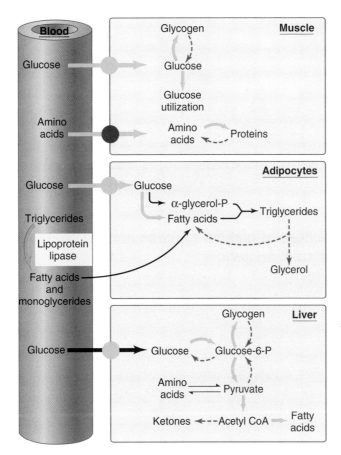

**Ilustration of the key biochemical events**
Figure 16.6

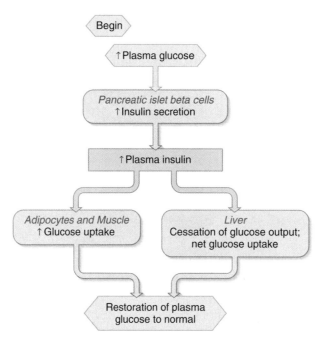

**Nature of plasma glucose control over insulin secretion**

Figure 16.7

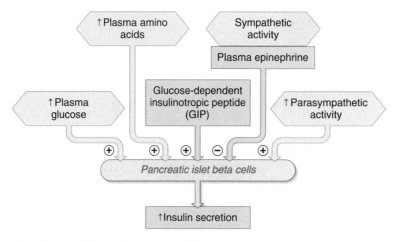

**Control of insulin secretion**

Figure 16.8

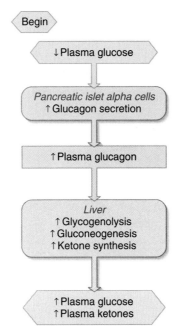

**Nature of plasma glucose control over glucagon secretion**
Figure 16.9

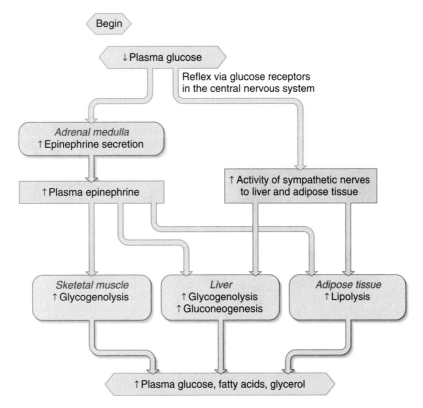

**Responses to low glucose**
Figure 16.10

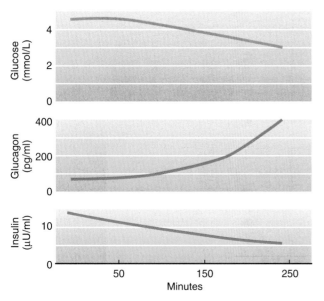

**Plasma concentrations of glucose, glucagon, and insulin during prolonged (250 min) moderate exercise at a fixed intensity**
Figure 16.11

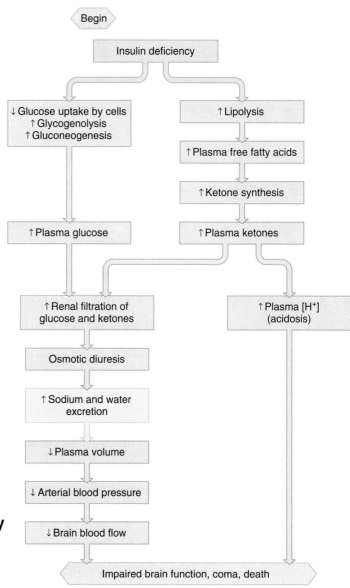

**Diabetic ketoacidosis: Events caused by severe untreated insulin deficiency in type I diabetes mellitus**
Figure 16.12

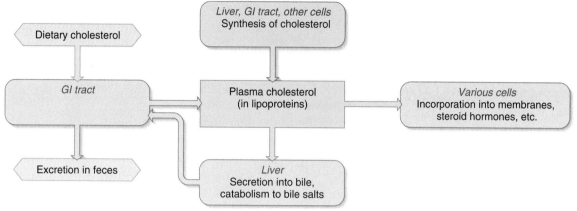

**Cholesterol balance**
Figure 16.13

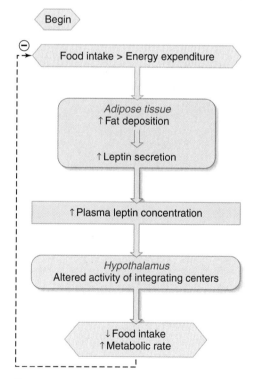

**Postulated role of leptin in the control of total-body energy stores**
Figure 16.14

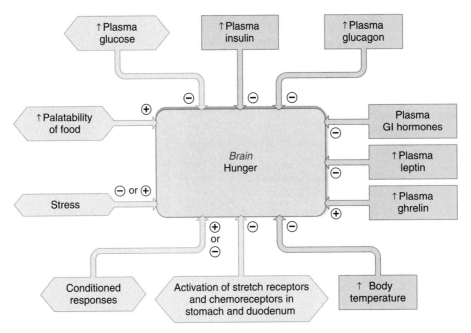

**Short-term inputs controlling food intake**
Figure 16.15

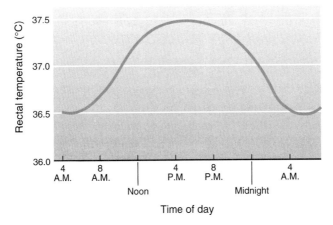

**Circadian changes in core body temperature**
Figure 16.16

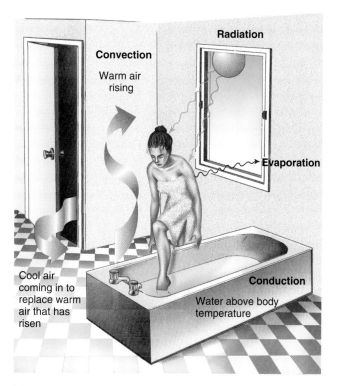

**Heat transfer**
Figure 16.17

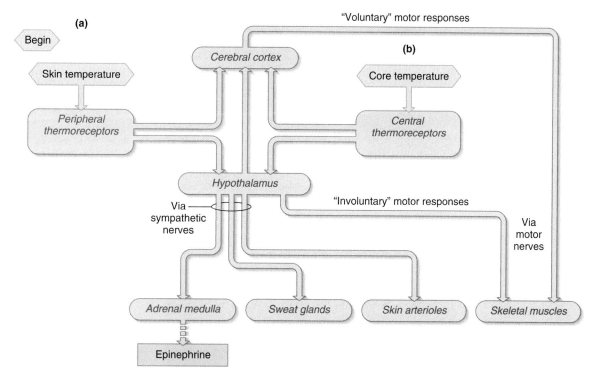

**Summary of temperature-regulating mechanisms**
Figure 16.18

Infection

Liver
Macrophages
⇓
Secrete
endogenous pyrogens
(IL–1, IL–6, ? others)
⇓
↑Firing of neural
receptors

Multiple organs
Macrophages
⇓
Secrete
endogenous pyrogens
(IL–1, IL–6, ? others)
⇓
↑Plasma IL–1, IL–6, ? others

Vagus
nerve

Systemic
circulation

Hypothalamus
↑Temperature setpoint

Skeletal muscles
Curl up,
put on clothes
Shivering   and blankets

Skin arterioles
↑Vasoconstriction

↑Heat production

↓Heat loss

Heat production greater than heat loss

Heat retention

↑Body temperature

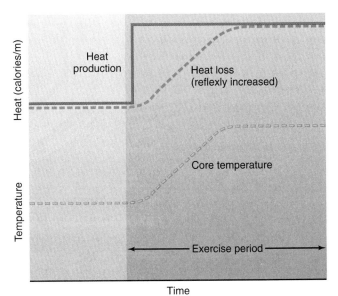

**Thermal changes during exercise**
Figure 16.20

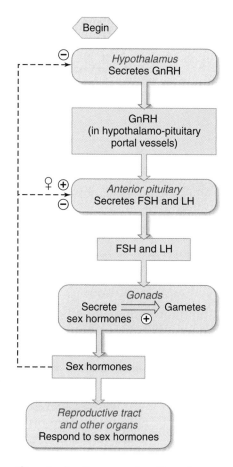

**Control of reproduction by hormones**
Figure 17.1

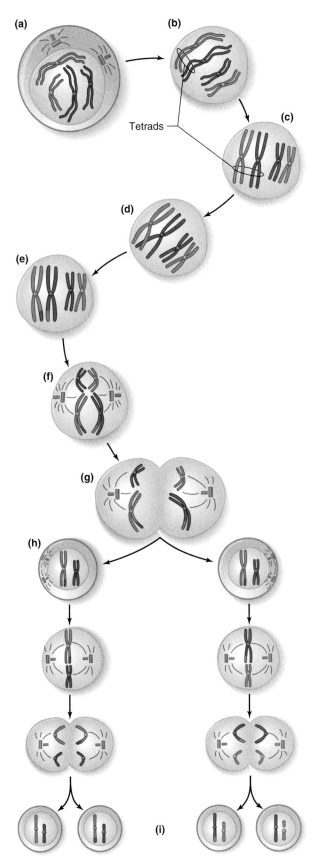

Tetrads

**Stages of meiosis in a generalized germ cell**

Figure 17.2

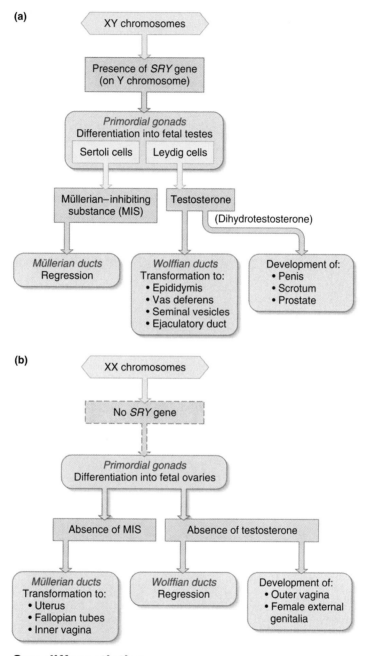

**Sex differentiation**

Figure 17.3

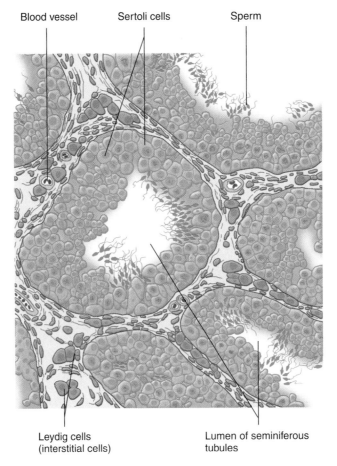

Blood vessel    Sertoli cells    Sperm

Leydig cells
(interstitial cells)

Lumen of seminiferous
tubules

**Cross-section of testis**
Figure 17.4

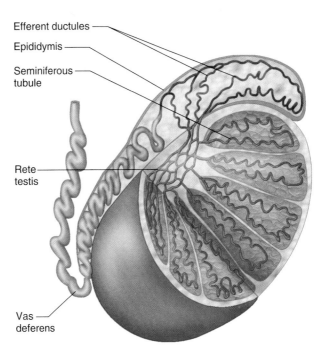

Efferent ductules

Epididymis

Seminiferous
tubule

Rete
testis

Vas
deferens

**Testis and associated structures**
Figure 17.5

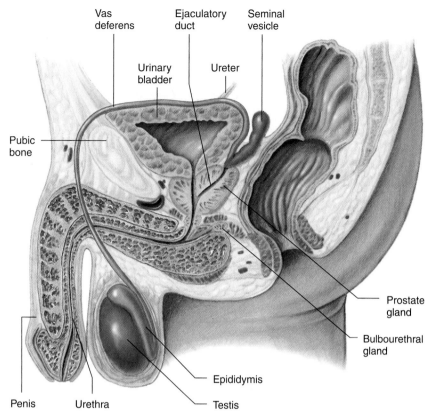

**Anatomy of male reproductive tract**
Figure 17.6

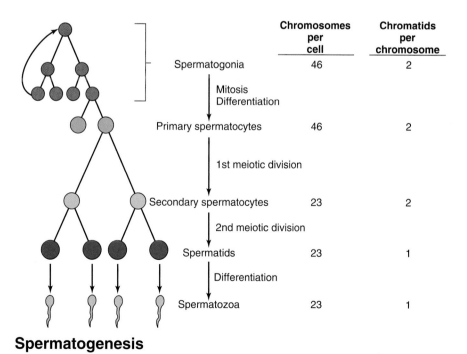

| | Chromosomes per cell | Chromatids per chromosome |
|---|---|---|
| Spermatogonia | 46 | 2 |
| *Mitosis Differentiation* | | |
| Primary spermatocytes | 46 | 2 |
| *1st meiotic division* | | |
| Secondary spermatocytes | 23 | 2 |
| *2nd meiotic division* | | |
| Spermatids | 23 | 1 |
| *Differentiation* | | |
| Spermatozoa | 23 | 1 |

**Spermatogenesis**
Figure 17.7

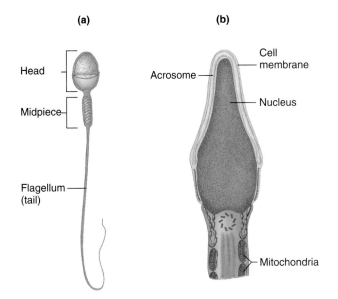

**Diagram of a human mature sperm**
Figure 17.8

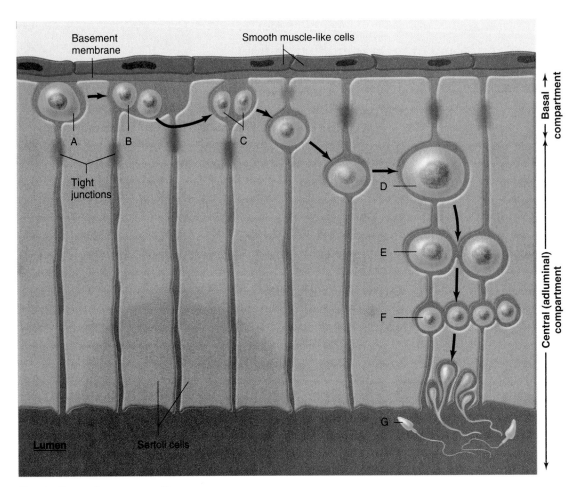

**Sertoli and germ cells**
Figure 17.9

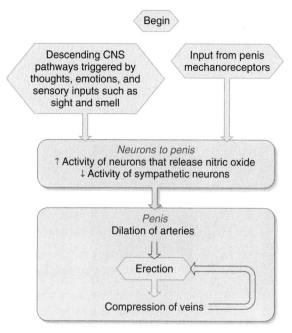

**Reflex pathways for erection**
Figure 17.10

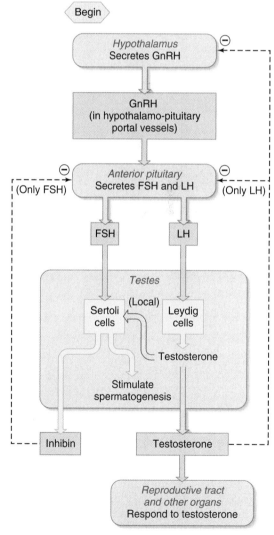

**Hormonal control of male reproduction**
Figure 17.11

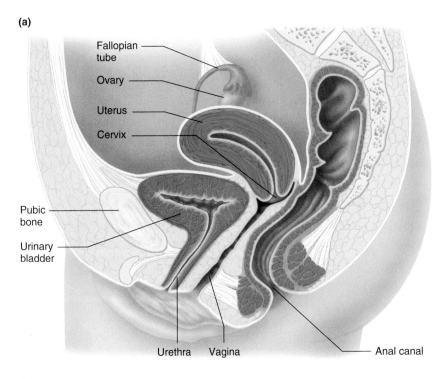

(a)

Fallopian tube

Ovary

Uterus

Cervix

Pubic bone

Urinary bladder

Urethra    Vagina    Anal canal

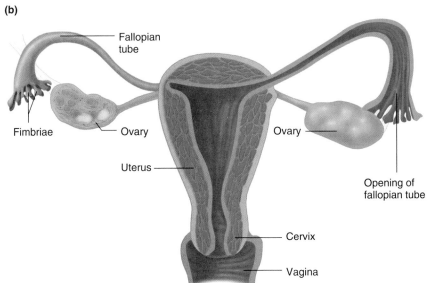

(b)

Fallopian tube

Fimbriae    Ovary

Uterus

Ovary

Opening of fallopian tube

Cervix

Vagina

**Female reproductive system**
Figure 17.13

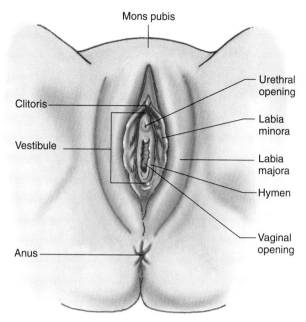

**Female external genitalia**
Figure 17.14

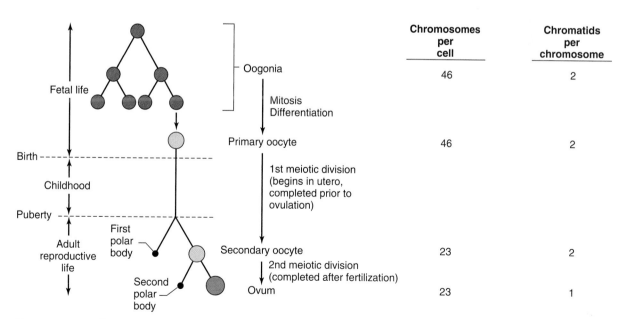

**Summary of oogenesis**
Figure 17.15

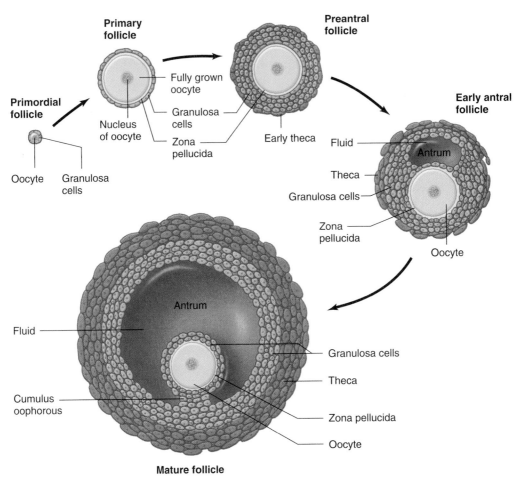

**Oocyte and follicle development**
Figure 17.16

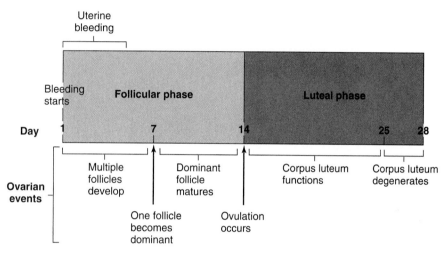

**Ovarian events during menstrual cycle**
Figure 17.17

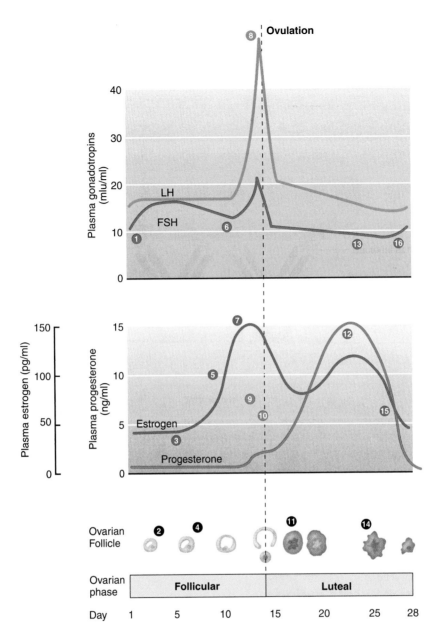

**Events during the menstrual cycle**
Figure 17.18

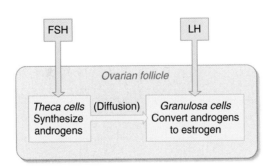

**Control of estrogen synthesis**
Figure 17.19

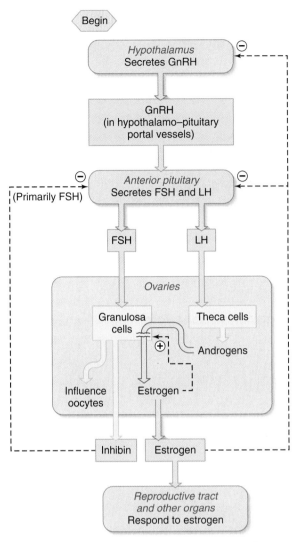

**Hormonal control of ovarian function**
Figure 17.20

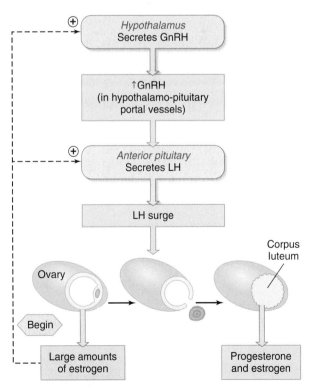

**The late follicular phase**
Figure 17.21

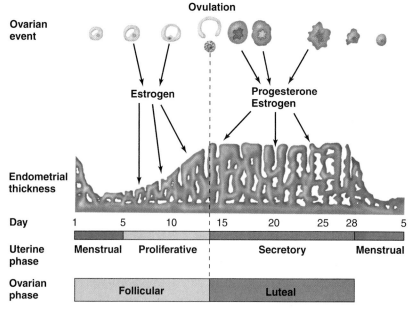

**Ovarian and uterine changes during menstrual cycle**
Figure 17.22

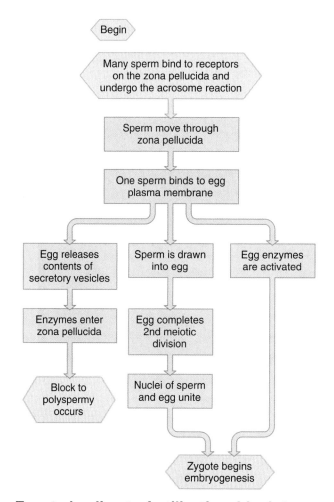

**Events leading to fertilization, block to polyspermy, and the beginning of embryogenesis**
Figure 17.23

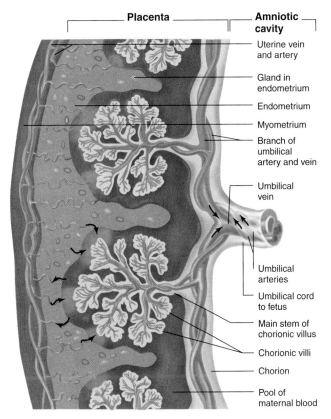

**Placenta** — **Amniotic cavity**

Uterine vein and artery

Gland in endometrium

Endometrium

Myometrium

Branch of umbilical artery and vein

Umbilical vein

Umbilical arteries

Umbilical cord to fetus

Main stem of chorionic villus

Chorionic villi

Chorion

Pool of maternal blood

**Formation of placenta**
Figure 17.26

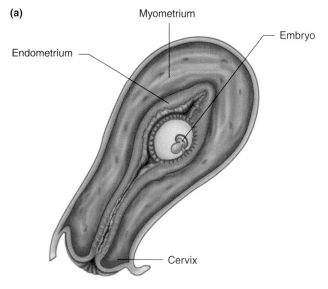

**(a)**

Myometrium

Endometrium

Embryo

Cervix

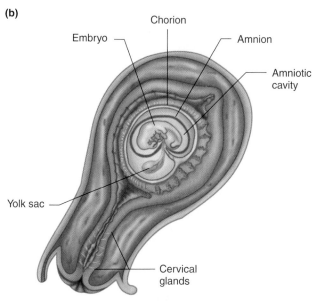

**(b)**

Chorion

Embryo

Amnion

Amniotic cavity

Yolk sac

Cervical glands

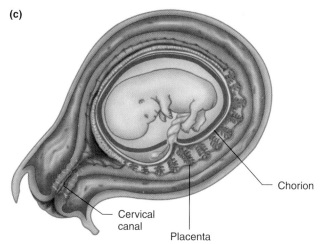

**(c)**

Chorion

Cervical canal

Placenta

**Embryo development at 3, 5, and 8 weeks**
Figure 17.27

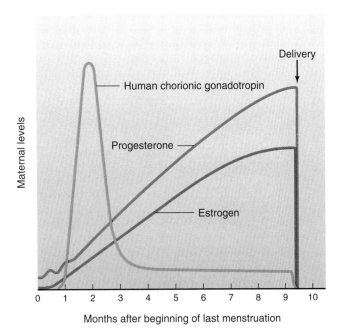

**Maternal hormone levels**
Figure 17.28

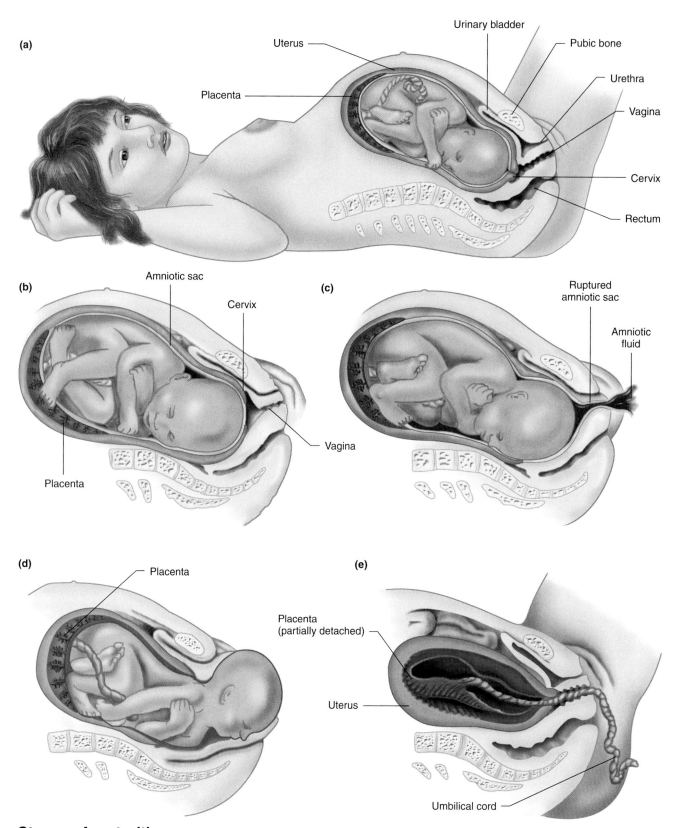

**(a)**

Uterus

Placenta

Urinary bladder

Pubic bone

Urethra

Vagina

Cervix

Rectum

**(b)**

Amniotic sac

Cervix

Placenta

Vagina

**(c)**

Ruptured
amniotic sac

Amniotic
fluid

**(d)**

Placenta

**(e)**

Placenta
(partially detached)

Uterus

Umbilical cord

**Stages of parturition**
Figure 17.29

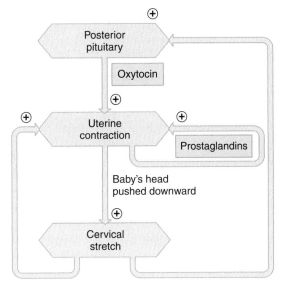

**Positive feedback during parturition**
Figure 17.30

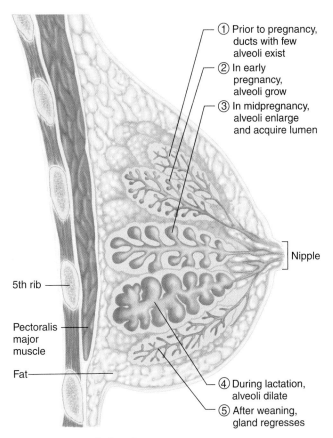

① Prior to pregnancy, ducts with few alveoli exist

② In early pregnancy, alveoli grow

③ In midpregnancy, alveoli enlarge and acquire lumen

Nipple

5th rib

Pectoralis major muscle

Fat

④ During lactation, alveoli dilate

⑤ After weaning, gland regresses

**Anatomy of the breast**
Figure 17.31

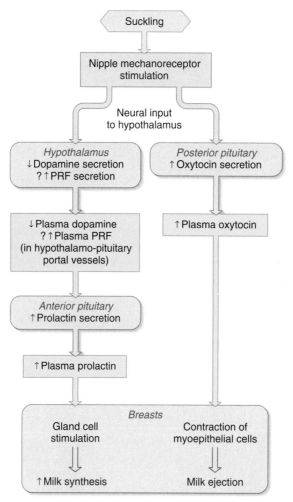

**Major controls of the secretion of prolactin and oxytocin during nursing**
Figure 17.32

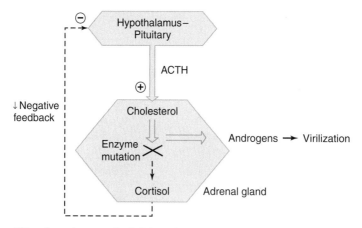

**Mechanism of virilization in female fetuses with congenital adrenal hyperplasia**
Figure 17.33

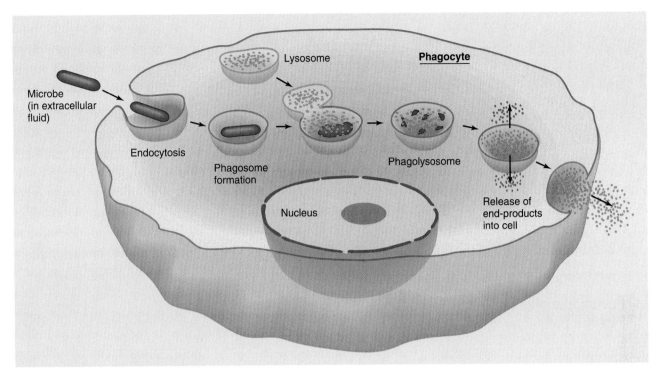

**Phagocytosis of a microbe**
Figure 18.2

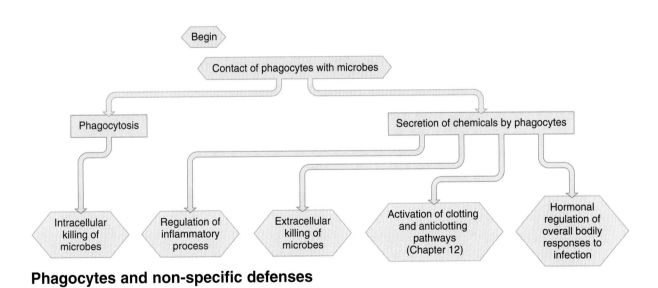

**Phagocytes and non-specific defenses**
Figure 18.3

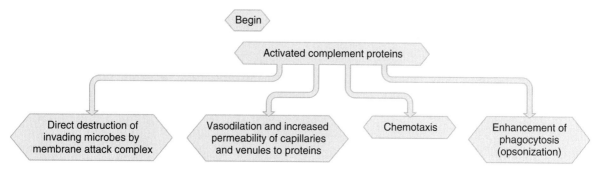

**Functions of complement proteins**
Figure 18.4

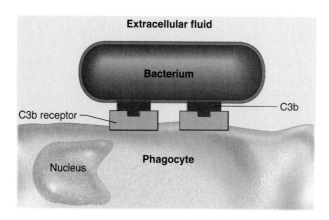

**Complement C3b as opsonin**
Figure 18.5

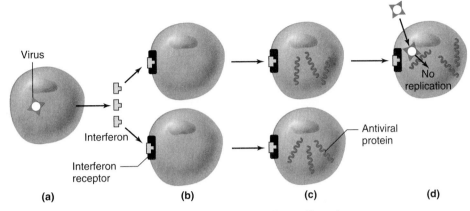

**Role of interferon in preventing viral replication**
Figure 18.6

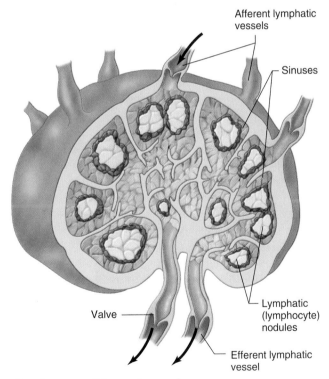

**Anatomy of lymph node**
Figure 18.7

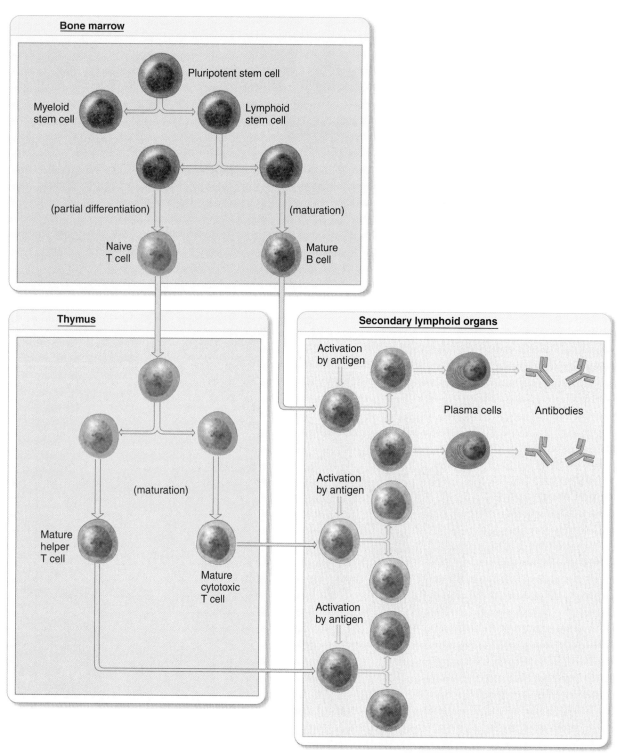

**Derivation of B cells and T cells**
Figure 18.8

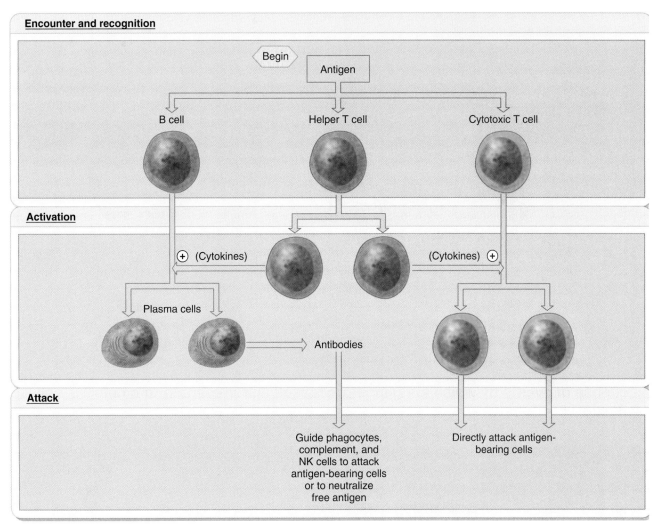

**Summary of roles of B, cytotoxic T, and helper T cells in immune responses**
Figure 18.9

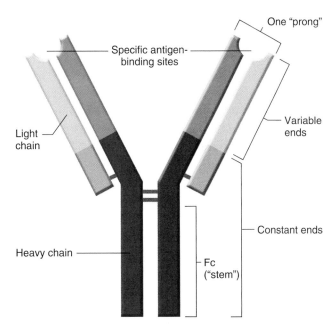

**Immunoglobulin structure**
Figure 18.10

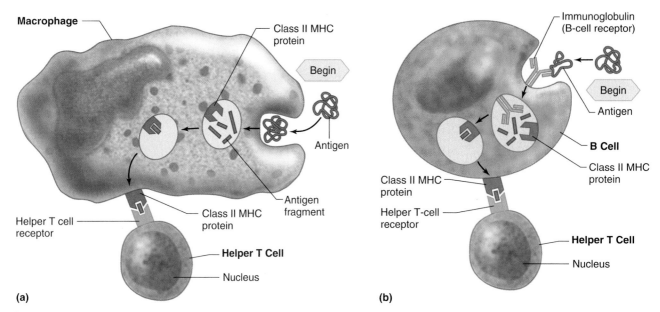

**Sequence of events by which antigen is processed and presented to a helper T cell**
Figure 18.11

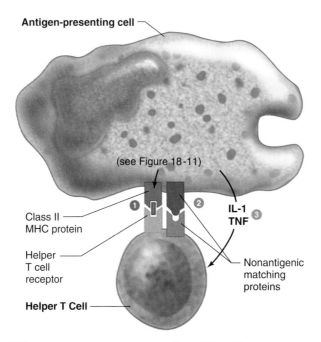

**Three events are required for the activation of helper T cells**
Figure 18.12

# Processing and presentation of viral antigen to a cytotoxic T cell by an infected cell

Figure 18.13

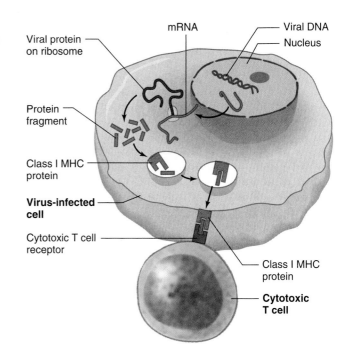

mRNA

Viral protein on ribosome

Viral DNA

Nucleus

Protein fragment

Class I MHC protein

**Virus-infected cell**

Cytotoxic T cell receptor

Class I MHC protein

**Cytotoxic T cell**

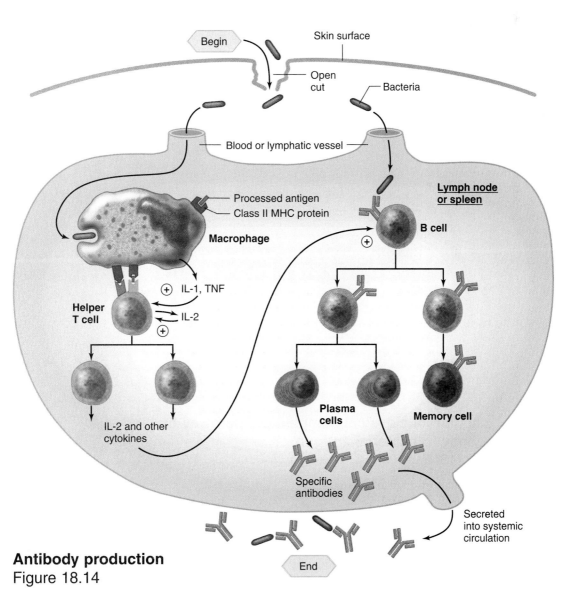

Begin

Skin surface

Open cut

Bacteria

Blood or lymphatic vessel

**Lymph node or spleen**

Processed antigen

Class II MHC protein

**Macrophage**

**B cell**

⊕

⊕ IL-1, TNF

IL-2

**Helper T cell**

⊕

IL-2 and other cytokines

**Plasma cells**

**Memory cell**

Specific antibodies

Secreted into systemic circulation

End

**Antibody production**

Figure 18.14

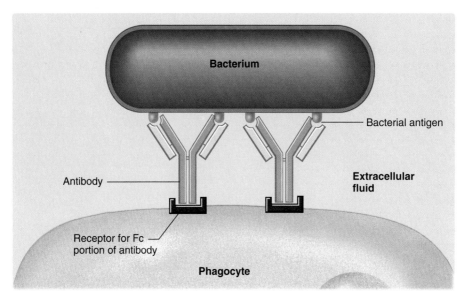

**Antibody-mediated phagocytosis**
Figure 18.15

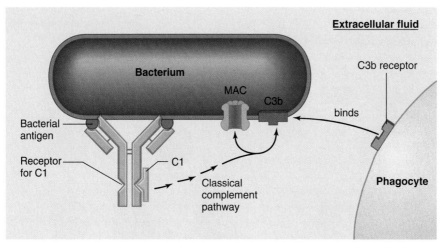

**Activation of classical complement pathway by binding of antibody to bacterial antigen**
Figure 18.16

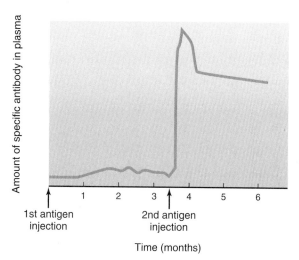

**Rate of antibody production**

Figure 18.17

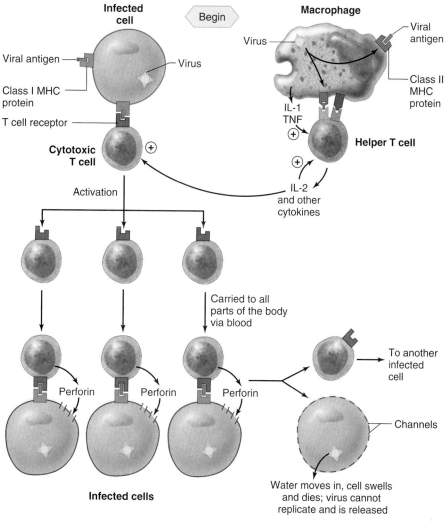

**Blood groups**

Figure 18.18

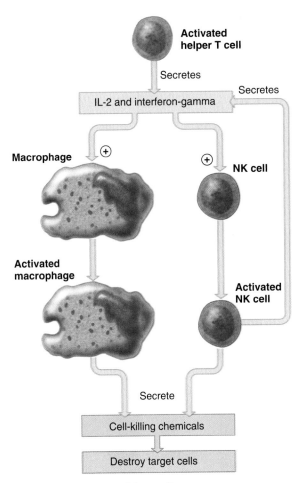

**Activated
helper T cell**

Secretes

Secretes

IL-2 and interferon-gamma

**Macrophage** ⊕

⊕ **NK cell**

**Activated
macrophage**

**Activated
NK cell**

Secrete

Cell-killing chemicals

Destroy target cells

**Role of IL-2 and interferon-gamma**
Figure 18.19

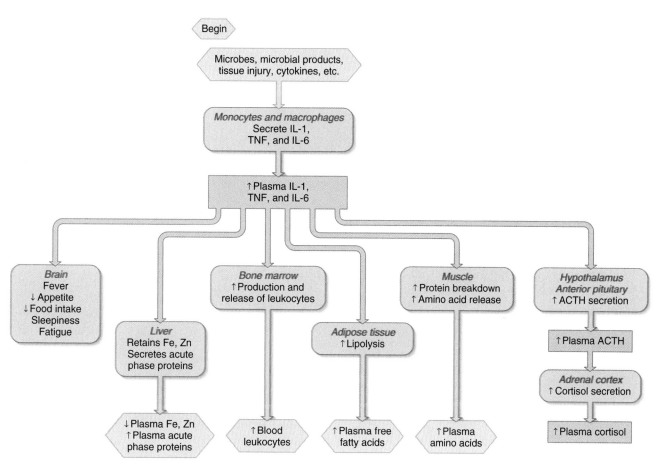

**Systemic responses to infection or injury**
Figure 18.20

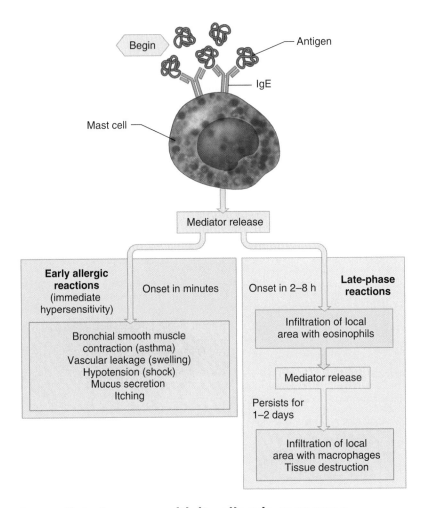

**Immediate hypersensitivity allergic response**
Figure 18.21

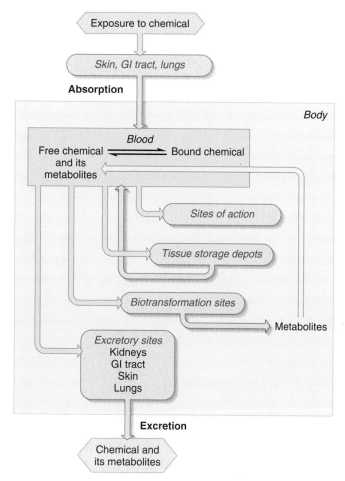

**Metabolism of foreign chemicals**
Figure 18.22

# Notes

# Notes

# Notes

# Notes

# Notes

# Notes

# Notes

# Notes

# Notes

# Notes

# Notes